W9-AUG-912

RUSSIAN RESEARCH CENTER STUDIES · 45

ACCOUNTING IN SOVIET PLANNING AND MANAGEMENT

ACCOUNTING IN SOVIET PLANNING AND MANAGEMENT

ROBERT W. CAMPBELL

HARVARD UNIVERSITY PRESS

CAMBRIDGE, MASSACHUSETTS · 1963

The Russian Research Center of Harvard
University is supported by grants from
the Carnegie Corporation, the Ford
Foundation, and the Rockefeller Foundation. The Center carries out inter-
disciplinary study of Russian institutions
and behavior and related subjects.

This volume was prepared in part under
a grant from the Carnegie Corporation of
New York. That Corporation is not, however, the author, owner, publisher, or
proprietor of the publication and is not to
be understood as approving by virtue of
its grant any of the statements made or
views expressed therein.

Distributed in Great Britain
by Oxford University Press, London

Library of Congress Catalog Card Number: 62–20245

Printed in the United States of America

TO LAURA

ACKNOWLEDGMENTS

My study of Soviet accounting began nearly a decade ago, and in the intervening period it has benefited greatly from the help and encouragement of numerous institutions and persons. While writing the doctoral dissertation from which the book grew, I was supported by the Russian Research Center of Harvard University. Revision for publication was made possible by a Faculty Research Fellowship from the Ford Foundation. The financial assistance of these organizations is much appreciated.

Soviet accounting was first suggested to me as a subject for research by Professor Alexander Gerschenkron of Harvard. My first reaction to this proposal was tinged with dismay; the subject seemed full of mysteries outside my experience or preparation. But Professor Gerschenkron's suggestion has proved to be a fruitful one; I have found accounting to be an extremely useful point of departure for understanding the functioning of the Soviet economy. Revising my original conclusions to keep up with the changes that have been taking place in some areas of Soviet accounting, and to develop the ideas that grew out of and virtually overturned my original approach, has been a frustrating process. That I have persisted owes much to the encouragement of Professors Abram Bergson of Harvard and Gregory Grossman of the University of California, to whom I am very grateful.

June 1962   R. W. C.

CONTENTS

TABLES

ACCOUNTING IN

SOVIET PLANNING

AND MANAGEMENT

INTRODUCTION

THE IMAGE which the Soviet drive for industrialization conjures up in the minds of most of us is an eventful history in which brutal ruthlessness, utopian vision, and tragic social upheaval dominate the narrative. Against this dramatic background a preoccupation with the bookkeeper's routine of debit and credit must seem incongruous. Moreover, the relevance of accounting to an understanding of the Soviet system is not immediately obvious. The author of a book on Soviet accounting is therefore under a particular compulsion to make clear the rationale of his study. Certainly accounting by itself, the process of recording data on stocks, flows, claims, and other business operations, contains more routine than drama. But in the aggregate it has an incalculable impact on the operation of an economic system. Accounting is an indispensable tool of management in any modern economy, but in the management and control of the giant corporation constituted by the Soviet economy its role is much more crucial than in any capitalist economy. Viewed in relation to the effective management and control of this economy, even the small details of accounting — the rules, the routines, the plan of accounts, the form of documents and reports — acquire great meaning and interest.

The objective of the present book is to discuss Soviet accounting in relation to various problems of economic planning and management. Such a statement of intent, however, is deceptively vague. The scope of the accounting function has so expanded in today's world, both in the minds of its theoreticians and in the practice of business, that the statement actually constitutes a hunting license to consider almost every aspect of the organization and administration of the Soviet economy. The first task of this introduction must be to define more precisely the boundaries of the inquiry.

The appropriate scope for a study of Soviet accounting is not easily obvious, but that is not surprising. Even a cursory examination of either Soviet or American accounting journals will disclose an unending argument about what constitutes accounting and about what the scope of the accounting function should be. Because accounting is so intimately bound up with other facets of planning and management, it is extremely difficult to establish a definition of accounting which has both unity and specificity. That is, it is hard to define the limits broadly enough to encompass all the questions that concern accountants without at the same time bringing under the umbrella of the definition many aspects of management where accountants are involved only peripherally or not at all. Accounting is closely connected with problems of organization, for example. Accounting information has to be used by someone, and its usefulness depends as much on whether there is someone in a position to make use of it as on how it is compiled. Accountants are therefore often cautioned to think carefully about responsibility and authority and channels of communication before they get down to the more technical problems of keeping track of numbers. In another direction, accounting is scarcely separable from problems of planning. Ex post accounting data become useful for control purposes only if they can be related to some standard or norm, and one of the biggest problems of accountants in the past several decades has been to integrate the processes of setting standards and keeping records. But the establishment of standards is essentially a part of planning.

Another difficulty in delimiting the problems to be considered is the fact that accounting data are only one among several kinds of quantitative information generated by the record-keeping operations of business units. The conventions that separate accounting information from other kinds frequently have a customary rather than an analytical justification. This point can be illustrated by the Soviet terminology for record-keeping. The general word for recordkeeping is *uchet*, but this is subdivided by a series of descriptive adjectives into account-ing (*bukhgalterskii uchet*), statistics (*statisticheskii uchet*), and technical records (*operativno-tekhnicheskii uchet*). All of these different kinds of information are supposed to be generated by a single set of primary documentation within the enterprise, and so they have at least a genetic homogeneity. Moreover, the lines between them are uncertain — a class of information called accounting at one stage may be transformed into statistics at another, such as data on costs. Accounting information can, however, be distinguished by the fact that it is in value terms and is integrated within a single set of concepts and accounts by the use of the principle of double entry. This is essentially what is meant hereafter by the data of bukhgalterskii uchet.

The broadest conceptions of accounting become, in applica-tion to the Soviet Union, an all-embracing framework for de-scribing and evaluating the operation of the entire economy. If one defines the accounting function very generally as involving the preparation and interpretation of quantitative information for the purposes of management, then the substitution of ad-ministrative organization of the allocation process in the Soviet Union for the market organization in the United States means that the province of accounting is enlarged to include responsibility for generating *all* economic information. If the extension of the accounting function along another dimension is accepted (namely, its involvement in the tasks of setting standards, clarifying responsibility, and so on), then a shift from the market economy to the administrative economy implies that the whole process of preparation and control of national economic plans comes within the scope of accounting. Furthermore, responsibilities that come within the competence of enterprise accounting in the market economy escape those confines in the Soviet Union. Many traditional accounting problems take on a form and configuration in the Soviet economy different from those to which we are accustomed, and, if the accountant is to keep them in his purview, he must broaden his approach to include some very general problems of national economic organization and administration. The problem of inventory control may be cited as an illustration. Because the supply and marketing system of the Soviet economy is so different from that of the market economy, the planning of inventories and the responsibility for inventory control must be removed in part from the firm and given to other units in the system.

An approach based on such broad conceptions of accounting may ultimately prove very useful in studying the operation of the Soviet economy. The evolution of accounting thought in the United States may provide the concepts and the generalizations from which one might create a unified interpretation of Soviet planning and administration. Certainly economists working on the Soviet system need some such approach — they have found it impossible to proceed very far in applying to the Soviet system of economic organization the familiar models they have developed to explain the market economy. This book, however, has no such vast ambitions and will be limited primarily to some of the more conventional conceptions of accounting in their

4

application to the Soviet Union. The major limitation will be with respect to the kind of data involved, namely, the data of bukhgalterskii uchet, as defined above. This limitation is established only for the sake of convenience — and in spite of a vivid awareness that there is nothing fundamentally distinctive about accounting information from the viewpoint of those who need to make economic decisions or those whose job is to analyze and control the performance of economic units. Indeed, if one were asked to identify the concertmaster in the Soviet informational symphony, he would probably settle on statisticheskii uchet. Precisely for this reason, however, a broad range of questions involved with the creation, reporting, evaluation, and use of the data of statisticheskii uchet has already been studied by those interested in the operation of the Soviet economy. Consider, for example, the many studies of the planning of physical limits and directives, of the generation and use of output data in physical terms and in "quasi-physical" aggregations, such as output in 1926–27 prices, and of the organization of statistical reporting. Many general studies of planning and management also have adventured into the borderland shared with accounting to consider questions of organization, channels of information flows, and setting of standards, which might equally well be defined as accounting questions. This research has generally been done by economists rather than accountants and has not always been couched in the terminology of accounting, but inevitably it reflects concern for the kind of questions and approaches that would preoccupy accountants.

The area that has not yet been carefully explored, however, is the use of accounting information proper — the data of bukhgalterskii uchet — in the process of planning and management. The purpose of this book, then, is to fill in this part of the foundation on which an accounting interpretation (and here I mean accounting in the broadest possible sense) may ultimately be based. Nor will planning be discussed in any comprehensive way. There are many areas of planning and management in which it is possible to proceed with virtually no reference to what the bookkeepers do, and much of what the bookkeepers do is never echoed in the reactions of managers or planners. My references to planning will involve only fragments of the total picture of planning. Even within these limitations what follows will be quite selective. It might better be described as a series of essays on some representative Soviet accounting problems than as a survey of Soviet accounting. The common denominator of all these problems is that they involve the interaction of accounting data as defined above and problems of planning and management.

It may also be wise to add a second prefatory warning — that I have approached the subject of Soviet accounting as an economist rather than as an accountant and without the detailed knowledge of a practicing specialist in the field. This circumstance defines my interests and, unfortunately, also my limitations. It has several important implications. First, the judgments made tend to confront Soviet accounting with some ideal accounting system (perhaps some self-professed Soviet one or, given the nature of the system studied, perhaps with the abstractions of economic theory) and not with personal experience in the operating realities of some existing system, such as accounting in this country. Second, no comparative evaluation of Soviet and American accounting is intended, even though at many points the evaluation of Soviet accounting draws on the principles and practices described in American accounting literature. Such a comparison is obviously of interest, but it must wait for the efforts of others. Finally, it must remain for practical accountants to determine whether accounting in the Soviet Union has developed any concepts and techniques that could be usefully applied in the accounting of a country like the United States. My general feeling is that it has not. At the same time, any acquaintance with Soviet accounting reveals it as a rich museum of experience. If American accountants with the requisite technical skill could be encouraged to study that history of varied experiment, the process would surely be suggestive of useful innovations, even if no ready-made, transferable, formulas were found.

Accounting serves two extremely important functions in the modern economy. On the one hand, it is the source for much of the information needed for economic decision making; and, on the other, it provides the information needed by managerial officers for checking and controlling subordinates. In the Soviet economy in particular, centralization of planning and control implies a heavy reliance on accounting, and the activities of Soviet enterprises are covered by a system of accounting probably more comprehensive than that of any other economy in the world.

Particularly important in fulfilling these functions is cost accounting. Chapter 2 describes the vital interrelation of Soviet cost accounting with price formation, economic decision making, and economic efficiency. In the Soviet economy the data of cost accounting are translated more or less directly into prices without the interpolation of a complicated market mechanism. The Soviet economy is an economy virtually without markets in the usual economic sense, and most prices are fixed by the state on the basis of cost-accounting reports. Because of the use of cost-accounting data for pricing purposes, it is of interest to know whether the cost-accounting rules are correct from the economic point of view — whether the costs they determine are accurate measures of cost and value. The interesting problems here are essentially those of allocation. The assignment of given outlays to separate accounting periods or outputs involves complicated theoretical problems, and my purpose is to see how Soviet accounting handles these problems. Soviet methods of valuing and depreciating fixed assets are treated in Chapters 3 and 4, and Chapters 5 and 6 take up a number of problems of allocating expenses among enterprises, products, and time periods. In Chapter 7 the impact of Soviet accounting errors on economic decisions is illustrated with some examples of the interaction between accounting data and decisions made within the enterprise.

The second aspect of Soviet accounting to be examined is its effectiveness as an instrument of managerial control. The accounting records of an enterprise display in value terms all aspects of the performance of an enterprise and of its individual parts. Cost accounting in particular has been developed as the most important technique by which managerial personnel evaluate and control the efficiency of operation of the units under their administration. In the Soviet planned economy great emphasis has been given to this function of cost accounting, and cost performance is taken as the most important indicator of the general efficiency of enterprise performance. The effectiveness of Soviet cost accounting in serving this objective is discussed in Chapter 8. Another aspect of enterprise behavior which is controlled primarily by the use of accounting data is inventory behavior, discussed in Chapter 9.

Closely intertwined with both the control functions and the information functions of accounting is the technical efficiency with which it is carried out. The bookkeeping work of a modern economy involves a large commitment of resources and is an important industry in its own right, although it is fragmented and scattered among the other industries. Therefore, the technology of the accounting process holds a certain interest in itself, just as would the technology of any other industry. The main reason for including a discussion of technical efficiency in this study, however, is that it is closely related to the two problems already described. The usefulness of cost accounting depends not only on the economic relevance of the concepts which it employs, but also on the accuracy with which the utilization of resources can be documented and the detail with which the data can be processed. The usefulness of cost-accounting information for purposes of control also depends on the detail and speed with which the data can be recorded, analyzed, and reported to the responsible officials.

To keep it within manageable proportions, the study has been limited in two additional dimensions — with respect to the time period covered and the area of the economy treated. Throughout, the emphasis will be on contemporary accounting practice. It may be added, however, that there appears to be considerable continuity in Soviet accounting over the last two decades. Much of the present system has its roots in the thirties or earlier. On the other hand, there have been notable changes in certain respects, as, for instance, in the treatment of depreciation. Indeed, it might be very interesting to consider the development of Soviet accounting as a process of adjusting the accounting system inherited from capitalism to the needs of a planned economy, but any detailed attempt to do so is probably precluded by a lack of precise information for earlier periods. Changes in Soviet accounting practice over time will be discussed only when these changes help in understanding the nature of the present system or when they are of some intrinsic theoretical interest.

With respect to the area of the economy covered, emphasis will be on the industrial sector. The question underlying the first half of the book is the relation between cost accounting and price determination, and it is in the industrial sector that this interdependence is most clearly expressed. It is here that some of the most complicated questions of cost allocation arise and where price formation is most directly tied to cost accounting. Also with respect to the second focus of interest — cost accounting as a control instrument — it is in the complex enterprises of large-scale industry that cost control becomes a difficult problem in administration.

The sources on which the present study is based consist mostly of official Soviet laws and instructions and Soviet accounting handbooks and textbooks. The fact that Soviet accounting is carried out on the basis of a highly formalized system of rules and instructions, and is characterized by a high degree of uniformity, makes it relatively easy to find out how any given accounting problem is handled and to draw broad generalizations. There are a number of very general laws and regulations which lay down rules for cost accounting that are applicable to all enterprises in the Soviet economy. There are, for instance, general rules prescribed by the Council of Ministers for valuation of the items of the balance sheet, detailed decrees specifying how depreciation is to be estimated, and even economy-wide rules for the allocation of expense between finished and unfinished production. General descriptions of Soviet accounting practice are also available in the great flood of textbooks on accounting. More detailed information for individual branches of the economy is given in the form of specialized textbooks prepared as training aids and reference books for accounting personnel who work in those branches. In addition to these purely accounting sources, there is often a great deal of discussion of accounting practices in general economic journals, in the technical periodicals of individual branches, and in the financial periodicals. These auxiliary discussions are particularly valuable, since they often contain critical discussions of Soviet accounting, which provide a useful counterweight to the more or less normative nature of the legal materials and the textbook discussions. The discrepancy between the official image and informal reality is a problem in all Soviet research. In the case of accounting it will not be overcome until non-Soviet accountants have a chance to inspect Soviet practice at firsthand.

To complete this introduction, it will be useful to describe briefly some of the general features of Soviet accounting. From the formal point of view, Soviet accounting is virtually identical with traditional capitalist accounting. This has not always been so. In the early postrevolutionary period, there was some uncertainty as to the forms which accounting should take in a socialist state. During the first few years of the Soviet regime, conventional accounting was more or less abandoned. Such recordkeeping as there was centered on the problems of recording the movement of physical goods and of accounting for budgeted expenditures. This degeneration of accounting was in part the natural result of the objective economic conditions (inflation, rationing, and the reversion to barter operations), but it was also assisted by the prevailing notion that socialism would involve a moneyless economy. For instance, one early accounting book bristles with statements like this:

The authors consider that the misfortunes which have befallen us in the matter of organizing accounting are explained mainly by the fact that the existing capitalist bookkeeping has been taken as the basis for the solution of the problem . . . The socialist state operates not with commodities and their monetary measures, but with material goods, products, raw materials — in general with material resources which serve for the satisfaction of all needs . . . We pronounce the death sentence on the double-entry system of accounting and assert that the principle of the double-entry system and the whole science of accounting have outlived themselves in the conditions of the socialist economy.[1]

This identification of capitalist double-entry bookkeeping with the use of a monetary measure of value is completely erroneous, of course. The essence of double-entry bookkeeping lies

11

in its dual description of a collection of values and in the principle that every operation must be reflected on the accounts in equal debits and credits. Thus, the only prerequisite for its use is that there be a rationale for the dual description and a common unit of account. Indeed, at the time when it was thought that money would be abandoned and that the labor unit (*tred*) would become the unit of account, there were a number of proposals for translating the whole double-entry system into labor units.[2] This kind of thinking persisted for only a short period, however. The introduction of the New Economic Policy, the enunciation of the principle of *khozraschet* (see below), and the reorganization of state industry in 1921 clearly implied the use of traditional bookkeeping in monetary terms, and in 1923 the party spoke out clearly for traditional bookkeeping:

In the conditions of today, a single and reliable empirical check on the correctness of the interrelationships of the enterprise, trust, and state, and of the correctness of the whole management, can be given only by its material results as they are revealed *in the commercial balance sheet*. Without correct *bookkeeping*, embracing the state economy from top to bottom, without scientifically designed cost accounting, determining the real cost of the products of state industry, there is no guarantee against the gradual dispersion or wastage of the nationalized property, and in this case the trusts would become channels for the transfer of state property into private hands.[3]

No departure from the principle of double-entry bookkeeping has been suggested since that year. There are occasional suggestions in the works on the theory of accounting that the unit of account will eventually be the labor unit, but it is recognized that this does not imply the abolition of double-entry bookkeeping.

The wholesale transfer of capitalist accounting to the service of the planned economy has been greatly facilitated by the Soviet administrative invention of *khozraschet*. Under this principle the enterprise is given the status of a corporation with powers of employing the property assigned to it, of making contracts, and of carrying on economic activities. Its transactions with the rest of the economy are settled through the use of money, and in general its expenses are supposed to be recouped by its revenues. Thus, from an accounting point of view, it is little different from a capitalist enterprise, and its activities can be accounted for by a conventional set of accounts. Nearly all production enterprises in the Soviet economy operate on this basis. Of course, because of the peculiar milieu in which the Soviet enterprise operates, the economic interpretation of the accounting magnitudes is distinctive. The Soviet enterprise has a profit, but the interpretation of this profit differs from what it would be in the capitalist balance sheet because of the different degree of autonomy which the enterprise has in disposing of it. The kinds of values embraced by accounting are also somewhat different — the Soviet balance sheet does not show land or other natural resources, since these are not considered by the Russians to constitute value. Nevertheless, the formal essence of capitalist bookkeeping has been applied to the Soviet enterprise with no difficulty whatever.

Despite the formal similarity between Soviet and capitalist accounting, however, the former shows fairly clearly the strong influence of centralized planning and control. In the planned economy, as Soviet writers point out, accounting ceases to be a technique oriented toward the needs of the individual enterprise for internal management and takes on the more general functions of providing the information which is needed for planning and control from above. The planners need a huge volume of information as the basis for prospective planning, and those who check on the fulfillment of planned assignments must have detailed information on the actual achievements. In this situation it is necessary that the enterprise accounting be designed to produce information in the form needed by the central authorities. The concepts and categories used in the enterprise accounting must be assimilable to the planners' concepts and categories.

This point can be illustrated by the example of wage payments. One of the aggregates in which the planners are vitally interested is the magnitude of money payments to the population; whatever classification of outlays the enterprise may find suitable for its internal needs, it must set up its outlay accounts in such a way as to distinguish money payments to the population. Similarly, from the control point of view, accounting reports can be used to check plan fulfillment only if the cost classification and allocations are handled according to the same rules as those used in drawing up the plans.

In order to satisfy these needs of a centrally planned economy, Soviet accounting practices are prescribed from above and are characterized by a high degree of uniformity and standardization. The first steps to standardize accounting were taken as early as 1926, when the Supreme Council of the National Economy (VSNKh) issued instructions for uniform cost accounting in individual branches of the economy. In 1926 there were adopted the first standard rules for drawing up the balance sheet and for valuing its component items, and in the early thirties the first uniform plans of accounts were worked out for Soviet industry. The most important drive to redesign accounting to fit the needs of planning came in the early thirties, in connection with the beginning of the industrialization drive. Under the decrees of May 9, 1929, and December 17, 1931, the Gosplan and later the Central Administration of National Economic Accounting was given the task of working out a "unified system of national-economic recordkeeping" (*edinaya sistema narodno-khozyaystvennogo ucheta*), which would integrate and standardize all recordkeeping on the basis of a single set of original documentation within the enterprise.[4] In accordance with this task, the Gosplan and later the Central Administration of National Economic Accounting (TsUNKhU) were given the responsibility for checking and approving all accounting instructions and forms introduced by the individual branches. Other legislation at this time required that each enterprise create a distinct bookkeeping department, headed by a chief bookkeeper, which would be responsible for carrying out the instructions prescribed from above, and the rights and responsibilities of the chief bookkeeper were carefully defined.[5] Most of these pieces of original legislation have been superseded and replaced by more recent decrees, and the Ministry of Finance has been brought in as a third agency which must approve all accounting legislation, but the general principle of centralized control of bookkeeping practice laid down in the early thirties has remained the same in its essentials right up to the present day. Such imposition of uniformity is essential for a planned economy, though, as will be shown, it often has an adverse effect on accounting by making it primarily an instrument for outside control and impairing the flexibility that might make it a more effective tool of management at the enterprise level.

THE RELATION BETWEEN

COST ACCOUNTING AND

ECONOMIC CALCULATION

ACCOUNTING in general and even some of its narrower specific forms, such as cost accounting or inventory accounting, serve a multitude of purposes. These may be control, evaluation of the behavior of subordinates, and ascertainment of costs for economic calculation or determination of income. The adequacy or usefulness of an accounting system depends on the objectives it is to serve, the kind of organization involved, and the setting within which it works. The first seven chapters of this book are concerned primarily with the adequacy of Soviet accounting procedures in generating information about costs as a basis for economic calculation. The environment within which cost accounting works in the Soviet economy differs radically from the market economy, and the first step must be to describe this setting and explain the peculiar demands which it places on cost accounting. Only then can criteria be specified for evaluating Soviet cost accounting from this point of view.

One distinctive feature of the Soviet economy is that nearly its whole system of prices and costs is determined by accounting alone without any help from market processes. For many purposes, it is useful to consider the Soviet economy as a single giant corporaton embracing nearly all the productive activity of the economy. Its unity from an accounting point of view is based on the fact that its various parts are linked not by market behavior but by administrative direction from the center. The various production units are not autonomous in their actions and decisions, but are supposedly subject to a single will and purpose. The transactions between any two enterprises are not, as in the capitalist economy, an interaction between economically sovereign powers. They fit instead the cliché of the left hand dealing with the right. The frontiers of this corporation lie at the point where it deals with households and with firms in other countries. These are frontiers because they involve a large element of market behavior rather than administrative direction.

Cost accounting in this giant corporation is a fundamentally different animal and has a different relationship to the problem of economic calculation and resource allocation than does cost accounting in the capitalist economy. In the latter, cost accounting is an instrument of private firms. There is no need to go beyond a purely parochial point of view in evaluating the cost accounting of an independent capitalist firm. The concept of cost to the firm is the only concept of cost that is relevant. Cost accounting is related only indirectly to the allocation of resources, and it would make no sense to ask whether costs as computed within firms correspond to national costs so that the economy as a whole can make rational economic decisions.

Rationality in the capitalist economy involves two separate questions. Economists are concerned with the efficiency of market structures as these affect the allocation of resources; the value concept used in their theorizing is price. Accountants are concerned with the efficiency of accounting — that is, their concern in evaluating cost accounting is whether it enables firms to act like the maximizing units which the economist assumes them to be. Although both questions must be considered in evaluating the efficiency of a market economy, they can obviously be discussed completely separately. In the unified firm constituted by the Soviet economy, however, this distinction between price formation and accounting is blurred. Formally, two kinds of value tags can still be distinguished, depending on whether they involve the numbers computed by accountants for intraenterprise activity or those attached to interenterprise transactions. We may call the first cost figures and the second, prices. From the larger point of view, however, that of the head office in Moscow, this distinction is not particularly meaningful. It is not based on a distinction between market behavior and the conventions of accounting within firms, but only on whether the value tag attached to a particular flow has been set by application of an accounting rule within subordinate units or by an accounting convention wielded by the accountants in the central office. The cost of coal is determined by the accounting rules employed at the level of the enterprise, the price by a rule applied by some higher level of authority. Price formation in this economy is only accounting writ large: it is a process in which the cost results of enterprise accounting are amended by accountants at a higher level.

The implication of this conception of the Soviet economy, for our purposes, is that questions of rationality in cost calculation cannot be neatly divided between the accountant and the economist. The problem constitutes a borderland in which both the economist and accountant will find the terrain unfamiliar and their conceptual tools often inappropriate. The economist, for instance, will find it difficult to apply his ideas about value to a system which lacks markets and in which price tags are determined essentially by accounting procedures. The account-ant, on the other hand, will find that, when he is dealing with a firm so large as to embrace the whole economy, he must add a large dose of economic theory to the concepts and insights brought from his experience with cost accounting used as an enterprise instrument.

Rational Planning and the Role of Value Indices

In this problem of interpreting and evaluating Soviet cost accounting, the first task is to clarify the objectives of cost accounting in the Soviet economy and their general relation to the vast problem of economic calculation.

Viewed in the most general terms, the problem of the Soviet planners is the universal "economic problem" of allocating scarce resources efficiently. On the one hand, they face a set of production possibilities defined by the state of the arts and the resources at their command. Faced, on the other, by the objectives they want to accomplish, economic rationality on their part lies in maximizing in the marginalist sense. The planners should make the marginal rates of substitution between preferred final goods equal to the marginal rates of transforma-tion of these goods as defined by the production possibilities. Obviously, much of the apparatus of modern value theory is applicable, *mutatis mutandis,* to the Soviet planned economy. Corresponding to the optimum allocation of resources, there is a set of values for all the components of final output. Further-more, imputation from the equilibrium set of values according to production functions determines value-cost magnitudes for all intermediate outputs and primary resources. These are the values which the pricing and accounting rules should be designed to approximate.

It is conceptually possible for the regime to approach its problem of maximizing without any reference to monetary notation. If the central planners had enough information concerning the production possibilities of their economy, such as might be provided by a detailed input-output table or the various programming models of production, they could determine the marginal rates of transformation between final goods in physical form and match them against the marginal rates of substitution of these goods derived from their preference function. Moreover, a plan for allocation of all resources in physical terms could be determined from the system of production relationships. In such a system, the category of value would be a fifth wheel. A set of value indices would be implicit in the solution but would have no obvious planning usefulness. Prices might still be attached to goods at every point of transfer, but, since they would not affect any planning decision, they could be set in any arbitrary way. And if prices were a fifth wheel, traditional double-entry bookkeeping and cost accounting would be a sixth. Bookkeeping reports could still be compiled, but if the planners had done their work well, on the basis of accurate production functions, bookkeeping costs would be gratuitous from the point of view of measuring costs against benefits (although traditional double-entry bookkeeping in monetary terms might still serve as a control instrument). It might be useful to have bookkeeping costs compiled ex post so that the planners could check on the accuracy of their planning. But the paradox is that, if mistakes had been made in planning, bookkeeping costs compiled ex post would not reveal true costs. From the economic point of view, real costs are opportunity costs, and there is no way for bookkeeping to account for costs in terms of opportunities foregone.

Despite the conceptual possibility of such a physical approach to the problem of allocating resources, it is not technically feasible for the Russians, at least not at the present time. It is true that the Russians do a great deal of planning in physical terms, such as in the material balances and in the allocation of manpower. But this physical planning is really concerned only with ensuring the mutual compatibility of different parts of the plan and has nothing to do with the problem of optimization. It is also true that locating decision making above the level of the individual enterprise makes it possible for planners frequently to disregard some prices as parameters and to widen greatly the area within which the choice between alternatives can be made on a purely technological basis. An interesting illustration of such a repudiation of prices in favor of physical optimizing is found in a book describing the economic calculations associated with planning ore-enrichment plants. The planners must decide the quality point below which an ore source cannot be treated to ensure profit. The cost per unit of the desired mineral in the enriched ore rises as its content in the raw ore falls. It would appear that no ore-enrichment plant should be based on an ore source so poor that the cost per unit of the mineral in the enriched ore exceeds its price. However, recognizing that the price may not be an objective criterion of value, the planners decide whether or not to enrich a given ore only on the basis of the entire process extending from mining to finished metal. Taking the output of metal and correspondingly the ore-mining margin as given, the ore-enrichment process is extended to the worst ore source where it can still effect a saving of resources in the total process.[1]

Nevertheless, value measurement must enter into every economic decision at some point in the calculations. The use of monetary indices of cost and gains is compelled by the impossibility of completely centralized planning. Since any planner not at the center is unable to judge what effect his choices will have on the achievement of the aggregate optimum (the maximum attainment of the ends of the state), he must make partial optimizations, and this requires calculations in terms of generalized indices of cost and value. It is this circumstance that makes it imperative for the management of the corporation to install a cost-accounting system.

Some observers take the position that economic decision making in the Soviet Union relies very little on prices. They emphasize the restrictions which physical allocation and detailed planning from above place on the management of individual enterprises and the important influences of nonmonetary criteria on managerial behavior. The implication is that, since planning depends very little on price considerations, the accuracy of the pricing system is a question of little practical importance. There is some truth in this position, but the irrelevance of price can be exaggerated. The mechanisms by which prices affect economic decisions are different from those of a market economy, but this does not mean that prices have no influence. For instance, prices play a very different role in the achievement of quantity equilibria in the Soviet economy than they do in the market economy. In general, the degree to which local units are permitted to determine their output programs on the basis of price calculations is very limited, but planners at various levels *do* depend on price calculations in deciding how to produce any given output program.[2] Under this system, quantities from the supply side are determined not by the reactions of individual producers to prices but by a process in which the quantities from the demand side are added up at the center or at intermediate levels of planning and the output program which they require is then assigned to the individual producers. Thus the quantity equilibria are still ultimately based on reactions to prices. Moreover, the Soviet manager's failure to be influenced by prices in his behavior is largely a reflection of the fact that so many decisions are made at higher levels; but the decisions of the higher unit can still be based on price calculations. Despite all the features of the system which interfere with reliance on prices as guides to decision making, it is undeniable that planners at all levels are constantly being confronted with alternatives, and their usual response is to make choices on the basis of calculations in value terms. The choice between production variants is one of the most important themes in Soviet technological literature, and choices are always framed in terms of cost alternatives. It should not be a matter of indifference to the regime whether the costs and prices its accountants determine provide an accurate reflection of national economic cost.

If, then, the problem is to establish a system of internal cost accounting for this unified firm, what are the "correct" concepts of cost? How should the accounting rules employed by enterprise management and by people higher in the administrative hierarchy be formulated so that the combination generates price tags for outputs and actions on which the directors and their subordinates can rely in making decisions about resource allocation? To put the question thus betrays, of course, the perspective of a bourgeois economist rather than that of the Marxist planners themselves. Lacking any theory concerning value in relation to the problem of the allocation of resources until recently, they have never been able to formulate the objectives of cost accounting at all coherently. Nevertheless, one can glean from their discussions something rather like the above formulation of what information cost accounting should supply

Criteria for Costing and Pricing

The major difficulty in specifying the kind of cost data Soviet accounting practice should be designed to produce arises from the fact that there are many concepts of cost, each economically valid in the appropriate situation. The choice among alternative concepts of cost depends on the decisions involved and the functions to be served. If the function of prices is short-run allocation of resources, then prices should reflect current scarcity relations. If they are to be used as the basis for long-run decisions about allocations of resources for some time into the future, then short-run influences ought to be disregarded. If the decision involves the choice of a general policy at a fairly high level within the structure, such as the emphasis as between two competing kinds of fuel, then it might be possible to ignore much of the differentiation in cost among producers. On the other hand, if it is a short-run scheduling decision about assigning an output goal among producers of a given fuel, then differences in cost from producer to producer could not be ignored. For some decisions it would be correct to ignore fixed cost and concentrate only on variable cost, but clearly this would not do in undertaking to settle issues concerning growth and long-run allocation. Given the nature of this giant corporation, which of these kinds of costs are most useful, or to what extent should it try to generate all of them? These questions cannot be settled definitively, but in what follows I shall try to point out some of the distinctive features of the Soviet economy which bear on them.

First, it is obvious that the Soviet system of pricing and costing must satisfy other objectives in addition to facilitating correct economic decision making. This is a centrally planned economy in which it is desirable for administrative reasons to have prices that remain fixed over fairly large jurisdictions and fairly long time periods. This is almost indispensable for ease of planning and control.

Second, it should be emphasized that the Russians do not assign to their price system the task of short-run allocation. They rely very little on prices to bring short-run supply and demand into equilibrium. This is particularly true with respect to output decisions. The utilization of capacity and the composition of output are only slightly responsive to prices. This limitation on the function of prices in itself rules out the relevance of many of the intricacies of the market-price model from which Western economists draw their insights about the meaning of "cost."

The impact of prices on economic decisions in the Soviet economy is most obvious in the area of relatively long-term decisions made at relatively high levels of planning. Many choices concerning what material to use, how much transportation to employ, the degree to which capital goods should be substituted for labor, which of several alternative processes to choose, are effectively made for long periods of time by the decisions of planners above the enterprise level. The location of a plant, its layout, and the equipment installed frequently fix these decisions for some time and eliminate much of the possibility of choice among current inputs.

Finally, it should be emphasized that the Soviet economy is characterized by rapid growth and intensive utilization of capacity. This fact places some limitations on the distinction which played so important a role in the theory of socialist pricing of the 1930s between fixed cost and variable cost, between long-run average cost and marginal cost. In the Soviet economy, those who make production decisions which will require the consumption of electric power must base their decision on the long-run average cost rather than on the marginal cost of power, since their requirements will be met not by higher utilization of existing capacities with low marginal cost but by newly constructed capacity. The general argument applies to many other situations as well. All of these circumstances suggest that the emphasis should be on such general cost concepts as full cost, long-run costs, and average cost.

On the other hand, even if the peculiarities of the Soviet system are recognized, it is obvious that in many situations

2 5

planners have sufficient latitude for maneuver to require value indices embodying subtler distinctions. At more detailed levels of planning over smaller areas of the economy and over shorter time horizons, the Soviet price system, typically based on branch and regional averages, on long-run average costs, and characterized by considerable temporal rigidity, will be misleading. The interesting thing is that Russian planners seem well aware of this and in particular cases try to use subtler concepts of cost, although they must usually derive them on their own outside the routine system of cost accounting established by the head office. They are quite willing to ignore actual prices in favor of ingenious alternative estimations of cost that may be relevant to a particular decision. When a decision rests on some cost magnitude within the enterprise, they are willing to ignore the traditional average-cost concepts which the accountants compute and report in favor of more appropriate cost concepts. For example, they may recognize the importance of distinguishing between fixed and variable cost in a particular decision and attempt to derive variable cost figures from the basic data. Success in these attempts depends on the ease with which the accounting system devised by the head office can be so adapted. The suitability of Soviet cost accounting for handling some of these problems will be discussed in Chapter 7.

It should be obvious, without belaboring the point further, that the nature of this economy mutes the importance of many of the distinctions to which we are accustomed in economic theory. In terms of its capabilities in perceiving alternatives, making policies, and executing decisions, it is a clumsy economy. This probably explains the fact that the directors of the Soviet production establishment seem to be content with a cost-accounting system which embodies much less subtlety and sophistication in its definition of cost than an economist acquainted with the market economy might consider desirable.

To summarize the argument so far, the Soviet cost-accounting system is established by what is in effect the head office of a single firm, to serve the needs of the head office. These needs include, among others, the determination of a set of cost indices for all components of output, for purposes of economic calculation. The cost figures generated reflect two levels of accounting. (1) Each enterprise, taking the cost of the inputs it acquires from other units, figures the cost of its output. (2) The costs that finally emerge, however, involve more than cumulations and allocations of input costs as goods flow through the production process. At various points in the system, the head office amends the costs computed by the enterprises by levying charges and by interpolating price-cost differentials at the transfer points where goods are written off the accounts of one enterprise and onto the accounts of another.

To make this total accounting system the subject of inquiry for this book would be overambitious. It would have to result in a general theory of Soviet economic organization. It seems reasonable to expect that the theory of the Soviet economy will one day be built on such a concept, but the goal here is more modest, being limited primarily to the accounting practices of individual enterprises. Because of the artificiality of that limitation, it seems in order to consider, however briefly, the accounting practice of the central authority. So brief a survey cannot settle all the issues it raises, but perhaps it will be suggestive as an approach to the Soviet economy and will clarify the limitations of what can be learned by looking at enterprise cost accounting alone.

Accounting above the Level of the Enterprise

Consider the activities of the central office of the Soviet firm (again, "firm" meaning "the economy") and the accounting associated with it. The head office has two primary functions. First, it performs some production activities which cannot well be allocated to khozraschet firms — such as administration, research, provision of some general services. Second, it shares with the board of directors of any corporation the prerogative of disposing of income. Accounting for these activities is essentially a problem of recording on an appropriate set of accounts these outlays and the sources by which they are covered. There is an important distinction between the two kinds of outlays and they require distinctive treatment in the accounting. Outlays benefiting current output are costs incurred in producing the income and should ultimately be allocated among all the components of that income. In accounting for these outlays, the head office in effect takes cost figures as computed by enterprises and, by various fiscal devices, converts these into a set of prices which can be interpreted as a set of national economic costs to be used in decision making. Here, obviously, the problem is to establish allocation rules which will assign these outlays on a reasonable basis to the various kinds of output involved.

The disposition of income in the form of outlays for such purposes as military programs, investment, and so on, must be charged against some sort of income account. The interesting issue is how the revenues of this income account arise and how they are reflected in enterprise cost calculations. We may perceive a normative standard for this process by asking ourselves what are the sources of income for the corporation. Its income arises primarily from two sources. The first is its relations with the household sector of the economy. In these transactions it receives "surplus value" in the literal Marxist sense. The regime obtains from the household sector an amount of labor resources considerably in excess of the amount of labor resources required to produce the goods returned to households in exchange. This is, in fact, the main resource of the Soviet regime. However, it also has a second source of income in the form of various surpluses within the production establishment. These comprise such items as differential rent on natural resources, the opportunity costs of capital, the transient rents which arise as windfalls or because of imperfect foresight. (These are offset to some extent by various losses.) Opportunity costs should be included in the costs of those subordinates within the establishment who enjoy the advantage of using the resources involved.

The above is theoretical and normative. Its purpose is to clarify the issues. The section which follows will explain how the Russians carry out this accounting at the center and will consider to what extent their practice fits the properties of the normative model. First, let it be said that there is a certain amount of institutional correspondence between the model and reality. The Russian head office does have a set of accounts on which it records outlays for production and disposition of its income. The Russians call this set of accounts the financial plan. It consists of two parts: the state budget and the consolidated income and disposition accounts for all enterprises. (The Soviet set of accounts does not fit our model, however, in that it does not distinguish between allocation of income and outlays in support of current production. Both are lumped together on a single set of outlay accounts.) These outlays are, in fact, included in the cost of output of enterprises by two devices — explicit charges levied on enterprises and price-cost residuals, that is, a difference between the cost which an enterprise figures for its output and the cost of that output as charged to other enterprises within the system. (The existence of these cost-price residuals is the result of the impossibility of completely centralized cost accounting. Costs are figured in the enterprises and cannot be calculated simultaneously by all enterprises because each must know the costs of its inputs before it can calculate the costs of its output. To make possible any decentralization of cost accounting, the regime must establish something in the nature of a "standard cost" or "planning cost" for each output. Soviet prices should be interpreted in this way as intrafirm accounting standards, not as something analogous to the prices of a market economy.)

These alternative devices for passing on the central outlays to enterprise accounting do not fit our model in that they bear no correspondence to the distinctions made above between income and costs of production or between different sources of income. For example, the turnover tax is designed *primarily* to collect the income arising in the relations of the regime with households, but it does not collect it all and, moreover, is also used in some places to collect producer surpluses.

Accounting for surplus value. The starting point in the general accounting structure of this economy considered as a single firm is the cost of labor. The level and structure of wages is the main determinant of costs throughout the system. Labor cost is the element in the cost structure of the economy which comes closest to being market-determined rather than administratively determined. The value indices established for this input are much less affected by accounting conventions than by supply and demand. Superficially, the Soviet labor market does not seem to satisfy the requirements of a free market. The government specifies wage scales which must be adhered to by enterprises, and the mobility of labor has been considerably restricted at times by administrative controls. Despite these restrictions, however, the Soviet labor market in many ways works as a free market. The legal restrictions on mobility frequently remain uninvoked and workers do move about a great deal. On the other side of the market, enterprises find many ways of varying the wages they offer their employees, despite the wage scales fixed at the center. What the government actually specifies for most industries is a series of wage scales showing a basic daily pay rate for workers in each of a number of skill categories. But these scales do not actually define wages very precisely. A worker can be shifted from one category to another in order to vary his earnings. Moreover, 75 percent of all industrial workers in Soviet industry are paid on a piecework basis and the pay specified in the fixed wage scale is for fulfilling the piecework norm by 100 percent. Since the setting of the piecework norms themselves is an enterprise function, it is always possible to vary the norms so that actual earnings are above or below the specified daily rate. In certain other directions, such as between piece workers and time workers or between branches of the economy, the restrictions are probably more effective. But even to the extent that the government does succeed in imposing a planned wage pattern, its objectives are similar to those of the capitalist labor market. The most thorough study of Soviet wage-setting policy which has been made to date concludes, on the basis of data relating to the thirties, that Soviet wage differentials approximate those in a capitalist economy and that "the principles of relative wages in the Soviet Union are also capitalist principles." [3] Therefore, the presumption is that with respect to this factor of production, quantitatively the most important input in any economy, price varies in proportion to productivity. The relative price of labor is a more or less correct measure of national economic sacrifice.

The absolute level of wages, on the other hand, appears at first glance to be above the actual worth of labor. The amount which state enterprises pay out to the population in the form of wages far exceeds the factor cost of the goods which the planners allocate to provide for the sustenance of the population. This divergence, however, does not imply any irrationality in the price of labor from the point of view of the regime. Since surplus value is the most important resource of the regime and the planners want it husbanded carefully, they should make a charge for it against any user of labor. When it comes to the point of implementing this objective in terms of concrete pricing methods, the state has the choice of two possibilities. The first would be to set the average wage rate so that the aggregate money incomes of the workers would just suffice to cover the outlays of enterprises on the production of consumer goods. Surplus value could then be included in cost by a separate explicit charge levied on payrolls against all the users of labor. The second alternative would be to set the average wage rate at a level so that the aggregate incomes of workers would be adequate to buy all the final output of the economy. It would then be necessary to extract the monetary equivalent of surplus value from the workers by some other means.

The Russians have chosen the second method and equate purchasing power of the population to the factor cost of consumption by means of the fiscal devices described above. These two alternatives are completely identical in terms of the wage-rate pattern which each would set, and so from the point of view of cost accounting it matters not at all which one is used. It should be obvious that in this aspect of their accounting the Russians in the head office do a reasonably effective job in the sense that all the charges which generate this portion of income are sooner or later charged against the households. Accuracy in this part of the accounting is compelled by the fact that this is a market relationship rather than an administrative relationship. Failure to equate charges against households with the real income realized by exploitation of households would lead to financial disequilibrium with repressed inflation, erosion of incentives, and many other obvious difficulties. The weakness of their accounting here, however, is that they do not collect surplus value and add these charges into the price system just at the point where transactions are made with house-holds. Rather, I suspect that much of it is collected further back in the production process in the form of turnover tax and profits on the output of intermediate producers. The result is a distortion of the cost system.

Overhead costs. The Russians have done their best to eliminate the problem of overhead costs incurred at the level of the head office. From the accounting point of view, Soviet organizational history can be interpreted as a process of trial-and-error search for a way to move cost accounting out of the head office and into firms, to avoid accounting for outlays as general overheads in favor of their precise assignment to the output involved. The principle of khozraschet, by making individual units financially independent, also made it possible for cost accounting to be largely decentralized. At the same time, this device has limitations and may not always work effectively as a cost allocator, as we shall see below.

For accounting, khozraschet has a dual purpose. It not only makes it possible practically to charge costs to the appropriate activity; it also to some degree substitutes a market mechanism for an accounting determination in the valuation of flows. This point can be illustrated with the case of research organizations. Research is a classic example of an overhead expenditure — difficult to allocate because its benefits are so diffuse and unpredictable. The Russians have accordingly established research as a function of the head office — if not precisely at the center, still at a fairly high level in the administrative hierarchy. This status means that it is most conveniently financed from the budget and its outlays are reflected in the cost system through overhead charges. In recent years, however, the Russians have found deficiencies in this approach. Research organizations are said to be too independent, too unresponsive to the needs of producers, and so there has been an effort recently to convert research to a khozraschet basis. This involves reducing the amount of financing by the budget and requiring research organizations to pay their own way by charging the beneficiaries for services rendered. This improves cost calculation because the cost of research is now included in the cost of appropriate output. At the same time, it replaces administrative decisions about the use of resources and accounting determination of the value of output with something like a market relationship. The purchaser of research services now has to evaluate the services to determine whether they are worth the cost, or he must ask how the services might be made more useful. Thus khozraschet both puts economic calculation at a lower level and concurrently provides cost data on which this calculation can be based.

On the other hand, there are dangers in trying to be too precise in the allocation of cost through khozraschet. If the benefits from some outlay are, in fact, rather widely spread, then carrying khozraschet in cost allocation too far will cause trouble. This is illustrated by recent decisions on the accounting for product-development expenditures. Until recently, development outlays made at the level of the enterprise were accounted for under very strict regulation. Because of some control problems, discussed in a later chapter, the general principle was that these expenditures had to be charged to output over relatively short periods, usually two years or less. This procedure has come in for a great deal of criticism recently in the Soviet discussion of the obstacles to technological progress.[4] In the Soviet administrative system, producers have very short time horizons. Both producers and users of new equipment focus on the immediate period, and this overprecise allocation of outlays to the early portion of the stream of output which benefits from them hinders the introduction of new technology. The suppliers are reluctant to undertake new kinds of production which would involve high cost even temporarily, and the users may conclude that the economic case for the new equipment is weak.

To overcome this problem, a new scheme has been instituted in which a tax is levied by some higher organ (now usually the *sovnarkhoz*, or territorial administrative body) on the appropriate enterprises (usually machine-building enterprises).[5] Development costs are then charged to this account rather than directly to specific new outputs. This can be thought of as a case where the cost accounting was generating a concept of cost irrelevant to the kind of decision involved. The decision to produce new equipment should take account of the development expenditures required. But once a decision has been taken, it would be foolish to let those costs discourage further action. Product-development outlays must be covered somehow, but it is important that they be distributed in some more or less neutral fashion so that they do not bias the price structure in a way that frustrates execution of a decision.

It should also be recognized that in particular cases khozraschet can be formulated in a way that is satisfactory from the administrative point of view but not necessarily from the point of view of reasonable allocation of costs. The Gosbank is a case in point. The Gosbank is essentially an organ of administration in the Soviet economy. It combines planning, recordkeeping, and control functions much like those which the Ministry of Finance, the Central Statistical Administration, and the Gosplan also perform. Unlike those institutions, however, which are supported out of the budget, the Gosbank is a khozraschet organization financed by charges against enterprises. The reason for the difference is an interesting question in itself, but the relevant point here is that Gosbank charges do not really allocate this part of overhead on any reasonable basis. Most of the work of the Gosbank is essentially the settling of transactions, which it does for all organizations, but its income arises predominately from charges made for short-term credit accommodations given to a relatively limited group of firms.

There is also a very interesting case where outlays, even though made by the higher office rather than by the purchaser, are still recorded in the cost accounts of the purchaser. There was a decade of the postwar period in which the Russians financed directly from the budget the organizations which draw up the specifications, blueprints, cost estimates, and so on, for new projects. The purchaser, accordingly, did not see these as costs of a project to be met out of his investment funds. Nevertheless, when the finished facility was valued for the balance sheet of the organization operating the facility, these costs were included. This case serves as a reminder that the allocation of costs for determination of value tags need not be the same as the allocation that is most desirable for purposes of measuring and controlling performance. This is a technique which the Russians could probably use much more than they do.

In the end, of course, however carefully the Russians try to allocate costs by the principle of khozraschet, they will always find some activities that can be performed effectively only by the head office or some other organization above the level of the enterprise. And usually these will have to be financed out of the budget. Their benefits are so general as to be unassignable, and their outlays are accordingly charged in the first instance to general overhead rather than to specific industries or classes of output. The main consideraton in this allocation ought to be to spread outlays widely. The rationale is not so much that each good is responsible for some of the overhead, but rather that overhead distribution should not be allowed to distort the structure of costs that *are* allocable. At a minimum, this means that all outputs should be charged some overhead — either by an explicit charge or by being priced high enough to earn some profit. But this is a principle which the Russians have never explicitly acknowledged or espoused.

Producer surpluses. Producer surplus is an economic rather than an accounting concept, and one would not expect the Soviet accountants in the head office to distinguish this element of income or to be concerned with how the corresponding charges should be reflected in the cost system. Furthermore, since Marxist value theory (with the one exception discussed below) denies the validity of the concept altogether, there is no reason for Soviet economic theoreticians to amend the deficiencies of the accountants' view. In conformity with the labor theory of value, during most of the Soviet period there has been no charge for the use of capital or for the use of land. It is common practice for Russian investment planners to use some form of interest charge in deciding on the degree of capital intensity of a given project, but with a few minor exceptions no charge for capital is included as an element of accounting cost or as a charge to be included in price. Marxist value theory is somewhat vague with respect to differential land rent, and there are a few cases in the Soviet economy where an explicit rent charge is made. These include rents for timber, for ubiquitous construction materials, and for peat. In the case of timber, the charge is the stumpage fee which is said to be varied in such a way as to extract differential rent.[6] Actually this fee is quite small and does not even cover the cost of forest management, but the variation in accordance with differential productivity is said to be a fact. Apparently at the time of the 1949 price increases, it was intended to make the stumpage fee a real charge for differential rent. But under the 1950 reductions in prices, the fee was sharply reduced as one method of reducing lumber prices and (nominal) construction costs. The rent charge made for peat and for ubiquitous construction materials, such as gravel and building stone, is supposed to have the same characteristic of variation in accordance with differential productivity.

The question we are to consider here is whether or to what extent the turnover tax and the cost-price residuals are in practice set to extract producer surpluses. To anticipate my conclusion, the Russians are often led by some administrative consideration to add a charge or to set a price above the average cost of producers for the purpose of extracting a surplus.

In the case of petroleum, for example, a high turnover tax can be interpreted as an implicit charge for rent. The cost per calorie of producing petroleum and petroleum products is so much below that for coal and other substitute fuels that, if these costs were taken directly as a basis for economic calculations, the demand for petroleum products would far exceed the supply. Cost calculations alone would have encouraged Russian decision makers to use petroleum as fuel in many places where they now use coal. The discrepancy between cost and "value" is so obvious here that the price setters could not ignore it. In this case, as in many others, Marxist conceptions of value are offset by another traditional Soviet bias, inspired by the engineering mind. The high price for oil is often rationalized as necessary to forestall "inefficient" decisions about the use of oil, in particular to forestall burning oil under boilers. The source of this idea is that, since the thermal efficiency of internal-combustion engines is above that of many steam engines, petroleum fuel should be used only in the former and the price should be set so high as to discourage its use for boilers.[7]

A recent book on pricing mentions some interesting uses of the turnover tax to make the use of alternative raw materials a matter of indifference to producers.[8] On the basis of procurement costs alone (these are the arbitrary prices at which the state acquires output from the agricultural sector), it used to be advantageous for vegetable-oil mills to use sunflower seed and cotton seed rather than other oil-bearing seeds. The producers were reluctant to process other oil-bearing seeds since this would raise their cost. To remedy this, part of the turnover tax was removed from vegetable oil and levied instead on the sale of sunflower and cotton seeds. Through extraction of the economic surplus associated with use of the superior raw material, the producers were confronted with prices that encouraged them to conform to the prior decision concerning input mix.

In the alcohol industry, two raw materials, potatoes and grain, were priced at very different levels. This made it difficult to persuade producers to use both materials as planned and also made it difficult to interpret cost performance by the enterprises in this industry. The level of cost in a given enterprise was determined more by the proportions of the two raw materials than by the technical efficiency of its operations. Both these problems were remedied by use of a turnover tax set to extract the surplus.

In the case of cost-price residuals, the rate of profit in the Soviet economy has traditionally been extremely heterogeneous. The Russians have never simply marked up all goods by a fixed percentage over the accounting cost. This point can be illustrated by Table 1, which lists the planned rates of profit for a number of branches of the economy in 1938. (Such information for the postwar period is not available in the same systematic form, but we know that there still exists great variation in the markup rates.) What are the Russians trying to accomplish by such a differentiated markup rate? What is their rationale for setting prices to earn very high profits for some products and to cause losses for others?

Much of the heterogeneity in profit rates flows from an inability to foresee cost movements at the time prices are set. The prices set by the accountants of the head office are usually intended to remain in effect for an extended period of time.

TABLE 1. RATES OF PROFIT OR LOSS IN SELECTED INDUSTRIES PLANNED FOR 1938

Industry	Percent	Industry	Percent
Electric power	26.3	Automobiles	39.2
Special steel	14.2	Tractors	151.0
Chemicals	21.5	River shipbuilding	3.7
Dyes	18.0	Diesel engines	4.6
Plastics	26.6	Motorcycles and	
Ferrous metallurgy	4.9	bicycles	41.2
Steel pipe	3.1	Machine tools	4.6–5.3
Iron-ore mining	1.1	Metal products	
Aluminum	2.7	Machinery repair	28.2
Coal	Loss	Agricultural machinery	3.7
Peat	Loss	Timber haulage	2.4
Lead	Loss	Construction materials	.5
Nickel	Loss	Cement	.3
Gold	Loss	Wood products	9.1
Petroleum[a]	27.1	Rubber products	3.7
Abrasives	29.4	Rubber footwear	200.0
Electrical machinery	27.4	Automobile tires	−30.0

[a] 1937 plan.

Source. L. Vilenski, "Finansovye voprosy promyshlennosti," *Planovoe khozyaystvo,* no. 10, 1938. The percentage given is the ratio of the profit or loss to the cost of output. The figures relate to glavki, which may produce a number of products in addition to the one from which they take their name. Accordingly, there may be further differentiation of the profit or loss rate on commodities within the individual glavki.

If these prices are to fulfill their function as standards to be used in accounting, it is a great convenience that they remain stable over several planning and accounting periods. Soviet central planners deal with highly aggregated magnitudes and, unless prices remain stable, they are uncertain of the relationships between these value aggregates and the physical magnitudes they represent. Moreover, because of the interdependence of prices, price changes usually involve simultaneous adjustments of prices over a large part of the economic system. In a market economy, this problem is taken care of continuously and automatically by the market behavior of individual buyers and sellers, but in the Soviet system an overhaul of the price system presents a large administrative problem. Moreover, the planners have no assurance that, once prices are changed throughout the whole system, the new set of prices will actually be very close to actual costs.[9] Finally, price changes are very disruptive to control and planning. It is much more difficult to control costs in enterprises if the managers are always able to plead increases in prices as the cause of rising costs. It also greatly complicates the work of cost planning, investment planning, and other kinds of financial planning if the plans have to be reworked constantly to take account of price changes. The freezing of these standards by the head office for fairly long periods inevitably means that they depart more and more from actual costs as essentially unpredictable and random cost changes occur.

One could make out a strong case that, given the nature of the Soviet economy, the resulting cost-price residuals are indeed surpluses (or losses) and that their inclusion in the internal cost-accounting system is not inappropriate. In the first accounting period, obviously the high profits or the resource saving on some good, relative to original expectations, are clearly a windfall or a surplus. In an important sense, moreover, they *continue* to be a surplus for a number of consecutive accounting periods. It takes a while for the surprised planners at the top to grasp the idea that conditions have changed so as to falsify their expectations. Even when they have acknowledged this change, they are incapable of marshaling the forces of the economy quickly to take advantage of it. When it turns out that some material is cheaper relative to another than was assumed at the time the standards were set, the Soviet system is not easily capable of redrawing plans and reorienting lower-level administrators to the new perspective. It is a clumsy system with poor capabilities for diffusing or assimilating a new view of the terms on which alternatives are being offered and for reacting to changes in possibilities.

Unexpected price changes are only one explanation of the highly differentiated price-cost residuals. The Russians also consciously attempt to differentiate the markup rate at the time prices are set. Although there is considerable discussion of price policy in Soviet economic literature, most of it is not very enlightening. Many of the discussions never get beyond such broad generalities as "price is a weapon used to achieve the ends of the state" or "in determining prices on separate kinds of goods and services, the Soviet state, proceeding from the general tasks of economic policy, permits divergence of prices from value, setting the price higher or lower than cost." [10] But some more concrete discussions of the problems of price setting reveal some clues to the thinking of the Russians about how the markup rate should be determined. They sometimes speak of the unity and internal consistency of the system of prices,[11] but they lack a general theory of pricing and in actual practice seem to be thoroughly eclectic in the choice of pricing criteria. Despite this confusion, however, their price setting often reveals a sensitivity to the kind of considerations that American economists would consider relevant. It is said that in the 1949 price reform the price of electric power was raised from average branch cost plus 5 percent profit to average branch cost plus 8 percent profit, specifically for the purpose of permitting most producers to earn a profit or at least break even.[12] Another writer says that the same consideration lies behind the relatively high markup in light industry compared to that in heavy industry; there is greater cost variation among enterprises in the former.[13] In both cases the motive behind the policy is a desire to eliminate losses, and thus improve the effectiveness of khozraschet, but the result is to include producer surpluses in prices.

Price manipulations are often justified as a way of enforcing some prior decision. According to one writer, prices for a series of truck models should be set so that price rises less rapidly than capacity. He argues that the cost per ton-kilometer of haulage falls with increases in truck capacity, so that the price should be manipulated to encourage the use of bigger trucks.[14] The same writer suggests that the price of replacement parts and of new machines should be manipulated to encourage repair rather than replacement. These arguments have a provocative implication. They suggest that planners at a high level can arrive at the right decision on some issue of allocation but that, through some defect in administrative efficiency, those who are to fulfill the decision at a lower level would calculate the outcome differently and would also have enough maneuverability to frustrate the planned outcome. If this were indeed the situation, it would make sense to juggle prices to offset the biases of the executors of the decision and so make it enforceable. In these particular cases, however, it seems more likely that the central decision is unenforceable without price juggling only because it is a wrong decision. The central planners' decision in favor of large-capacity trucks overlooks the fact that many users cannot fully utilize such trucks.[15] In the case of repair, it is now recognized, even in the Soviet Union, that there is already too much repair relative to replacement. The cart has been put before the horse. Having taken decisions which ignored the question of cost, the planners must then distort the picture of real costs to enforce the decision.

Finally, there is often an implication in discussions of price policy that the markup rate should be varied between branches in such a way that each branch will be able to earn enough profit to finance the expected expansion in working capital and a large share of the expected investment in fixed assets.[16] The need for fixed investment and working capital to expand output in the future is clearly not a cost of current output. The Russians are assigning the price system the task of distributing and earmarking funds in addition to its role of indicating costs and values, without realizing that these two functions may be contradictory. This idea concerning the role of price seems to be characteristic of Soviet economic thought; the notion that accumulation is an element of cost is frequently found in discussions of value.[17]

Conclusion

The foregoing discussion carries several implications for any attempt to understand and evaluate Soviet cost accounting as a source of data for economic calculation. Clearly, it is impossible to treat the question of whether this system generates adequate measures of value in isolation from all other aspects of administration. The presence of tremendous administrative friction means that "value" in the Soviet economy may often depart from the normative concept. The Soviet system is a ponderous one with great limitations on the ability of managers to envisage alternatives, to discriminate among them, and to give effective orders based on the decisions taken concerning these alternatives. Accordingly, there is no need to try for a degree of finesse in cost accounting which assumes more perceptive and reactive sensitivity than the system actually possesses. For example, I suspect that the price tag which the system has placed on petroleum over most of Soviet history has been higher than it should be in a properly functioning economy. From their position at the top, Soviet planners should have been able to make petroleum less scarce and expensive than they told their decision makers it was. At the same time, however, if one considers why the Russians failed to make oil cheaper and more abundant, it appears that the Soviet system of administration and planning was incapable of getting oil found and produced, because the responsible planners were unable to comprehend the advantages of finding the oil or because they were not able to convey this information to the authorities or because the authorities were unable to get their directives carried out. Given this impotence, oil was more valuable than a mere adding up of resource inputs would imply, and so perhaps the large turnover tax placed on it had a rationale.

One can easily understand why evolution has not provided the human organism with an optical system that could discriminate bacteria — they cannot be swatted as mosquitoes can. This is not just a facetious analogy. It suggests how one ought to approach the Soviet national cost-accounting system and, indeed, how the Russians themselves approach it. The economist tends to evaluate Soviet costing and pricing on the basis of an assumption that the theory of value derived to explain the market system is universally valid, that the Soviet system for generating these value tags should generate the same kind of values. If it is pointed out that the Soviet economy is not designed to react fully to any such system of values, his defense is that the economy should be redesigned so as to validate the concept. Figuratively, he is saying that a "good" optical system would enable us to see bacteria and that we ought to be reorganized so that we could swat them.

Men with an accounting background would probably take a rather different view. They would be inclined to recognize the validity of more than one set of value indices for economic decision making, depending on the purpose in hand, and would be concerned with devising a system for the flow of information such that each decision maker within the system received a set of value tags appropriate to the particular decisions he had to make. On the basis of an analogy with the large capitalist firm, he would be prepared to accept transfer prices as accounting conventions and would not be worried that they were invalid for some purposes. He would be less concerned to perfect them than to see that the appropriate kind of cost data *was* made available to those who ignore accounting convention in favor of rationality.

I suspect that neither of these two conceptions is quite adequate. To some extent, the Russians already follow the accountant's conception. There are many cases in which Russian decision makers cheerfully disregard the prices which their system generates in favor of other measures of value. Probably the best known case is the use of "coefficients of deficitness" used in planning calculations to discourage the use of scarce materials.[18] By the use of such coefficients, the planner builds into his calculations the assumption that steel, say, is really three times as costly as its price tag indicates. In making decisions about the allocation of freight among carriers and the relative economic advantage of different forms of transportation, the Russians have made special studies to correct the costs of these services as determined by conventional cost accounting.[19] In such recalculations, they add in charges which were not covered in the traditional accounting and remove some price-forming elements which were included. The examples which the Russians have described impress one as rather crude, but the new Soviet infatuation with mathematical economics may well make them much more sophisticated. Some have proposed that, for purposes of calculation, they bypass the system of transfer prices in favor of a new set of value indices calculated in the head office by input-output techniques.[20] In effect, this proposal would recentralize the internal cost accounting, at least as far as economic calculation was concerned, though the transfer

4 6

prices might still be accepted as the accounting conventions in enterprise cost accounting. There are even some hints that this centralized costing procedure might include charges for capital and rent, and some of the proposals imply the simulation of market behavior to include demand considerations in the setting of the values.

The economist is right, however, in his suspicion that there are limitations on how far one can differentiate systems of value indices and keep the attention of each executive focused on the set of prices that is appropriate to each decision. Any set of prices is extremely pervasive in its impact, and it is very difficult to limit its use to only one kind of decision. The Russians have already had one disastrous experience along these lines. The use of the fixed prices of 1926–27 was supposed to be limited to the problem of aggregating output for the construction of an output index to be used by external controllers. In fact, however, it got mixed up with decision making within the firm and ultimately had an unhealthy impact on decisions about output mix, industrial organization, and many others.

The economist's suspicion is also borne out by the recent discussion of the theory of value. Led by an economist and a mathematician, the Russians are beginning to emancipate themselves from the simple cost theory of value which Marx left them. L. V. Kantorovich, the mathematician, and V. V. Novozhilov, the economist, have approached the theory of value and economic calculation from different directions, but both have shown that value is explained not only by the amount of labor embodied in a commodity but also by its productivity or utility.[21] They have also clarified the question of value as it interacts with the question of resource allocation. In their vision of how the new theory of value and allocation can be used to improve the operation of the economy, they do not see the central planners taking the quantity variables generated by such a system of calculation and instructing everyone what to do. Instead they say that one of the greatest virtues of a theoretically correct set of value indices is that it will at last make khozraschet work perfectly. Once all decision makers from top to bottom have proper value indices to which they can refer decisions, it will be possible to specify rules of behavior which will lead each decision maker to act in a way that is consistent with the national optimum.

DEPRECIATION ACCOUNTING:

A GENERAL DESCRIPTION

THERE ARE few practical or theoretical difficulties in accounting for certain kinds of costs. Direct labor costs and material costs, for instance, are easily determined, and the accounting periods and the individual products to which they are assignable are usually self-evident. Other kinds of costs present the accountant with much more difficult problems. This chapter is concerned with one such problem: the costs of capital consumption. Fixed assets such as buildings, structures, and machinery supply productive services over a long period of time, and so it is necessary to make some allocation of their costs over a number of accounting periods. It is necessary to estimate somehow how much of their cost should be attributed to producing the output of a given accounting period. Also, because fixed assets have long service lives, their value is subject to change through changes in the general price level and through obsolescence. The determination of the value of fixed assets and the allocation of this value over time present complex theoretical problems.

These allocations are usually made by depreciation charges.

The original cost of fixed assets (or some other measure of their value) is distributed over successive accounting periods at a rate that is intended to assign fully their cost to the output produced during their useful life. Soviet accounting uses a similar device in its amortization deductions (*amortizatsionnye otchisleniya*). These are very much like the depreciation charges of capitalist accounting, but differ in that they are intended to recover not only the value of an asset but the costs of major repair on it as well. The purpose of this chapter is to describe Soviet depreciation practice and to make some judgment about the appropriateness of Soviet depreciation charges.

The Rationale of Soviet Depreciation Charges

Since depreciation charges can serve a variety of purposes, it is important to make clear what the Russians think they are trying to accomplish by their depreciation accounting. Otherwise we shall lack proper criteria for evaluating Soviet practice. In the abstract, two different purposes might be distinguished for which estimates of depreciation are commonly employed. (1) The first is to determine the income of production organizations. In the background there is always some question of equity or of the relation of a given unit to the rest of society. The problem may be the determination of taxable income, preventing the distribution of capital as dividends, or recovering from the rest of society enough resources to replace fixed assets when they wear out. Controversies about depreciation accounting in the United States most often involve this kind of problem. (2) To a lesser degree, depreciation accounting is used for purposes of internal calculation within the firm. Decision makers want some idea of costs of individual kinds of output inclusive of capital consumption for pricing and output decisions. These two purposes are closely interrelated but differ in the degree of aggregation.

In the Soviet economy, determination of enterprise income loses most of the importance it has in capitalist economies. Since the firm is not fully independent financially, its income constitutes only a vague constraint on its access to resources, few decisions turn on it, and whether it is positive or negative is not of overriding importance. This semidependent financial status is reflected in depreciation accounting in the following way. As stated earlier, the depreciation charge in the Soviet economy involves two components: a charge intended to recover the value of the asset over its useful life and a charge to accumulate resources for intermittent major repair of the asset. (The Russians call the latter capital repair. For a full explanation of the term and how it is reflected in the accounting, see Chapter 4.) The portion of the charge destined to recover the value of the asset is not left under the control of the enterprise but is centralized as one of the incomes of the head office. It is merged into a central pool of investment resources. The distribution of this pool of resources between replacement and new investment, between firms, and between sectors of the economy is made by the head office — that issue is not left to be decided by depreciation charges.

The other part of the depreciation charge, intended to generate funds for the financing of capital repair, was long treated in the same way. Until 1938 these funds were extracted from the enterprise along with the funds for replacement, and capital repair was financed from centralized sources. The defect of that system was that enterprises lost the ability and incentive to take responsibility for capital repair, and in 1938 the procedure was changed to leave the capital-repair funds within the enterprises. Under this system it is intended that the repair needs of the enterprise will be met out of self-accumulated resources.[1] Even today, financial self-sufficiency in capital repair is far from an ironclad rule in practice. The resources which an enterprise accumulates in this way may be supplemented by transfers from the central pool, and in other cases they may be extracted from the enterprise and redistributed. It is broadly true, however, that in respect to capital repair the concept of enterprise income has some relevance. It is considered administratively desirable to have enterprises finance capital repair out of their own earmarked resources, and depreciation accounting should accordingly be organized to achieve fairly close equality between needs and resources.

At the level of the head office, of course, the concept of income does mean something, and estimates of depreciation may be necessary for determination of income at that level. But there is little evidence that this has been the dominant consideration in organizing depreciation accounting in the Soviet economy. If an estimate of depreciation were needed only for the purpose of determining net income for the economy as a whole, that could be done much more simply by a few entries made in the national income accounts. More fundamentally, there is little need to distinguish between gross and net income at the level of the head office. Covering depreciation is not an operational constraint since the Russian planners are not really bound to replace specific assets that wear out. There is no analytical distinction separating the problems of investment in replacement and investment in new capacity.

Conceivably the planners in the head office might be able to use depreciation information for specific kinds of assets in planning the output of capital goods. For example, in planning the supply and demand balance for trucks, they might want to know how many old ones will be scrapped and, therefore, how much of the gross output of trucks must be committed to replacement. But depreciation charges in value terms are too vague to be of much help in this kind of calculation, and even if depreciation information were usable at all for this purpose (if there were no difference between replacement and depreciation, for example), the calculations would have to be made in physical terms. Soviet planners sometimes speak of the usefulness of depreciation accounting for this kind of planning calculation, but I see little evidence of their doing much with it in actual practice.

Soviet depreciation accounting has been influenced by considerations of controlling and evaluating managerial behavior only to a very slight extent. Depreciation is treated in accounting as a cost over which enterprise management has no control. The charge is determined by application of a rate assigned from above to a stock of assets assigned and valued from outside, and it is invariable with respect to managerial actions. Since it is a fixed cost, it provides some incentive for the enterprise manager to increase output to minimize unit costs of depreciation, but it is not arranged in any way to encourage him to conserve the capital allotted to him. As will be explained later, management is never penalized by a poor showing on cost performance for failing to make assets serve out the lives envisaged in the depreciation rates. Even if he incurs much more capital consumption and capital repair than can be covered by the depreciation charges, the difference is never included in his cost reports or even in his profit and loss accounts.

My conclusion, then, is that in the Soviet setting depreciation charges are retained as part of enterprise accounting less for purposes of income determination and distribution, and more for cost-accounting purposes, than in the capitalist economy. The accountants of the head office recognize capital consumption as a real cost, differentiated by firms, sectors, and products; and they want this cost included in their internal cost-accounting system. Soviet discussions of depreciation accounting are not always necessarily consistent with this interpretation. Some writers imply that there is no need for depreciation on individual assets or for individual firms to be an accurate measure of capital consumption, as long as enough depreciation is charged in the economy as a whole. It is the national-income accounting objective which is paramount. Furthermore, one recent book proposes that there be a uniform rate of depreciation applied to all assets in the economy, set at a level that would generate enough funds to finance all capital investment.[2] However, the real intention of that suggestion is to introduce a charge for capital into the Soviet accounting system, although the change is offered for doctrinal reasons under the label of amortization. This is fairly clear since the author starts out by saying that one of the main deficiencies in the present system is that depreciation charges on very long-lived assets, such as hydroelectric stations, are too small to reveal the true costs of the output produced by them.

But ignoring these diversions, and looking at the whole history of action and commentary on depreciation accounting, it seems clear that depreciation accounting has always been intended primarily as a way of including costs of capital consumption in the cost-accounting system. It is against this standard, accordingly, that Soviet practice should be measured.

The Valuation of Fixed Assets

The first requisite for the determination of the costs of capital consumption is the correct valuation of the fixed assets which are to be depreciated. For a number of reasons, fixed assets in the Soviet economy have generally been valued in the enterprise accounts at less than their real worth. Consequently, even if the rates at which these assets are depreciated reflect their service lives accurately, the depreciation charge will be less than an adequate indication of the cost of capital consumption.

The most general cause underlying the inadequacy of the book values of fixed assets has been persistent price-level changes which have made replacement costs of assets far different from the historical cost at which they are shown on the books. From the theoretical point of view, it is the replacement cost which should be considered for purposes of cost accounting. The costs relevant to economic decision making are opportunity costs, and, if price changes lead to a situation where book values differ from replacement costs, it is the latter which measure real costs in the framework of existing scarcity relationships. Until about 1950 a continuing inflation led to a steady rise in the costs of investment goods and construction. There is not yet available any definitive index of the changes in investment costs in the Soviet economy for these years, but there can be no doubt that it has been a serious inflation. It has been estimated on the basis of very detailed study of prices of investment goods that costs of investment had risen by 1950 to almost six times what they had been in 1928.[3] Since 1950 the costs of investment have declined. Together with the fact that the absolute levels of investment have risen greatly over the period of the five-year plans, this means that undervaluation of the capital stock as a whole by the end of the fifties was not particularly large. According to one authority, the commonly accepted estimate among Soviet economists around 1957 was that the value of the fixed assets of the Soviet economy at replacement costs would be approximately one third more than the value shown on the books.[4] A much more serious problem is the heterogeneity which this extreme variation in the price level has caused in the valuation of similar assets. As an extreme example, one author mentions the case of a Moscow machinebuilding plant that had on its books before the 1960 revaluation two more or less identical lathes, one valued at 1,800 rubles and the other at 22,000 rubles.[5]

Soviet accountants and economists have usually recognized the desirability of basing depreciation charges on the replacement costs of assets rather than on the original purchase costs. For instance, L. M. Kantor, one of the most competent Soviet authorities on accounting, says in a discussion of depreciation policy that "the method of valuation of fixed assets at replacement value is in principle the very best and most correct method." [6] Moreover, the Russians have acted on this belief. Aware that the use of historical costs was leading to errors in cost accounting, they have from time to time carried out revaluations of fixed assets in certain areas of the economy. Until that of 1960, these revaluations have generally been limited in scope, and even in the areas of the economy covered the newly established values have been outmoded fairly rapidly by continuing inflation. The first revaluation of assets was made in the twenties in connection with the establishment of a new currency.[7] Book values of assets in existence previously had been expressed in prerevolutionary rubles, in the depreciating currency of the period of War Communism, and in the chervonets ruble introduced in 1922. The aim was to bring some uniformity into the valuation of these existing assets. Two important stocks of assets were involved. All the fixed assets of large-scale industry in existence prior to 1923 were inventoried in 1925 and were revalued at reproduction cost as of October 1925.[8] The fixed assets of the railroads were also revalued in 1925, but this revaluation was considered unsatisfactory and another was made in the years 1928–31. The results of the second revaluation were shown on the books but were not judged to be completely satisfactory, and still another revaluation was made in 1935. The 1935 revaluation was completely rejected, and apparently the results of the 1928–31 calculation remained on the books.[9]

Inflation during the period of the first two five-year plans, and the consequent divergence of book values from replacement values, again raised the question of a general revaluation;

in the years just before World War II, a second series of revaluations was begun.[10] Apparently it was intended to revalue
all the fixed assets of the state sector and of the collective farms,
but because of the outbreak of the war only a small portion
of this program was actually completed. The assets revalued
at this time included (1) those of the People's Commissariat of
Agriculture, (2) the state housing fund and other urban buildings and the buildings owned by collective farms and private
persons, (3) the fixed assets of the People's Commissariat of
Fishing Industry, (4) the fixed assets of the People's Commissariat of Communications. A new revaluation of the fixed assets
of the railroads was also made at this time, but it differed from
those in the other sectors of the economy in that it was never
reflected on the books of the railroads.[11] The program of an
economy-wide revaluation was not taken up again at the end
of the war, but fixed assets in the regions which had been
occupied by the Germans were inventoried and revalued as the
areas were retaken.[12] The new values were figured in terms of
the prices and norms of 1941. The revaluation seems to have
covered all the fixed assets of the state sector, whatever the
branch involved. In view of the fact that the area occupied by
the Germans had included something like one third of the fixed
assets of the economy before the war, this must have been quite
an extensive revaluation.[13] Finally, in 1960 there was an inventory and estimation of current values for nearly all the assets
of the economy (discussed below).

A second factor leading to understatement of the real costs
of fixed assets is the arbitrary nature of the Soviet procedures
for valuing new investment. Furthermore, because the degree
of understatement varies from project to project, these procedures lead to heterogeneity of valuation among different
aggregates of assets. The most important peculiarity in figuring
the cost of new assets is connected with the existence of two

57

alternative administrative systems for carrying out capital investment in the Soviet economy.[14] Under the first, called the own-account method (*khozyaystvennyi sposob*), the organization making the investment organizes the work itself: it hires the labor, acquires the construction materials, supervises the work, and so on. Under the second, called the contract method (*podriadnyi sposob*), the work is let on contract to a specialized construction enterprise. Under the own-account method the cost of a finished project is calculated as the sum of the outlays on it and is taken onto the accounts of the operating enterprise at this value. Under the contract method, on the other hand, the amount to be paid for the work is specified in advance in the contract, and it is this price at which the completed project is capitalized. Because of the interpolation of this price link, there arises the possibility of a divergence between the actual outlays on a project and the value at which it is finally shown in the fixed-asset accounts.[15] Under Soviet investment-planning procedures, the contract prices have been determined on the basis of fixed input prices and official input norms, whereas costs to the construction organizations were actually rising. Consequently, the contract construction organizations have generally made large losses and new assets produced under the contract method have been shown on the books at less than the cost of producing them. No attempt can be made here to specify precisely the magnitude of these losses in different years, but it is a commonplace in the literature on the construction industry that the losses are significant.[16] For one year, 1951, the amount of the loss was announced, and it turns out to be something like 4 percent of the volume of work done.[17] Moreover, this average undoubtedly conceals a great variation in the rate of profit or loss for individual construction organizations. Because the output of the construction organizations is so diverse, and because different organizations work under very different conditions, it is extremely difficult to make an objective estimate of what a specific project should cost, even given fixed prices and input norms for some of the major aspects of the work. There is apparently a great deal of arbitrariness in determining the contract prices for individual projects, with the result that some organizations make losses far above the average while others make considerable profits.[18]

Certain kinds of investment outlays, moreover, are never capitalized in the book value of completed assets, no matter what method of construction is used.[19] These include some of the expenses of planning a project, such as drawing up preliminary specifications, geological and engineering studies, legal expenses of getting title to the site, compensation for property destroyed in clearing a site, land surveying; and some of the expenses connected with getting the plant started, such as the cost of training new workers, technical inspection of the plant when it is finished, and maintaining the directorate of the plant during construction. Even taken all together, these expenses make up a fairly small fraction of total investment outlays,[20] but they could be significant in individual cases. For instance, the omission of geological and prospecting studies in the extractive industries must surely result in a significant undervaluation of the enterprises which finally engage in production. In the oil and gas industry, for instance, in 1955, prospecting and drilling costs written off rather than capitalized amounted to 3.226 billion rubles. The reported cost of oil produced in 1955 was only about 3.2 billion rubles.[21] In view of the rapid growth of oil output, it is likely that the amount of reserves added by drilling and prospecting in 1955 was greater than actual 1955 output but, even so, the result is a drastic understatement of the real cost of finding and producing oil.

Another category of investment outlays omitted from the book value of completed assets is outlays on abandoned construction and expenses connected with a change in the design of a plant. The Russians consider these losses rather than costs and so do not capitalize them. To the extent that they are indeed unforeseeable losses, this treatment of them is unobjectionable, but it is said that there is a tendency to write off in this way expenses other than real losses so that the reported cost of construction is kept down. Such a practice is also strongly suggested by the warnings in the auditing books to be alert for such falsifications and by a special order of the Commissariat of Finance issued in 1945 outlining a strict system of control over such writeoffs.[22]

Another peculiarity frequently mentioned by Soviet writers relates to the valuation of imported machinery and equipment in Soviet fixed-asset accounts. Ruble values for such equipment are figured by converting the value of the item in foreign currency into rubles at the official exchange rates.[23] (Until 1960 this was four rubles to the dollar. It is now ninety kopecks to the dollar. Other curriencies are assigned exchange rates proportionate to their value relative to the dollar.) But it seems likely that the ratios of the internal Soviet prices for various kinds of machinery to prices of similar foreign machines are widely dispersed around the official exchange rate. This has been clearly shown for Soviet-American comparisons in a study of the ruble-dollar price ratios made by the RAND Corporation;[24] presumably, comparisons with the prices of other countries would show the same general kind of results. Thus an imported machine is often given a ruble value far different from the value of a similar domestic machine. An appreciable portion of the equipment and machinery on the books of Soviet enterprises must be foreign machinery. There are no explicit statistics on the share of imported machinery and equipment in total machinery and equipment assets, but the data on imports of machinery and investment outlays on machinery and equipment for a number of years, shown in Table 2 below, provide

TABLE 2. THE RELATION OF MACHINERY IMPORTS TO INVESTMENT OUTLAYS ON MACHINERY

Year	Value of machinery imports (billion rubles)	Investment outlays on machinery (billion rubles)	Ratio of imports to outlays (percent)
1929	1.115	1.161	100
1930	2.065	1.899	100+
1931	2.473	3.023	81
1932	1.651	3.870	43
1933	.633	3.559	18
1934	.248	5.104	5
1950	1.578	30.9	5.1
1955	3.7	49.4	7.5
1956	3.6	63.0	5.7
1957	3.8	73.0	5.2

Notes and sources. All the prewar figures for imports are from S. N. Bakulin and D. D. Mishustin, *Vneshniaya torgovlia SSSR za 20 let, 1918–1937 gg.* (Moscow, 1939), p. 81. For 1950 there is a statement in TsSU, *Dostizheniya sovetskoi vlasti za 40 let v tsifrakh*, p. 31, that total imports were 5.824 billion rubles, and a statement in TsSU, *Narodnoe khozyaystvo SSSR*, p. 217, that the share of machinery and equipment in total imports was 27.1 percent. The figures for 1955 through 1957 are taken from Ministerstvo Vneshnei Torgovli SSSR, *Vneshniaya torgovlia soyuza SSR za 1956 god*, and from the 1957 version of this same handbook.

The figures for investment outlay on machinery have been culled from much conflicting information. Figures for total investment outlays for 1929 through 1934 is given in Norman Kaplan, *Capital Investments in the Soviet Union, 1924–1951* (Santa Monica, 1951), p. 41. He also gives the share of this total accounted for by outlays on construction. The residual is mostly expenditures for equipment. For 1933 and 1934 the share of equipment in total investment costs is given explicitly in Gosplan SSSR, *Narodno-khozyaystvennyi plan na 1935 god* (2nd ed., Moscow, 1935), p. 309, as 23.3 and 21.2 percent respectively. So we have estimated the outlays on machinery by taking these percentages for 1933 and 1934 and a figure of 20 percent for the earlier years. The postwar figures for outlays on machinery and equipment are taken from *Narodnoe khozyayistvo SSSR v 1956 godu*, pp. 173, 174.

an indirect indication of the relative importance. These figures are far from precise measures of the magnitudes we are interested in. Some of the machinery imports may be military items and other such items that do not go to investment. Similarly, the basis of valuation differs as between the import figures and the investment figures — imports are shown f.o.b. the border of the country of origin, whereas the investment outlays are inclusive of freight and handling charges. And few of these figures are unambiguous — for many of them it is possible to find alternative figures in Soviet sources that may differ considerably. But in any case the general picture is correct. The share of imported machinery and equipment in 1929 and 1930 was extremely high but fell sharply thereafter to something like 5 percent in 1934. In the postwar period imported machinery has remained small in terms of relative importance, but it has by no means been negligible. There is enough foreign machinery in the Soviet stock so that the peculiar approach the Russians use in valuation of this equipment will affect appreciable blocks of assets.

To summarize, throughout most of Soviet history, inflation, piecemeal revaluation, and arbitrary rules in the cost accounting of investment have combined to make the book values of fixed assets in the Soviet economy an inadequate index of their value. Moreover, the degree of this understatement is not uniform for all assets. More or less identical assets might be shown on the books of different enterprises at widely divergent values depending on the year in which they were acquired, whether they were domestic or imported items, whether they were produced under the contract method or the own-account method, and whether they were covered by one of the revaluations. This heterogeneity of valuation has confounded cost accounting, interfered with the provision of funds for capital repair, and made it difficult to compare relative costs and profits in different plants producing a given output. Complaints about these limitations have been repeated again and again in Soviet accounting literature.

To remedy these deficiencies, it was finally decided in the postwar period to undertake a general revaluation of all the fixed assets of the economy. This was first mentioned in 1953, was planned at one time for the end of 1959, and was finally accomplished as of January 1, 1960.[25] The revaluation was extensive in scope, covering the assets of all enterprises in the socialist sector of the economy in which depreciation is calculated (the important omissions were budget organizations and collective farms). Within these enterprises the revaluation embraced all categories of fixed assets except a few negligible elements such as library holdings and tools. Revaluation was not the only objective — fixed assets were also inventoried to ascertain whether book data were accurate in physical coverage. With this kind of approach, it was possible to revalue assets item by item rather than aggregatively by use of price indices.

The revaluation was made by local commissions using centrally produced instructions and price books. The first step was to estimate a replacement value, or "value when new" figure, for assets. Buildings and structures were revalued by the application of gross planning cost norms in current prices (such as cost per cubic meter of space enclosed) to existing assets. These norms were differentiated by type of construction, by regions to allow for variations in the cost of construction, and by other dimensions. In addition, a number of special instructions made it possible to adjust these values for application to nonstandard buildings. For the revaluation of machinery and equipment, handbooks were prepared giving the actual prices for all types of machines currently produced, as well as prescribed values for the most common types not currently produced, and for foreign equipment. Again, for items not covered, local decisions were to be made on the basis of analogy.

In determining replacement values for fixed assets, correction was made for obsolescence. In those cases where obsolescence involved only a difference in capacity, a simple coefficient was all that was needed. An old tractor with less horsepower than a modern one was given a reduced value in proportion to its smaller capacity. Obsolescence may also involve higher operating costs on old machinery relative to new, and in dealing with this problem the Russians showed considerable confusion. An accurate approach would be something like the following. Obsolescence means essentially that the old asset wastes current inputs as compared to the possibilities offered by more modern replacement possibilities. The magnitude of this waste is the measure of obsolescence. Thus, if an old asset is comparable with a new one in all respects except that it costs more to operate, its replacement value might be estimated by subtracting from the value of the modern asset the value of excess resources required in using the obsolete asset over its remaining service life. This is a fairly straightforward, common-sense notion, and several Russians have suggested it as the proper approach in the valuation of obsolete assets.[26] In the actual revaluation, however, the approach was to correct for this kind of obsolescence by means of a coefficient. For example, if the cost per ton-kilometer of transportation in an old truck was one third more than in a new one, the value of the old truck was figured as three fourths that of the new.[27] It is not clear why this formula was used when it is so obviously incorrect. Perhaps the answer is that the correct approach would disclose that many Soviet assets have negative values; the approach actually employed would never give this result. If the valuation procedure were to show such results, the planners would have a puzzling contretemps on their hands.

All assets were to be valued first in terms of their replacement value when new, but the revaluation was also to involve an expert estimate of the actual physical condition of the assets and was to express a judgment as to the percentage of the original value which had been lost through depreciation. The guidance on this issue provided by the instructions was extremely vague and consisted essentially of two recommendations: (1) to estimate remaining service life or degree of depreciation by expert estimate and (2) to compare years of service with some norm of total service life for the kind of asset concerned. The latter approach was probably used for most machinery and equipment, though in individual cases it would be inapplicable, as when past service already exceeded the service norm. For more complex assets, such as machines with many components (for instance, a drilling rig) or buildings, it was recommended that the average for the item be the weighted average of estimates for each of the main components. The application of these principles would have to be extremely subjective, and one may well be suspicious of the estimates of depreciation that were made.

The result of the revaluation was to raise the book value of all assets in the revalued sectors by 12 percent.[28] This is rather less than previous statements about the undervaluation of fixed assets had implied, but it is explained by the assertion that since 1949 the trend of prices has been downward and, in the case of machinery, by the large loss of value due to obsolescence. The impact of the change was quite different as between sectors of the economy and types of assets. For machinery, replacement value in current prices turned out to be about 10 percent less than the value shown on the books, while for buildings the revaluation led to an increase in value of a little over 20 percent. The revaluation reduced somewhat the original book value of assets of industry but increased the value for assets in transportation by nearly a third. The greatest hetero-geneity, however, was that between enterprises. No general data on this subject were published, but it is said that one steel plant had its value raised by 36 percent while the book value of another was reduced by 20 percent.[29] The differentials be-tween enterprises were great enough to cause significant altera-tions in relative cost patterns, at least in those branches where depreciation is a large fraction of total cost, such as the oil industry. It is estimated that as a result of the revaluation the cost per ton of oil produced in the Azerbaidzhan SSR will rise by 11 percent, whereas that in the RSFSR and Turkmen SSR will decline by 7 percent.[30] For individual oilfields, the range would undoubtedly be very much greater.

Another result of the revaluation was to reveal that the fixed assets of the Soviet economy were far more worn out than the amount of depreciation shown on the books would indicate. The revaluation showed an average degree of depreciation for the whole economy of 25 percent, which is twice what the books showed before the revaluation. (More will be said about this result in the next chapter.)

The principle of revaluation has also been extended to the fixed assets of the collective farms, which were inventoried and revalued as of January 1, 1962.[31] For the collective farms, how-ever, the objective is not so much to improve depreciation charges as it is to get fixed assets inventoried and valued so that depreciation will become possible. Up to the present time, col-lective farms have not calculated depreciation on their fixed assets and, indeed, until recently have not even used cost accounting.

Determination of Depreciation Rates

The accuracy of Soviet depreciation charges has been further prejudiced by errors in the determination of the rates of depreciation. The estimation of service lives for fixed assets and the setting of depreciation rates is, in the nature of things, somewhat of a guess in any economy, but some specific features of the Soviet economy have made the depreciation rates used by Soviet enterprises notably inaccurate. First, since the Soviet depreciation rate is intended to cover capital repair in addition to replacement, setting the rates involves a guess about what the general level of these expenditures will be for a fairly long period into the future. Second, in the interests of tighter control, depreciation rates in the Soviet economy are not determined at the enterprise level, as they are in the capitalist economy, but are established centrally and assigned to the enterprise. The result has been a systematic bias in favor of depreciation rates which are too low and great arbitrariness and heterogeneity in the rates assigned to individual enterprises. The method of determining the rates used in individual enterprises will be discussed here, and some statistical evidence is introduced in Chapter 4 to demonstrate that the general level of rates is too low.

Soviet enterprises have always used officially prescribed rates of depreciation. The first official rates were established by a decree of the VSNKh in 1923, and these were later replaced by a more complete set under a decree of 1930.[32] In both cases the decrees set up class rates, that is, separate rates for different kinds of assets set in accordance with differences in the average length of service life. Under this system the individual enterprise determined its depreciation charge by application of the separate rates to the value of each class of fixed assets. Both sets of rates suffered from two deficiencies: the general level of rates was too low and, more important, the asset classes were far too broad to be even approximately homogeneous with respect to service life. Subject to these qualifications, however, the system of class rates permitted the construction of an average rate of depreciation for each individual enterprise which would reflect the structure of its assets.

In 1938 there was a radical change in depreciation policy. Not only was part of the depreciation charge earmarked for capital repair and left in the hands of the enterprise; in addition, the former system of class rates was abandoned in favor of a system of composite rates for separate branches of the economy and for individual enterprises. (By composite rate is meant an average rate for a collection of assets heterogeneous in type and service life.) Under this system the depreciation charge in any given enterprise was calculated by applying to the aggregate value of its fixed assets a single composite rate assigned from above. The composite rates were set in the first instance for entire commissariats (later renamed ministries), and this general composite rate was to be differentiated and passed down through the chain of subordinate units within the commissariat until composite rates for individual enterprises were arrived at. The rates for individual enterprises were to be set so as to take account of differences in asset structure, but the rates for individual enterprises taken together were to be consistent with the composite rate for the commissariat as a whole. It must also be explained that the 1938 composite norms were not simply derived from the 1930 class rates, since the general level of the 1938 rates was higher.[33] Nor has there ever been worked out a new set of class rates corresponding to the 1938 composite rates. In this situation, it was impossible for the commissariat to determine rates for individual plants simply by averaging class rates, and it had somehow to proceed from the top downward in making the differentiation.

The accuracy of the composite rate assigned to a given plant under this system obviously depends on how a commissariat differentiated its composite rate among its constituent enterprises. As long as the composite rates as between commissariats and as between individual enterprises within the commissariats are made to reflect accurately the difference in asset structure (and the associated differences in service life and needs for capital repair), differentiation from the top is as good as aggregation from below. But apparently this condition has not been fulfilled. There are three important deficiencies in the practice of differentiating the norms.

First, at the official level it appears to be recognized that the differentiation should be made so that the final plant rates (in the portion of them that is to cover replacement) reflect differences in the average composite service life in different plants. Technically this could be done simply by increasing all the 1930 class rates proportionately to a level consistent with the 1938 composite rates, and then using the corrected class rates to determine a rate for each enterprise.[34] However, there are numerous suggestions by Soviet writers that as a practical matter the commissariat or glavk, in making the differentiation, may consider not only the relative average service life in individual plants but also the current need for funds for investment in each plant. One writer says specifically that there are frequent cases in which two plants with identical physical assets are assigned different rates since one of them has a larger capital-investment program than the other.[35] Presumably the motivation for such a distortion is that it is easier to get an investment plan approved if it is financed out of local resources than if it has to be financed out of the state budget. To differentiate the rates in this way is clearly incorrect; it completely subverts the purpose of the depreciation charge.

The rates assigned to the lower units might also be distorted to meet the need for funds for capital repair. After 1938 the depreciation rate was really the sum of two percentages, one a rate for replacement and one for capital repair. The costs of capital repair were always in terms of current prices, of course, rather than the prices in which the values of assets were expressed, and because of the inflation older enterprises with undervalued assets were not likely to get enough funds to cover actual needs for capital repair. Because of the extreme heterogeneity in the valuation of assets in different enterprises, the use of rates differentiated on the basis of relative average service lives in different plants would provide capital-repair allowances which were inadequate in the old undervalued enterprises and excessively generous in the new, contemporaneously valued, ones. In an effort to reconcile the funds provided through the amortization deductions with the actual need for capital repairs, it is standard practice for the division of the total rate into a repair rate and a replacement rate to be juggled between sectors and between plants so that old plants have a large share, sometimes all, of the total rate designated as a repair allowance and a small share designated as a replacement allowance. The new plants have rates distorted in the opposite direction. As an indication of how far this distortion may go, in the lumber industry the total rate of 3.9 percent was divided in 1955 into a rate of 3.4 percent for repair and a rate of only .5 percent for replacement.[36] This implies an average service life of two hundred years for the fixed assets of the industry.

Moreover, the heterogeneity of the valuation of assets is said to have been so great that sometimes allocation of even 100 percent of the total rate for the enterprise for capital repair would not provide sufficient funds,[37] and in such cases the total rate would often be distorted in the direction of larger rates for the undervalued enterprises. For instance, one writer cites the case of the Chief Administration of the Wool Industry, in which the average rate of depreciation is 6.5 percent but with a variation in rates for individual enterprises from 2.94 percent to 16.64 percent.[38] Such distortion may be desirable from the point of view of cost accounting, since it tends to make the amount of depreciation entered as a cost in similar but diversely valued plants more nearly the same, but its inevitable result is to make the depreciation charges for replacement lose any close connection to actual capital consumption. There are apparently many cases where these two manipulations of the depreciation rates do not provide enough repair funds, and it then becomes necessary to supplement them by transfers from other enterprises or from the state budget. Such transfers are often very large, amounting in the case of the coal industry and the ferrous-metal industry in recent years to about 20 percent of all capital repair funds and in other branches to smaller but often appreciable amounts.[69] This latter practice results in serious distortions of cost accounting, since such outlays are counted as costs in the enterprise which charges depreciation to produce the funds but not in the enterprise for whose benefit they are finally made. (This problem will be discussed more fully in the next chapter.)

Even in the absence of deliberate distortions, the differentiation of the 1938 composite rates is still subject to all the faults of the 1930 system of class rates. The 1930 decree sets forth only twenty-seven separate class rates and so is an inadequate base for differentiating rates to take account of all the variations in length of service life in individual enterprises. One Soviet writer puts it very well in the following statement, which is echoed again and again in the accounting literature.

The norms of depreciation established in 1930 . . . are extremely inadequately differentiated by branch and by enterprise, and under contemporary conditions do not satisfy the demands of accounting for and planning for the production of fixed assets . . . The technical equipment of all branches of industry is divided into only six groups. Here the period of depreciation of complicated automatic machines is mechanically equated to the period of depreciation of ordinary lathes, the period of depreciation of furnaces and coking ovens to that of a textile machine, the equipment of basic chemical industries, and so on. The groups given are too large, so that equipment is not sufficiently differentiated with respect to the period of depreciation.[40]

Finally, the composite branch norms of 1938, once set, remained in force during the entire twelve-year period from 1938 to 1950. The existence of these fixed rates meant that there could be no adjustment of depreciation rates to take account of changes in the composite service life of all assets within the commissariats resulting from a change in the degree of utilization, from changes in the class composition of assets, or from the introduction of new types of assets with service lives different from the previous average. Certainly during the war the degree of utilization was stepped up, and this would mean shorter service lives. Also it seems inconceivable that over a twelve-year period during which there occurred a large-scale destruction of assets, and then a large program of reconstruction under conditions of rapid technological change, there were no important shifts in the composite service lives of assets within the commissariats. Indeed, there are many statements by Soviet authorities that support this presumption. It is stated by one writer that the relative importance of buildings and such short-lived assets as machinery has been changing since 1938; another says with specific reference to the railroads that changes in the structure of assets have made the 1938 composite norms for the railroads inaccurate.[41]

In 1950, for the first time there were some adjustments made in the composite rates which had been set in 1938.[42] It seems unlikely, however, that the inadequacies listed above were really eliminated. The 1950 norms are always described as "temporary" and appear to represent a sort of stopgap adjustment pending a thorough overhaul of the whole system.[43] The fundamental problem, of course, is the determination of accurate rates for individual kinds of assets, and apparently the ministries were instructed early in the postwar period to go ahead and work out such detailed norms. It took a long time for this to be accomplished, but new norms have now been established, to go into force on January 1, 1963 (see below).[44]

Taken together, the errors in asset valuation and in the setting of rates mean that the determination of the depreciation charge ceased to be consistent with the actual composition of assets and the conditions of their use in each enterprise. It had come to be something like an arbitrary tax, distributed among enterprises with little regard to the underlying rationale of depreciation accounting.[45] As a result it could not achieve its principal objective of assigning the costs of capital consumption to the appropriate output; this was the most important motivation for the overhaul of depreciation accounting in the late fifties. The original announcement of the decision to revalue assets and to create new depreciation rates states as its main criticism that "the incorrect amount of depreciation charges leads in a number of cases to distortion of outlays on production and the cost of transportation." [46] Another writer says:

Incorrect calculation of amortization leads to distortions in cost, which in turn lead to the establishment of prices that are too high or too low, both on the means of production and on objects of consumption, to the distortion of the indicators of profitability of enterprises, and also of calculations concerning the effectiveness of capital investment and measures for the mechanization and automation of production.[47]

Unfortunately, such generalizations by Soviet writers are not usually illustrated with concrete cases of distorted prices and mistaken calculations. Consequently, it is difficult to get any general perspective on the quantitative importance of this aspect of errors in depreciation. But one writer cites facts in the case of the coal industry. He calculates that the loss on retirements in the coal industry in 1956 (which is a minimal estimate of the understatement of depreciation) would be 3 rubles, 50 kopecks, per ton if distributed over the total coal output in that year. That amount would be about 5 percent of the actually reported cost of 69 rubles, 93 kopecks, per ton.[48] He concludes the *rentabelnost* of the coal industry is considerably overestimated. *Rentabelnost* is a term which has no direct analogue in Western economic terminology, but it means in general economic advantageousness from the national economic point of view. So the statement implies that economic strategy has been confounded by the understatement of coal costs.

With the completion of the revaluation of fixed assets half of the problem has been settled. Because the average increase in the book values of assets for the economy as a whole is so small, and because the rates of depreciation have not yet been changed, there is still a considerable understatement of the costs of capital consumption. But by removing heterogeneity in valuation, the revaluation has made it possible for enterprises to be given enough capital-repair funds without the juggling of rates that was characteristic of the past, and it has also removed much of the spurious variation in cost between enterprises. The other part of the problem, the setting of new depreciation rates, is said to have been completed by the beginning of 1962, and the new norms are to be employed from January 1963 onward. These general characteristics of the revised rates seem fairly certain: they include allowance for obsolescence; they are based on much more study of factual asset lives and are much more differentiated by asset class (there are about 1,100 separate norms); and their general level is somewhat higher than the present rates.[49] When the new norms are ultimately introduced into the system, the overhaul of depreciation accounting will be complete.

SOVIET DEPRECIATION CHARGES:

A STATISTICAL APPRAISAL

So FAR we have considered the problems of asset valuation and the differentiation of a centrally determined depreciation rate among individual enterprises. The main emphasis was on the fact that heterogeneity in valuation and arbitrariness in the setting of the rates results in depreciation charges that are sharply distorted from firm to firm. The purpose of the present chapter is to go beyond this general description and consider the level of the depreciation charges, the construction of the rates, and the reflection of the deficiencies of depreciation accounting in the accounts of Soviet enterprises.

It seems quite certain that the charges for depreciation entered in Soviet cost calculations have always been far too low as estimates of capital consumption. This is acknowledged by the Russians themselves, and it emerges strikingly from a comparison of the share of depreciation in gross national product between the Soviet Union and the United States. As shown in Table 3, during the period of rapid industrialization depreciation charges have typically been less than 4 percent of the Soviet gross national product, whereas in the United States

TABLE 3. DEPRECIATION AS A PERCENTAGE OF GROSS NATIONAL PRODUCT

Country	1928	1934	1937	1940	1944	1948
United States	—	10.1	7.6	7.3	5.1	5.6
Soviet Union	5.1	5.4	3.9	3.6	2.7	2.3

Sources. The data for the United States are from the U.S. Department of Commerce, *National Income, 1954*, pp. 162–63 and 164–65. The data for the Soviet Union are from the following sources. For 1928, Oleg Hoeffding, *Soviet National Income and Product in 1928* (New York, 1954), p. 14. A figure representing depreciation in the state sector only has been chosen for the present table for comparison with those of later years. The figure for 1934 is from Francis Seton, "The Social Accounts of the Soviet Union in 1934," *Review of Economics and Statistics*, XXXVI (August 1954), 295–96, 301. The figure given in the source has been reduced to cover only the state sector of the economy. There is some reason to believe that even the adjusted figure is still slightly more comprehensive than those for the other years. For the remaining years, the sources are Abram Bergson, *Soviet National Income and Product for 1937* (New York, 1953), p. 20, and Abram Bergson and Hans Heyman, Jr., *Soviet National Income and Product, 1940–48* (New York, 1954), pp. 70, 190. In all cases the gross-national-product figure chosen has been in "adjusted rubles," a figure calculated in such a way as to eliminate the double counting resulting from the Soviet turnover tax.

they have never fallen below 5 percent and have usually been rather higher. It will be remembered that the Russian depreciation charge includes capital repair as well as replacement. The share of the Soviet depreciation charge intended for capital repair has varied slightly over time but has generally been about 50 percent of the total. When this difference in definition is taken into account, the share of depreciation in Soviet gross national product becomes comparatively very small indeed. The percentage figures for the United States are based on the depreciation charges allowed for tax purposes and, since the depreciation rates stipulated by the Internal Revenue Service are based on empirical studies of asset service lives, there is no presumption that the American depreciation charges are unrealistically high. Indeed, it is often claimed that these allowances are less than the depreciation counted as a cost by businessmen in their own calculations. The figures of Table 3, therefore, strongly suggest that the Soviet charges fall considerably short of covering the cost of capital consumption.

This understatement of depreciation relative to national product has several roots. First, in the large areas of the economy either no depreciation charge is made (as in the case of collective farm agriculture and in budget-financed institutions generally) or the depreciation charge is intended to cover outlays on capital repair only and not replacement (as in the case of most housing organizations).[1] Second, assets have traditionally been undervalued as a result of inflation. Finally, the rates themselves may be too low. Unfortunately, these last two points may be hard to separate analytically, as will be seen in what follows.

Accounting Entries

Before the evidence on the adequacy of Soviet depreciation charges can be discussed intelligibly, it will be necessary to digress to explain the accounting procedures more fully. The fact that the Russians have defined the concept of depreciation to cover both replacement of assets and capital repair complicates any interpretation of the evidence, makes it difficult to distinguish the various factors that have caused understatement of the charges, and, as we shall see, has led to much confusion in cost accounting and some dilution of administrative efficiency. At this point, therefore, I want to analyze in detail what it means to provide for both purposes with a single rate, how such a rate is determined, and how this procedure is reflected in the accounting entries.

Let us begin with a more precise definition of what the Russians mean by capital repair. For accounting purposes they make a distinction between capital repair and current repair on the basis of how frequently a given kind of repair operation is carried out, how completely the asset is torn down in the process of repair, and what proportion of its component parts are inspected and replaced if necessary. Typical examples of capital repair include overhauling a motor vehicle or locomotive, replacing the roof of a building, or rebuilding a machine. Such repairs are likely to be carried out not oftener than once a year, and often the period between successive repairs is much longer. The precise distinction between capital repair and current repair is usually laid down in detailed instructions issued by ministries (now by the economic councils). It is said that these instructions are often unclear, and as a result the decision as to the category of a given repair operation is often left by default to enterprise management. Moreover, the distinction between capital repair and current repair is far from uniform in the instructions used by different branches of industry,[2] and it is difficult to make generalizations about the precise scope of capital repair. Nevertheless, one attribute of the concept is perfectly clear — it does not involve additions to or improvements in existing assets. Capital repair does not improve the asset in the sense of raising its productivity, nor does it prolong the life of an asset beyond the period envisaged in the setting of the depreciation rates. (The practice, introduced in 1954, of permitting capital-repair funds to be used for modernization of assets in the process of repair should be noted as a slight qualification to the preceding statement.) Soviet accounting sometimes employs a special category of "restorative repair," which covers additions and improvements to existing assets. Apparently this kind of repair is financed from sources other than the repair portion of the depreciation allowance and, in any case, is capitalized as new investment. In the oil industry, for instance, investment in deepening a well to restore it to production is treated in this way.[3] This interpretation of capital repair also emerges clearly from the formula by which the Soviet writers assert that the depreciation rates were originally calculated.[4] Where r is the annual depreciation rate to be applied to the original value of the fixed assets, V the original value of the asset, R the total expenditure for capital repair which the asset is expected to require over its entire service life, and L the expected service life of the asset, the formula is: $r = [(V + R)/LV]$ 100. Thus, the expenditure of R for capital repair is one of the prerequisites for making the asset serve out its life of L years and is not a source for financing new investment. The practical rationale for providing capital-repair funds through the depreciation charge is that such expenditures are bunched in time, and this is a device for smoothing out their impact on cost of production over successive accounting periods. This is rationalized at a somewhat higher level of abstraction by the notion that capital-repair operations involve replacing worn-out parts of an asset and so are analogous in principle to replacement of the whole complex constituted by the asset.

Several implications of this formula should be emphasized. First, the depreciation rate is not simply the reciprocal of the planned service life, as it is when depreciation is intended only to recoup the original value of the asset. Second, one of the important assumptions is that it is possible to estimate the ratio of R to V. If this estimate is not made accurately, then the asset might, in fact, turn out to have precisely the service life envisaged, but the depreciation charge would not cover both capital repair and replacement. Moreover, two separate kinds of errors can be made. One might misjudge not only how many times the asset will need to undergo capital repair but also the prices of repair relative to the original prices in which the value of the asset is shown. Finally, the relative sizes of V and

R determine what share of the total depreciation rate is intended separately for capital repair and for replacement. Suppose, for instance, that R and V were equal; then if r as calculated by the formula is 10 percent, this would be split into rates of 5 percent for repair and 5 percent for replacement. If R is twice as large as V, then the 10 percent would be split one third for replacement and two thirds for repair.

Next, let us consider the whole cycle of accounting entries associated with the process of capital consumption as it is carried out in a Soviet firm. In the typical example on p. 81, each of the entries is shown on a set of accounts and each entry is identified by a number keyed to the text description that follows. (1) At the beginning of the accounting period the enterprise has, let us assume, 1,000 rubles worth of fixed assets which is just matched on the equities side of the balance sheet by a Charter Fund of 1,000 rubles. (2 and 2a) In the course of the accounting period the assets depreciate. Assuming an annual depreciation rate of 10 percent and assuming that half of this is for repair and half for replacement, the charge for the year is 100 rubles, and this is reflected in the five entries shown. The amount of depreciation is charged to the cost of production and credited to Depreciation. Concurrently, the same amount is debited to the Charter Fund and credited to Amortization to the extent of the portion intended for capital repair and to an account called Liability to Prombank (that is, the bank which collects and disburses investment funds) to the extent of the amount intended for financing new investment. (3) The output is sold and the depreciation is recovered as cash. (4) Once earned, the depreciation designated for replacement purposes is extracted from the enterprise by a payment to the Prombank. (5) To simplify the case somewhat, assume that the funds left with the enterprise for capital repair are actually spent for that purpose within the year. This operation will involve a

Cycle of Entries for Depreciation Accounting

Fixed Assets				Charter Fund			
(1)	1,000 R	100 R	(7)	(2a)	100 R	1,000 R	(1)
				(9)	20 R	50 R	(6a)
						75 R	(12a)

Cost of Production				Depreciation			
(2)	100 R	100 R	(3)	(6)	50 R	100 R	(2)
				(8)	80 R		
				(12)	75 R		

Cash				Amortization Fund			
(3)	100 R	50 R	(4)	(6a)	50 R	50 R	(2a)
(10)	75 R	50 R	(5)				
		75 R	(11)				

Capital Repair				Liability to Prombank			
(5)	50 R	50 R	(6)	(4)	50 R	50 R	(2a)
(11)	75 R	75 R	(12)				

Retirement of Fixed Assets				Financing for Special Purposes			
(7)	100 R	80 R	(8)	(12a)	75 R	75 R	(10)
		20 R	(9)				

credit to cash and a debit to an account called Capital Repair. (6 and 6a) When the capital-repair operation is completed, this is interpreted as having made good some of the depreciation on the asset, and to reflect this on the books the amount spent for capital repair is debited to Depreciation and credited to Capital Repair. At the same time, the expenditure of the funds reserved for capital repair is recognized by a debit to the Amortization Fund and a credit to the Charter Fund. Thus, when the capital-repair funds have been used for the assigned purpose, the depreciation account shows only the amount of depreciation for replacement purposes that has been charged on the fixed asset. At this point the capital-repair account is closed out, and the balance of the balance sheet accounts show no traces of the fact that the charge was to cover capital repair. Also at this point we can think of the enterprise as having converted part of its original endowment of fixed assets into cash through the depreciation charges and having been divested of this cash by a payment to the Prombank. Its fixed assets are still shown on the asset side of the balance sheet at their original value, but on the other side of the balance sheet the depreciation account shows by how much this value should be adjusted downward to recognize their actual value.

The entries thus far have involved assets, depreciation, and repair for the enterprise as a whole, but for some purposes these aggregates must be distributed among individual assets. It is contemplated in the accounting legislation and is apparently general practice that enterprises keep a "plant ledger," that is, a subsidiary set of accounts for individual items of fixed assets. These show the original value of each asset, of course, and in most enterprises the expenditures for capital repair of individual assets is recorded on the individual card in the plant ledger for the asset involved. It will be remembered, however, that the depreciation charge is determined in the first instance for the enterprise as a whole by applying to the fixed-asset total the composite rate assigned from above; apparently the depreciation charge is not generally distributed among individual assets and is not recorded on the individual asset cards. As will be shown, this leads to complications in retirement accounting.

When an asset is retired, the results are calculated on an account called Retirement of Fixed Assets. (7) The full original value of the asset being retired is transferred from the Fixed Assets account to the Retirement account. (8) The accrued depreciation on the asset is transferred from Depreciation to Retirement. (There are also some adjustments for scrap recovered and expenses involved in retirement, but these are irrelevant to the present problem.) The determination of the amount of depreciation charged on this individual asset is apparently not highly formalized, and considerable discretion is left to the accountant. Actual practice in this decision will be described below. The balance of the retirement account thus shows whether or not the depreciation charges for replacement have recovered the original cost of the asset. If depreciation charged exceeds the original value of the asset, there is said to be a gain on retirement and, if the opposite, a loss on retirement. (9) The amount of this loss or gain on retirement is then written off Retirement to the Charter Fund and so is never included in cost-of-production calculations or in profit and loss statements.

(10) As was explained in the last chapter, it often happens that funds earned through depreciation charges are transferred from one enterprise to another in order to finance capital repair. Such a transfer would be shown on the accounts as an increment in cash and on the equity side under a heading called Financing for Special Purposes. (In the enterprise from which these funds were extracted, the ultimate result after a number of intermediate entries would be a reduction in cash and a reduction in the charter fund.) It may also happen that funds for capital repair will be made available from still other sources, such as the state budget. These are handled in the same way, except that there are no entries in the books of another production enterprise. (11, 12, 12a) When the funds

so acquired are spent for capital repair, the whole cycle of entries previously described for this operation are again repeated, except that in this case one set of entries (12a) involves Special Financing and the Charter Fund rather than the Amortization Fund and the Charter Fund.

It should be obvious that, when capital repair is financed in this way, this particular outlay of 75 rubles has been included in the cost of output of the enterprise where it was originally earned, but will never be shown as the cost of the output of the enterprise in which it was actually spent for capital repair. This approach to financing capital repair also leads to an anomaly in enterprise accounts that is said to occur quite frequently. It may very well happen that expenditure on capital repair, financed from funds transferred from outside, will exceed the total depreciation shown for the assets. It is said, for example, that this was true of some petroleum refineries, specifically those in Moscow, Ishimbai, and Batumi. All of these are relatively old enterprises dating from the thirties and must be heavily depreciated, but before the revaluation of 1960 their accounts show them as completely undepreciated.[5]

The Underestimation of Depreciation

Against this background, consideration can now be given to some evidence on the adequacy of the depreciation charges. The evidence available refers mostly to industry, but it is in this sector, of course, that the largest part of Soviet depreciation charges originates.

The understatement of depreciation in industry in the thirties is strongly suggested by the data of Table 4. As the table shows, fixed assets and capital repair of fixed assets to the amount of 76,000 million rubles were taken onto the balance sheets of industrial enterprises in the period between January 1, 1928, and December 31, 1938, but the stock of fixed assets as shown

TABLE 4. FIXED ASSETS, RETIREMENTS, AND DEPRECIATION IN LARGE-SCALE INDUSTRY (MILLION RUBLES)

Year	Year-end value of fixed assets	Investments taken onto balance sheets	Implied retirements and capital repair	Depreciation charged
1927	9,018	—	—	—
1928	10,262	1,270	26	491.6
1929	11,389	1,818	691	541.3
1930	14,199	2,608	−202	575.7
1931	17,376	3,354	177	868.3
1932	22,627	5,431	180	1,100.1
1933	29,007	6,510	130	1,394.1
1934	35,340	8,327	1,994	1,737.3
1935	43,583	10,174	1,931	2,130.9
1936	50,384	12,331	5,530	2,584.1
1937	57,935	11,952	4,041	2,976.0
1938	68,000	13,185	3,120	3,780.0
Total	—	76,600	17,618	18,179.4

Notes and sources. *Value of fixed assets.* These data refer to the original value of fixed assets as shown on the books of Soviet enterprises of large-scale industry. They include only "productive assets"; that is, they exclude any fixed assets of the enterprise used for housing, education, cultural activities, etc. The figures for 1927 through 1937 are taken from Khromov, pp. 18–19. The figure for 1938 is computed as follows. According to one source (G. Kozlov, *Khozyaystvennyi raschet v sotsialisticheskom obshchestve*, Moscow, 1945, p. 29), the value of fixed assets in large-scale industry in 1938 was 63 billion rubles. The time reference of this figure is not clear, but it is taken to be an annual average figure, on the basis of the following considerations. The annual growth in the immediately preceding years was on the order of 7 billion rubles, and the 1939 year-end figure is given as 81.905 billion rubles (Kantor, p. 62). Therefore 63 billion rubles would be far too low for a year-end figure for 1938. The figure in the table is derived by multiplying 63 billion rubles by 2 and subtracting the 1937 year-end figure.

Investments taken onto balance sheets. These figures represent actual transfer of new assets and capital repairs to the operating balance sheets of enterprises. (The Russian term is "vvod v deistvie.") They refer only to productive assets and so are comparable with the stock figures of the preceding column. They apparently refer to all industry (rather than to large-scale only), but invest-

TABLE 4 (*continued*)

ments in small-scale industry must have been negligible in this period. The figures for 1928 through 1934 are from TsUNKhU, *Sotsialisticheskoe stroitelstvo* (Moscow, 1936), pp. 390–91. The figures for 1935 through 1938 were derived in the following way. Kaplan has computed investments in productive assets in industry for these years (N. Kaplan, *Capital Investments in the Soviet Union, 1924–1951*, Santa Monica, 1951, p. 217), and these have been converted into "vvod v deistvie" by applying the percentage of "vvod v deistvie" to investments for the Second Five Year Plan, i.e., 90 percent (E. L. Granovskii and B. L. Markus, *Ekonomika sotsialisticheskoi promyshlennosti*, Moscow, 1940, p. 346).

Implied retirements and capital repair. These figures are derived by taking the stock on January 1, plus the "vvod v deistvie" for the year, minus the stock on December 31.

Depreciation charged. The figures for 1928 through 1936 are from Arakelian, p. 27. The source does not state explicitly that the figures relate to large-scale industry only, but this interpretation is suggested by the fact that there is sometimes cited a series in which the amounts are somewhat larger (see, for instance, Sobol, p. 54). The figures for 1937 and 1938 are computed by applying to the annual average value of fixed assets the global rates of depreciation for industry, namely 5.5 percent in 1937 and 6 percent in 1938.

in the accounts of enterprises grew by only 58,982 million rubles. This leaves a gap of 17,613 million rubles which represents retirements, losses of fixed assets due to accidental destruction, and the part of investment that consists of capital repair (as explained above, this is not added to the book value of assets but is noted on the books of enterprises by reducing the amount of depreciation shown in the depreciation account). Total depreciation charged on these fixed assets over the period was only 18,179 million rubles and so covered capital repair and retirements with only a slight margin. Indeed depreciation charges probably did not actually cover retirements and capital repair in view of certain qualifications about the meaning of the statistics. The series on depreciation probably includes depreciation on "nonproductive" fixed assets of industry, and adjustment for this fact might lower the depreciation total by several percent. Furthermore, the growth of the fixed-asset series is the result not only of investment, but also of shifts into the category covered by the series and upgrading of small-scale industry to large-scale. No precise adjustment for this influence can be made, but there is little doubt that it was at work. Note, for instance, that in 1930 the figures imply negative retirements and capital repair. For 1931–33 also the official figures on retirements and capital repair exceed the implied magnitudes shown in the table for these years by something like 1,500 million rubles.[6] If it were possible to make allowance for all these factors, it would undoubtedly be found that the depreciation charges were less than capital repairs and retirements.

Moreover, on the basis of the following considerations, we must conclude that the inadequacy of the depreciation charges was even greater than is suggested by their relationship to repair and retirements. In a period of rising investment costs, such as the Soviet economy experienced throughout the 1930s, old assets will be shown on the books at smaller values than comparable new assets. Assets retired will thus tend to be those valued in prices relatively lower than the prices in which the aggregate stock is valued, and it is on this aggregate stock that depreciation charges are calculated. If the norms are correct, then, we would expect depreciation charges to exceed retirements and capital repair in this situation.[7] This would happen even if the stock were not growing at all in physical terms. Since this eleven-year period represents the so-called build-up period before the large additions of assets in the First and Second Five Year Plans had a chance to age, retirements and repair should have been far below straight-line depreciation charges if the norms had been based on actual need. But the discrepancy was probably in the opposite direction.

Although the above demonstrates that the rates were too low, the dual function of the Soviet charge means that there are two interconnected factors behind this result. (1) The service lives for assets used in working out the rates may have been longer than assets actually were made to serve, and (2) the amounts of R relative to V in the original equation may have understated the actual amount of repair. The second factor was obviously important — as inflation proceeded, the magnitude of R employed in the original formula turned out to be far less than what was actually required for capital repair. Whether the service lives were overestimated, however, remains unsettled.

The most interesting evidence on the adequacy of Soviet depreciation charges in the postwar period concerns the losses at the time of retirement of fixed assets. As part of their investigation of fixed-asset accounting, begun in the late fifties, the Russians surveyed the data and found that retirement losses were extremely large. This fact was undoubtedly known in a general way before — most accounting textbooks, for instance, say that the result of retirement of fixed assets is customarily a loss. But until the late fifties there was never any serious concern about these losses. It was not a subject for critical comment, and I have seen only one case in which the alarming size of these unrecovered amounts was explicitly mentioned.[8]

As a result of the surveys, many data on retirement losses were published, revealing that probably over half of the value of most fixed assets remained unamortized at the time they were retired. Table 5 shows the percentage of original value unamortized at the time of retirement for a number of branches of industry. This tabulation omits some important industrial branches — primary metals, machinery, and chemicals. Other sources, however, make it clear that there are large losses on retirement in them as well. One writer says that the rate of loss on retirement in machinery plants is 25 to 40 percent,[9] and examples of similar magnitudes are given for chemical plants.[10] In the nonferrous-metal branch, retirements as a percent of total fixed assets exceed the depreciation rate for replacement.[11]

TABLE 5. LOSSES ON RETIREMENT AS A PERCENTAGE OF ORIGINAL VALUE

Industry	1954	1955
Coal	76	72
Oil	27	24
Construction materials	49	47
Forest, paper, and woodworking	52	61
Meat and milk	36	29
Fishing	50	46
Light (shoes, apparel, etc.)	—	26
Electric stations	36	37
Production of industrial consumer goods	28	—
Production of food goods	41	37
Textile	—	26
Local (RSFSR)	—	45
Fuel (RSFSR)	—	45
Average	53	51

Source. Dodonov, *Amortizatsiya i remont osnovnykh sredstv v promyshlennosti*, p. 123.

Again, unfortunately, the meaning of these results is somewhat ambiguous. First, the ratio of losses to original value shown for the assets that happened to have been retired in these years cannot necessarily be accepted as a characteristic measure of the degree to which the stock of assets at the present time is being underdepreciated. Second, it is more or less impossible to untangle the amount of the loss on retirement caused by overestimation of actual service lives from the amount of excessive expenditure on capital repair caused by the rise in prices.

The difficulty in accepting these percentages as a measure of the degree to which assets are currently being underdepreciated arises from obscurities in the way Soviet accountants assign depreciation to individual assets at the time of retirement. It will be remembered from the earlier description that the accountant does not routinely distribute depreciation to individual assets as depreciation charges are calculated each month; he records it in a single total for the enterprise as a whole. This then means that, when the time comes to retire an asset, the amount of depreciation which has been charged on it is not explicitly available on its ledger card and the accountant must somehow allocate to this asset a portion of the accrued depreciation shown on the general books. Although in the actual calculation no specific rates were used for individual assets, the composite rate for the enterprise as a whole was based on some implicit assumptions concerning service lives for the separate kinds of assets and concerning the composition of assets. Although these class rates are never explicitly in evidence, they are obviously lurking somewhere in the background. If the accountant assigns to an asset being retired more depreciation than has actually been charged in the light of this implicit class rate, then it may very well turn out that there will be no loss on retirement.

Without discussing in detail the way in which the decision about how much depreciation to assign to an asset being retired is actually made, it is possible to state that the amount will often be either too much or too little. The rules for making this decision are not highly formalized and much latitude is allowed to the accountant. In fact, in most books on accounting no mention is even made of the problem. But there are some hints that the amount of depreciation assigned will tend to be too little. In many enterprises there has been a large volume of capital repair financed from sources other than the depreciation charges — that is, from capital-repair accumulations transferred from other enterprises, from an allocation of profits, or from the state budget. Whatever the source of funds in such cases, their acquisition is not reflected in the depreciation account. (The reader may wish to refer back to the earlier explanation of the entries which these operations generate.) Nevertheless, when these funds are spent for capital repair, the expenditures are ultimately debited to the depreciation account and so reduce the amount of depreciation shown for the enterprise as a whole. The result then is that the depreciation account can show an amount far less than has actually been charged as replacement depreciation in that enterprise. In fact, the older and more undervalued assets are, the more likely they are to have been repaired extensively from such funds, and the depreciation account may show negligible amounts. There are even cases where the depreciation account shows a debit balance; here there is not enough depreciation to go around, so to speak, and the accountant will be likely to assign assets being retired less than has really been charged on them.[12] Another factor that could lead to too small an amount being assigned to retired assets is the practice of figuring the amount of depreciation for an individual asset by using the composite rate for the enterprise as a whole.[13] Suppose, for example, that the composite rate for replacement for the enterprise as a whole is 5 percent and that one asset is being retired after ten years of service. The accountant in this case might simply calculate the amount of depreciation that has been charged on this particular asset as 5 percent a year for ten years. He would then conclude that only half its original value had been recovered by depreciation charges. In any situation where the stock of assets is growing or where the stock of assets had not fully "matured," assets being retired would always be those with less-than-average service lives, but they would be assigned depreciation based on the assumption that their expected service lives were the same as the average implied by the composite rate.

Alternatively, it is possible that the depreciation assigned could be too large an amount since the enterprise accountant might prefer not to show large losses on retirement. Obviously, he can eliminate losses on retirement simply by assigning to the asset being retired whatever portion of the total depreciation accumulation for the enterprise is necessary to balance the asset's original value. Because there is so little discussion and so little formality in the rules concerning fixed-asset retirements, it seems impossible to estimate the net result of the conflicting errors flowing from the decisions on the part of individual accountants.

There is another kind of evidence, however, bearing on the interpretation of the figures for losses on retirements. This is the relationship of the depreciation account to fixed assets as shown on the books of industrial firms. The Russians employ an indicator called the "coefficient of depreciation" (*koeffitsient iznosa*), which is the ratio of the amount shown in the depreciation account to the amount shown as the original value of the fixed assets. This should be a measure of the average degree to which fixed assets are worn out and should be equivalent to the ratio of the average age of assets to the average service life postulated in the construction of depreciation rates. (It will be remembered that the amount of depreciation recorded at one point includes charges made for capital repair; but when the capital repairs are actually made, the total of the depreciation account is reduced by the amount of repairs. Hence, the depreciation account at any given time should show the accumulated amount of depreciation for replacement purposes that has been charged on the fixed assets of the plant over their past life.) The average service life implied by Soviet depreciation rates can be estimated as follows. The annual rate of depreciation for replacement purposes in industry for 1955 was 2.7 percent. But for the years prior to 1955 it had not been quite so high; it was 2.3 percent in 1952 and 1954, for instance,

and 2.4 percent in 1953.[14] In some years before that it was
slightly higher, about 2.5–2.6 percent from 1938 to 1950.[15] So let
us use 2.5 percent as an approximate estimate of the average
rate at which depreciation for replacement has been charged
on the existing stock of assets in Soviet industry. Figures for
the coefficient of depreciation in industry for a number of postwar years are shown in column 1 of the following tabulation.[16]
If each of these numbers is divided by 2.5, the result is the
implied average age of existing assets shown in column 2. It is
virtually certain that the average age of the assets of Soviet
industry is greater than the implied figures in column 2 of the

Year	Coefficient of depreciation (January 1)	Implied average age
1950	17.30	6.92
1951	16.10	6.44
1952	14.40	5.76
1953	14.50	5.8
1954	14.50	5.8
1955	14.20	5.7
1956	15.40	6.2

tabulation. Admittedly, the fact that the absolute volume of
investment keeps growing rapidly, and that a large amount of
prewar assets were destroyed during the Second World War,
should exert a strong downward pressure on the average age.
Nevertheless, big flows of investment began thirty years ago,
and much of that early investment is still in use and on the
books. There are scattered statements that corroborate this.
For instance, Ia. B. Kvasha, who seems one of the most
thoughtful analysts and competent investigators of the depreciation problem, has stated that, of all the production fixed assets
of industry (probably in 1957), 42 percent were less than 5
years old, 54 percent were 5 to 27 years old, and only 4 percent

were older than 27 years.[17] Obviously these groups are too broad to permit the computation of a reliable weighted average, but the result is fairly high even if the average age within each group is assumed to be considerably less than the midpoint of the age interval. For instance, if the average age of the first group is taken as 2 years, that of the second as 11 years, and that of the third group as 30 years, then the average age of the whole stock would be about 8 years. The average age for the whole stock calculated in this way is very sensitive to the figure chosen for the average age of the second group, rising to about 8.5 years and 9.0 years if the average age of the second group is taken as 12 and 13 years respectively.

Certainly no precise conclusion about the average age of assets can be drawn from this evidence. But it is enough to suggest a considerable shortfall in the depreciation account, of an amount equal to perhaps a year or two's depreciation charges. This shortfall arises as a net result of two processes. The financing of capital repair from outside sources causes some of it, and the depreciation assigned to assets being retired increases or decreases it, depending on the direction of the error. The situation is also complicated by the fact that in some cases capital-repair funds accumulated through depreciation charges have been used for other purposes. During the war, for instance, virtually nothing was spent for capital repair and the funds generated by the depreciation charges for capital repair were transferred to the budget.[18] In the postwar period as well, capital repair funds have sometimes been transferred. (Transfers *between enterprises* of capital-repair funds accumulated by depreciation charges will have no effect on the aggregate depreciation account for all industry and so can be ignored here.) There are not enough data published to make possible an estimate of the net cumulative transfer of funds for capital repair into nonindustrial areas. But the shortfall in the amount shown in the depreciation account is not large enough to suggest that the amounts of depreciation assigned to assets at retirement have been excessive. Indeed, it is quite possible that the bias has been in the other direction, and the official statements of losses at retirement may actually be less than the actual losses.

Whatever the conclusion for industry as a whole, it is much more certain that rates for individual branches are far too low. This is true of the coal industry, for instance. For coal assets retired in a few recent years, the portion of the original cost of the assets not recovered in depreciation charges was 74.4 percent in 1952, 75.8 percent in 1954, and 71.1 percent in 1955.[19] Moreover, in this branch of industry the evidence seems to show fairly clearly that assets retired were assigned more depreciation than had really been charged on them. The coefficient of depreciation of fixed assets in the coal industry is stated to have been 8.1 percent in 1949, 4.3 percent in 1953, and 3.3 percent in 1955.[20] The rate of depreciation for replacement purposes in the coal industry was 3.2 percent under the 1938 norms, dropped to .9 percent under the 1950 norms, and rose to 1.1 percent under the 1952 norms.[21] The average rate might thus be somewhere between 2 and 3 percent. Together with the coefficient of depreciation for 1955 of 3.3 percent given above, this implies that on January 1, 1955, the average age of all fixed assets in the coal industry was only about a year and a half. This of course could not possibly be the case. Moreover, since 1949 there is not supposed to have been any budget financing of capital repair, and so the drop in the coefficient between 1949 and 1955 suggests that the accountants in the coal industry have been assigning an excessive fraction of the accumulated depreciation account to assets being retired. The ratio of losses to the original value of fixed assets that are being retired in the coal industry is, therefore, actually higher than the 70–75 percent that the figures show. It is stated that the same sort of situation exists in the lumber industry, in the textile industry, and in a number of others.[22]

Conclusion

This must seem a rather tortuous argument to bring so little in the way of conclusions. On the other hand, the frustrations of trying to interpret these accounts themselves suggest an important conclusion. If we cannot analyze the figures from the accounts associated with the consumption of capital (for example, fixed assets at original value, depreciation, expenditures on capital repair, and losses on liquidation of assets), the Russian planners surely face the same difficulty. This is one measure of the deficiencies in Soviet capital-consumption accounting. The various accounts lose any clearly defined meaning and lose much of their usefulness for analysis of capital consumption. This is true both at the level of the national economy and at the level of branches or enterprises. There may, indeed, be some argument whether the Russian planners have ever used the information in these accounts for purposes of aggregate economic analysis. They talk in a rather vague way about using the coefficient of depreciation, for example, as an aid in planning future capital investment, though I have some doubts that they have ever actually done this to an important extent. But that use does exist, both potentially and on paper, so that this seems an unimportant quibble.

Working through the meaning of these accounts also throws into sharper relief the main weaknesses of the Soviet approach to depreciation accounting and suggests how it might be improved. Much of the difficulty flows from assigning to depreciation charges the double problem of providing funds for capital repair and for replacement. In the foregoing I have sometimes found it convenient to think of depreciation as involving two separate rates and two separate charges, as do the Russians at times. At a number of points in the actual use of the rates, however, the two are effectively treated as one. This is true when the depreciation rates are originally worked out, for instance. What emerges from the formula is a single rate, and the other information utilized in the formula is simply discarded. If, at a later point, the charge is divided into separate repair and replacement allowances, that is an expedient afterthought, not necessarily consistent with the average length of service lives of the assets involved or the relationship between expenditures for repair (R in the formula) and the original value of the asset (V).

In some of the accounting entries of enterprises the distinction is preserved; in others it is not. The total charge for both purposes is accumulated in the depreciation account in a single total, for example. Finally, a charge serving the dual purpose links two items which are not homogeneous with respect to the administrative problems involved. In actual practice enterprise management is given considerable responsibility and authority over the conduct of capital repair. Capital repair is a process which is carried on more or less continuously, using resources (such as a repair shop and a special labor force) which are effectively under the control of management. To a considerable extent, it is the enterprise director's interpretation of the need for capital repair, rather than the availability of earmarked funds, that determines how much of it he is authorized to perform. In short, capital repair is a much more decentralized area of decision making than are new and replacement investment, but financing capital repair within the framework of a fixed total rate prevents the manager's repair activities from finding any reflection in cost-performance indicators and imposes a, perhaps intended, barrier to the freedom of financial maneuver.

All these problems (and they are ones that have turned up over and over again in the discussions of the past few years) would be simplified or eliminated by keeping the depreciation charge as a device to charge off the original value of an asset to production costs, and by letting capital repair be charged as a current expense, smoothed to some extent if necessary by some other technique. The rationale for a depreciation charge to accumulate funds for capital repair is usually explained by Soviet writers in terms of the uneven distribution over time of repair on individual assets. However, this would not be true for aggregates of assets, and it seems unlikely that within any Soviet enterprise the variation in capital-repair expenditure from year to year is very great. To treat capital repair as just another current expense might well show that the costs of production in old plants or with old assets is higher than in new ones because of the high repair costs. But this is an objective fact, and it makes little sense to treat cost in earlier years as burdened by the cost of restoring and repairing assets in later years.

The basic defect of the present approach can be explained from another point of view. It requires in the determination of rates predictions about matters that are essentially unpredictable. There are built into the rates some prejudgments which the planners should decline to make, notably about the repair-replacement decision. The formula assumes that the economic service life can be determined in advance, and the appropriate amount of capital repair required to achieve that life is predicted at the same time. This is basically the rationale for charging some of capital repair to the first years of use of the asset, although in fact at that time it does not require capital repair. The whole procedure implies, first, that the planners know what the repair needs will be from the beginning and, second, that enjoying this kind of foresight they should take them into account in their calculations. That implicit assumption is unrealistic: they do not have such foresight and ought to leave the repair question open for flexible decision as time goes on. Apparently this is not only a prejudgment in theory; it also apparently operates to some degree in practice, as will be shown in Chapter 7.

Thus, given the fact that obsolescence may dictate unexpectedly early replacement, that the relative efficiency of repair over replacement may change with time, and that general price-level changes may destroy the assumed relationship between repair cost and the original value of the asset assumed in the formula, it would be better to keep capital repair and depreciation separate. If they were, the Russians would not have to resort to such devices as juggling the replacement rates out of all relationship to average service life, transferring funds from one enterprise to another, and financing capital repair with outside resources, with all the adverse effects on the reliability of cost accounting which these manipulations involve.

The present arrangement also tends to encourage falsification in reporting. The borderline between capital repair and other types of repair is difficult to define. It is said that enterprises charge off to the capital-repair fund other kinds of repair expenditures which were actually intended to be charged to the cost of production.[23] In this way they show better cost performance than what was actually achieved. If capital-repair expenditures were treated as a current expense, this loophole would be closed. Managers would have cost responsibility for capital repair and would accordingly be motivated to make this operation as efficient as possible.

The Russians have recently started to deal with some of the difficulties involved here. For one thing, they have permitted enterprise management to employ the capital-repair funds with much less supervision than was formerly exercised by the Gosbank.[24] For another, they have recently allowed management to use some of the capital-repair funds for modernization of fixed assets rather than simply for repair. Only two choices — modernization or repair — are offered, but that is better than one.

It is difficult to know just why the Russians have been so firmly committed to their present dual conception of depreciation. It may have something to do with the terminology itself. The Russian words for depreciation (*iznos, snashivanie, iznashivanie*) are less vague than ours; they simply mean "wearing out." To describe obsolescence a special qualifier (*moralnyi iznos*) is added, which implies that this is a figurative wearing out. There is a Russian word much closer in connotation to *depreciation* — *utsenka* (loss of value) — but it is never used in the depreciation context. The rationale for the double charge always runs as follows. The objective of the charge is to recover in value terms the wear and tear on an asset. Since parts of the asset wear out from time to time, the charge should not only make good the final collapse of the asset, but also the intermediate, partial, wear and tear. This also supplies the rationale for debiting completed capital repair to the depreciation account; the repair has made good some of the physical wear and tear on the asset. The Russians, I think, have a hard time breaking away from this line of argument. Occasionally they do, of course, as when they are confronted with such absurdities as a credit balance for the depreciation account. Also more original minds can break away. Kvasha, for instance, declares unequivocally that capital repair and depreciation involve separate kinds of issues and that there is no need to provide for them both by a single charge.[25]

To judge from the way in which discussion of depreciation policy had evolved up to the present time, most Soviet accountants have had the good sense to recognize the importance of this distinction, and it is promised that in determining and applying the new depreciation rates the two concepts will be separated.[26] They will continue to be described jointly as depreciation, but the magnitudes, the rates, and the concepts will be kept apart at each step along the way, from the construction of rates, through their differentiation among enterprises, to the recording of amounts. If this change is in fact accomplished, it will be the answer to many of the most troublesome aspects of Soviet depreciation accounting.

SOME PROBLEMS OF

COST ALLOCATION

Since accounting units usually embrace a number of different production activities, and since accounting reports are drawn up for arbitrarily delimited time periods, cost accounting must have rules for allocating outlays among activities, outputs, and time periods. A basis for some of these allocations is self-evident, but for others it is not. The purpose of this and the following chapter is to examine critically the rules which direct Soviet cost accounting in this area.

The Distribution of Enterprise Overheads

Many of the outlays made by industrial enterprises, such as the wages of administrative personnel, costs of heating and lighting, outlays of service shops, depreciation and maintenance of plant, have no immediately observable connection with individual kinds of output. In his original recording of these expenses, the accountant does not assign them to any particular kind of output, but accumulates them in general accounts relating to the plant as a whole or to large units within the plant. But obviously these "overhead costs" must be charged to the cost of all the output taken together, and, in making cost calculations for individual kinds of products, the accountant distributes them among the different products and activities of the enterprise on some more or less conventional basis.

Before describing the Soviet treatment of overhead costs, it will be well to make a few preliminary remarks concerning the distribution of overhead costs. Is there any nonarbitrary method for assigning them to individual kinds of output? It is true that for some elements of overhead expense there will not be any obvious method of assignment. Certain expenses may, in fact, be invariant with respect to the composition of output or invariant with the scale of output. In such a case there is no putative causal relationship and no basis for assignment. In such circumstances the most important consideration is to allocate overhead so as not to distort the structure of costs that *are* allocable.

To what extent overhead will have to be treated in this way, however, depends to a large degree on the amount of organizational efficiency that can be achieved by the enterprise and on the amount of detail in cost accounting with which it can cope. There is often a technological connection that provides a basis for assignment, but it is discernible only if the accounts are structured so as to compute costs of intermediate outputs. For instance, the relationship between the outlays of the repair shop and individual kinds and parcels of output may appear to be very obscure. But if these outlays are charged in the first instance to cost centers or to such intermediate outputs as machine-hours of work, it becomes relatively simple to trace outlays to the output eventually benefited. This is simply an application of a proposition stated several times already. How precisely the upper levels of any organization can know the costs of their outputs depends primarily on the degree of administrative perfection they can achieve. The essence of effective administrative control in a production organization is to make the structure of responsibility and authority congruent with the pattern of technological causality. Areas of responsibility can be distinguished only on the basis of distinctions among processes. Since the various processes are to some degree interdependent, evaluation of the performance of the controller of any single one requires some measurement of its interaction with others. This ultimately involves some measure of its drain on the capacity of others or its contribution to the output of others. The more effective such organizational articulation is, the more clearly is the skeleton of technological interaction laid bare and the more evident becomes the relationship of any outlay to ultimate output. At the same time, the operation of the administrative scheme generates the actual data (that is, in the indices used in evaluating interdependence) needed for the allocation of costs. The general approach in accounting for overhead cost, then, should be (1) to distinguish those outlays which are invariant with respect to changes in the output and to distribute them in proportion to direct costs, and (2) to classify other elements of overhead with respect to the indicators on which their magnitude depends and distribute them accordingly. It may not be expedient to carry this process too far, since the increase in accuracy may not justify the additional work, but this is the ideal which the distribution method should try to approximate.

In general, Soviet overhead accounting is very similar to that used in American plants. Expenses not directly assignable to specific kinds of output are accumulated in accounts called shop expenses, general plant expenses, expenses of auxiliary shops, and nonproduction expenses.[1] These are subsequently distributed to smaller units of the plant and to different outputs on the basis of some conventional indicator.[2] What is distinctive about Soviet overhead accounting, however, is the large variety of outlays which are accumulated in the very general overhead accounts and the almost universal dependence placed on a single allocation method: distribution in proportion to production wages.

The most important overhead in Soviet accounting is shop expenses. The scope of the category varies from branch to branch, but usually it includes the expenses of operating machinery and equipment (depreciation of machines, cost of energy, wages of machine-maintenance personnel, current repair, and so on), the costs of intrashop transport, auxiliary materials, the wages of all supervisory and auxiliary personnel, depreciation of shop assets other than machines, depreciation of tools and dies, testing, and many others. In short, it includes nearly every expenditure made at the level of the shop except wages of direct production workers and the costs of direct materials and semifabricates.

With very few exceptions, this entire category of expense is distributed in proportion to the wages of production workers recorded for the separate kinds of output. The possibilities for error which this method of distribution opens up are suggested by the high ratios of shop expense to production wages characteristic of Soviet plants. Concrete figures are not often given in Soviet sources, but there is enough information to indicate that the ratio is very high. Before the war, in the machine-building branches, for instance, shop expenses were usually about four or five times higher than production wages.[3] Additional information on shop expenses is often found in planning handbooks and in "illustrative calculations" in cost-accounting textbooks and books on cost analysis. These usually show shop expenses that are two to three times higher than production wages.

This nearly universal dependence on wages as a basis for distributing all the components of shop expenses inevitably means serious distortions in cost accounting. Many of the items which the Russians include in shop expenses simply do not vary in proportion to wages, and to distribute them on this basis is completely arbitrary. Some of the outlays included in this account, particularly the costs of supervision and administration, may vary more or less in proportion to working time. As long as the hourly rates on different lines of production are the same, then wages are a fairly good measure of labor time and, accordingly, a reasonable basis for distributing these particular elements of shop expenses. But the correspondence between wages and labor time disappears when the workers on different products are paid at different rates. Certainly the Russians have an extremely differentiated wage structure, and it seems quite possible that there would frequently be differences in the average wage rate of workers on different kinds of output within the shop. The correspondence between working time and wages is further disrupted by the widespread use of simple and progressive piecerate wage systems in Soviet enterprises.[4] If the norms are fulfilled unevenly as between different lines of production, then wages are no longer proportionate to labor hours. Soviet accounting makes some allowance for this fact by excluding from the wage base used for distributing shop expenses the premiums paid to workers for overfulfillment of the norms under the progressive piecerate system (the so-called *progressivki*). The rationale for this system of payment is that a large part of shop expenses varies in proportion to labor time. Therefore workers who overfulfill the norms save overhead per unit of output, and the regime is willing to encourage overfulfillment by sharing the gain with the workers responsible. On this basis it would be incorrect to charge shop expenses to such an output in proportion to full earnings, and so the Russians exclude the progressivki from the wage base used in distribution of shop expenses. But these same considerations are equally pertinent under a simple piecerate system. Workers who overfulfill the norms save overhead and those who underfulfill them waste it, but the use of actual wages as a basis for distributing overhead masks this difference. When under the simple piecerate system the norms are fulfilled unevenly, overhead will be allocated incorrectly. It is said that such divergent fulfillment of norms is of frequent occurrence.[5]

Many of the elements of shop expenses could be distributed more sensibly on some alternative basis. This is certainly true of the expenses connected with the operation of machinery, for instance, which make up a very large share of the category. To distribute these costs in proportion to wages is especially undesirable, since the degree of mechanization of different processes within the shop may differ. In such a situation the labor-intensive outputs which benefit relatively little from the machines will be charged the greatest share of their costs. From what is known about the crudity of Soviet methods of capital allocation, the unevenness of the process of mechanization, and the relative lack of freedom of the manager to control his investment, it seems likely that there would be a heterogeneous level of mechanization even at the level of the shop. Indeed, the Soviet writers on accounting consider that such unevenness of mechanization is common and that distribution of machine expense in proportion to wages is one of the worst errors of Soviet cost accounting.[6] A better method for distributing these expenses is obviously on some sort of a machine-use basis. These expenses can be charged to the groups of machines involved and then to the output eventually benefited. Most Soviet textbooks describe various machine-use methods of distribution, but apparently these methods are not actually used in many enterprises. According to one writer, the first important attempt to introduce the machine-use basis of distribution came only in 1938, when the Commissariat of Heavy Industry attempted a reclassification of expense and the introduction of this method in its enterprises.[7] However, even these instructions seem to have left open the possibility of distributing most shop expenses in proportion to wages, and one author in 1944 stated that distribution on a machine-use basis is "in practice little used." [8] Apparently the separation of the expense of operating machinery into a special category in the cost estimates and cost reports has spread rapidly; by 1953 it was said to be universally required.[9] But the mere separation of these expenses into a special account has not been accompanied by a shift from the production-wage method of distribution. This would involve too much work. A 1953 source concerned with the machine-building branches, in which this method was first introduced and in which it is presumed to be most widely used, says that the machine-use methods are used "in some machinebuilding plants," but that the method of distribution in proportion to production wages is "the most widely used method." [10]

The second account in which overheads are accumulated in Soviet enterprises is general plant expenses. Included here are maintenance of general plant facilities, wages of general managerial personnel, cost of plant laboratories and design departments, maintenance of warehouses, losses, fines, and local taxes.[11] This overhead, like shop expenses, is nearly always distributed in proportion to production wages. Statements to this effect are frequently made and examination of the specialized branch accounting texts verifies them. There are some cases in which other methods are used, but these appear to be exceptions. The alternatives are distribution in proportion to raw-material cost, in proportion to shop value added, or in proportion to total shop cost. The method of distribution in proportion to total cost was once universal,[12] but with occasional exceptions it has now been replaced by the wage basis.

Technological bases for distributing these expenses are less obvious than for many elements of shop expenses. Nevertheless, some of the components could be more accurately distributed on some direct basis. For instance, the costs of maintaining warehouses could be charged to procurement operations and included in cost by way of materials. Similarly, the costs of maintaining laboratories and research facilities could no doubt be better charged to the particular kinds of output which these facilities service. The fines paid for violations of the electric-power contract are a cost of electricity, and so on. However, it is very difficult to argue that the majority of items of general plant expenses would vary in proportion to any conceivable technological indicator. This is true of the big category of administrative expenses, the fines and penalties, the various local collections and taxes, and others. Russian writers on accounting generally take this position.

As was said earlier, the proper method of distributing overhead costs depends on the manner in which they vary. Perhaps the most pertinent bit of evidence in this connection would be the view that the planners take of general plant expenses in their ex ante calculations. How do they actually estimate the amount of general expenses when they draw up cost plans? Unfortunately the evidence found on this score leaves the issue in doubt. The planning practices of the Russians seem to imply that they do not know how general expenses vary. According to one source, plant designers, in estimating costs in prospective plants, figure general plant expenses as a percentage of wages.[13] The literature on cost planning and cost analysis, however, seems to follow a different assumption. It devotes much attention to the behavior of these expenses and their division into those that are "constant" and "proportional," but the assumption throughout is that those which vary do so in proportion to the volume of output. For instance, one writer says:

The planning of indirect expenses should be based on the limits which are established for the plant by the glavk [ministry] and which specify the amount of each group of indirect expenses per thousand rubles of gross production and their absolute limits.[14]

If the project makers are right, then the existing treatment is correct. But if the others are right, the variable part of general plant expenses, at least, should be distributed in proportion to total shop cost.

In all these imperfections of Soviet cost accounting, there is probably no great harm. They only mirror clumsiness in administrative control and in cost planning. The ability of higher management echelons to predict the behavior of these costs at the planning stage, to distinguish responsibility for costs, and to check on the fulfillment of cost performance is so limited that the employment of more sophisticated methods in overhead-cost allocation would be superfluous. It will not often happen that at the fairly aggregative level, where decision makers are considering prices of alternative goods, any decisions of importance will turn on the allocation of overhead costs which has been made at the enterprise level. (At lower levels of decision making within the enterprise there may be some decisions which are so affected, as we shall see in Chapter 7.) This probably explains the Soviet tolerance for simple but erroneous allocation methods. At the same time, however, there are a number of cases where economic decisions or an issue of control *do* turn on the allocation of enterprise overhead costs, and in these situations the designers of the Soviet cost-accounting system have shown much more interest in allocation standards.

One of these cases involves the distribution of shop expenses and general plant expenses between finished and unfinished production. The general rule for this was laid down by an instructional letter of the Commissariat of Finance of November 29, 1940. General plant expenses and shop expenses are to be assigned to unfinished production only in the planned amount and the rest is to be written off to finished production. However, exceptions are made for special cases. In those industries in which increases or decreases in unfinished production are not specifically planned, *all* overhead costs go to finished production.[15] (It is often argued that all overhead should be charged to finished production in all industries.[16]) In those industries with large series production and mass production, overhead can be included in unfinished production at "standard cost," and in those industries in which large discrete units of output are produced, as in shipbuilding and turbinebuilding, unfinished production may include full actual overhead.

These procedures can lead to serious time distortions in the cost reports and in the valuation of unfinished production in the balance sheet. This will be true where overhead is assigned wholly to finished production, if there is any change in the stock of unfinished production, and also where overhead is included in unfinished production to the planned amount, if the change in the stock of unfinished production is significantly different from that planned. Such changes must surely be frequent in Soviety industry, especially over the short accounting period of one month, and this objection is in fact often made by Soviet accountants.[17] Moreover, the volume of unfinished production can fluctuate widely in different lines, even when the overall amount remains more or less constant. These rules simply do not allow for the specific conditions of individual plants, and by removing the decision from the local accountant they

111

lay the basis for some senseless allocations. One writer cites the following examples:

In those cases where such instructions are issued without the necessary qualifications, some plants permit distortions of cost through applying incorrectly the principle of standard cost valuation of unfinished production. Thus in one machine construction plant, producing small series output, actual expenditures on one series of ten units was one million rubles, whereas planned costs were . . . 500,000 rubles. . . . by the end of the accounting period only one unit had been completed. The accounting section valued outlays on the unfinished units at planned cost, that is at about 450,000 rubles, and wrote all the rest of the outlays, that is, 500,000 rubles, onto the one finished unit.

In another plant expenditures on one unfinished item exceeded the planned amount of outlays considerably; in drawing up the annual report the chief accountant could think of nothing else to do but write the amount of this excess onto the cost of finished items of a completely different type perhaps with the aim of "cleaning the balance sheet of unreal accounts."

Such impermissible distortions of the cost indicators unfortunately take place not in two or three enterprises, but are met with quite frequently.[18]

The reason for the adoption of these methods is that they facilitate control. There is a great temptation in Soviet enterprises to permit expenses to accumulate in the unfinished-production accounts for long periods rather than to report them as costs.[19] By setting up this very clear-cut rule as to how much expense is to be charged to unfinished production, such manipulations are forestalled. Rules of this kind, which distort the cost figures but strengthen control, are common in Soviet accounting. The principle of forcing pessimistic interpretations of cost results plays much the same role in Soviet accounting as the principle of conservatism in income determination plays in capitalist accounting. In both cases the rules may lead to unrealistic figures, but, because they are simple and objective, they remove certain questions from the possibility of local interpretation and so help to prevent willful misrepresentation.

Most enterprises carry on some auxiliary activities, and some overhead is assigned to these. Here also allocation affects a variable in which higher-level management is much interested (an evaluation of cost performance turns on it), and so the designers of the Soviet cost-accounting system have given much attention to that allocation. This is not to say that they will necessarily seek a sophisticated allocation rule but, rather, an easily defined and checkable one. As a corollary, one can almost predict that the rule they settle on will be a biased one for control and a crude one for cost calculation. Enterprises are often tempted to assign excessive amounts of overhead to capital-repair operations. Costs of capital repair are charged to the amortization fund or other sources of financing rather than directly to the cost of current output, and the assignment of overhead outlays to these accounts therefore makes the reported cost of output look better. The solution adopted to control this temptation toward falsification is to set limits, and these are expressed as a percentage of the wage outlay on capital repair.[20] The Commissariat of Heavy Industry, for instance, at one time set a fixed coefficient for the ratio of overhead to wages in capital-repair costs of 113 percent,[21] and the shipbuilding industry is said to have a coefficient of 33 percent.[22] Moreover, capital repair carried out by shops other than the repair shop may not be charged to shop expenses if it is in excess of the norms set up for the repair-mechanical or the repair-construction shops.[23] In effect planned costs are here being substituted for real ex post calculation of what it costs to repair machinery. As will be seen in Chapter 7, this may confuse the decision about whether to repair or replace equipment.

A third account in which overhead is accumulated is expenses of auxiliary shops, where the outlays of such service shops as power, repair, transportation, and others are recorded. In the past, expenses of auxiliary shops were usually included in general plant expenses and were distributed on the same basis. In recent years, however, there has been a tendency to keep them in a separate category and to assign them directly to the shops benefited. For most of these shops it would be fairly easy to find some direct method of distribution among the main production shops on the basis of services actually rendered, but it is said that the methods used are often arbitrary or inexact. Even in allocating the costs of power plants, where the consumption of energy by the different consuming shops should provide an exact basis for distribution, the lack of measuring devices prevents an accurate assignment. In as late as 1954 one writer says:

The majority of industrial enterprises at the present time do not provide the necessary accounting of all the actual expenditures of the shop. . . . the shops are not equipped with the control-measuring devices necessary to account for the expenditures of water, electric energy, air, and steam. . . . The expenditures of these cost items by khozraschet shops is made in some enterprises at planned norms, in others according to conventional coefficients, and in others according to the arbitrary directions of the department of the chief mechanic.[24]

Finally, overhead at the level of the enterprise includes non-production expenses (*vne-proizvodstvennye raskhody*). This category covers the expenses connected with selling, expenses for maintenance of finished-goods warehouses, expenses of the trust (the trust is a central administrative organ for several enterprises, not supported by the budget), "outlays on technical propaganda," expenses connected with standardization, and deductions for the support of research institutions. These expenses are distributed among outputs in proportion to total factory cost, both at the level at which the outlays of a trust are allocated among its constituent enterprises and at the level at which the plant assigns these costs to different outputs. I have found no Soviet rationalization for allocating this overhead on the basis of full factory cost, in contrast to the wage basis used for other overheads. Presumably it reflects some notion that it is a more general kind of overhead and should be distributed accordingly.

It is hard to imagine that any important distortions are involved here, especially since these expenses are relatively unimportant. The category is interesting rather because it indicates the contradictions in the theoretical bases of Soviet accounting. The original rationale for distinguishing these outlays in a separate category was that they were nonproductive expenses of distribution, which in Marxist economic theory are distinguished from outlays on production. Corresponding to this dichotomy, enterprise cost accounting distinguished factory cost, which is composed of all the outlays on production, and commercial cost, which is made up of factory cost plus the nonproduction costs. Presumably this distinction is necessary in computing national income according to Marxist definitions. In actual practice, however, the distinction has come to be completely meaningless, since many purely production costs are included in nonproduction costs and purely "commercial" expenses are included in the factory-cost concept.[25] In other words, this is a distinction which represents a somewhat confused obeisance toward Marxist economic theory, with no real practical justification.

It should be added that it is a fairly common practice in Soviet industry to distribute not only overheads but also direct expenses on a very arbitrary basis. In some enterprises, particularly in the branches of industry characterized by a wide assortment of outputs and in smaller plants elsewhere, all ex-

115

penses of an enterprise may be distributed among products in accordance with some predetermined formula rather than on the basis of any actual cost calculation. This is often called the "simplified standard" cost method or, quite aptly, the "kettle method" of cost calculation. The actual forms it takes are diverse, but in essence it operates as follows. During the month, outlays are accumulated in plant-wide expense categories such as material, wages, plant expenses, shop expenses, and so on. At the end of the month, the cost of each kind of output is computed according to the norms of the Gosplan, and the corresponding amounts are written off the plant-wide expense accounts. What is left in the expense accounts after this distribution is then assigned to the different outputs in proportion to the amounts determined by the planned norms. In other words, there is no real ex post accounting. Although the practice is often condemned, it appears to be fairly common. It seems to be used in the textile industry, the furniture industry, the shoe industry, the leather industry, among others. The method is obligatory for all enterprises under regional, city, and oblast jurisdiction and for industrial cooperatives.

In sum, the Russians have characteristically clung to methods of distributing overhead expenses which, although they are frequently arbitrary and seriously distorting, have the compensating virtue of great simplicity and exact definition. Soviet writers on accounting are well aware of the shortcomings of these methods, as can be seen from the following typical statement.

The imperfection of the method of distribution in proportion to production wages is beyond doubt. We may therefore suppose that in a number of cases life will force us to abandon it and to replace it with a more well-founded and a more perfected method.[26]

At the same time, it is perfectly clear why the Russians have failed to improve their methods. More detailed classification of overheads and more precise ways of distributing individual elements of overhead would mean a great deal more bookkeeping work and would require and permit more initiative on the part of the enterprise bookkeeping staff. The centralized control of accounting practice and the primitive technology of Soviet accounting compel the use of arbitrary, but at the same time simple, methods of overhead distribution.

Allocation of Cost among Joint Products

It frequently happens that a given production process produces several distinctive products concurrently, as in meatpacking, the refining of petroleum, or the mining and refining of polymetallic ores. This has always posed a puzzling problem for Soviet cost accounting. In these cases most costs cannot be considered to have been incurred solely on behalf of any of the outputs taken separately, and a cost-of-production theory of value will not suffice for calculating the value of joint products. This is a problem which can be understood only in the light of a market or other imputational theory of value. The bookkeeper can make an ex post distribution on whatever grounds he chooses, but the costs so determined will be arbitrary and, in the nature of the case, can never determine value. Unwilling to admit any such un-Marxist position, the Russians have entangled themselves in a circular argument. Theoreticians of value say that prices are based on the cost of production; on the other hand, accountants frequently state that in joint-product cases total costs are distributed between the products in proportion to their prices. The Russians have never been able to rationalize this contradiction or even consistently to elect one or the other horn of the dilemma. Occasionally they have adopted practices which imply acceptance of the fact that the value of joint products cannot be determined by cost accounting and must be determined by reference to demand, but at

117

other times they appear to consider the problem purely one of cost accounting and have attempted to solve it through completely irrelevant allocation formulas.

The accountants of capitalist firms, of course, also encounter joint-production situations that require cost allocation. However, it is generally recognized in the literature dealing with this matter that these cost allocations are only for the purpose of internal calculations; the accountants are under no illusion that they are determining "values." That problem is settled by market forces. They recognize that their allocations are essentially arbitrary and that the validity of any particular allocation approach depends on the use to be made of the cost data — for example, whether it is a decision about pricing, about varying the proportions between products, or about the feasibility of recovering a byproduct.[27]

In present-day Soviet accounting literature there is no clue to what the Russians might have as a theory of value in the case of joint products. The textbooks confine themselves to a bare description of the instructions for particular cases. One must look to discussions of earlier years for a theory of joint-product pricing. On examination, it seems that most of the current procedures are literal applications of these earlier recommendations. The most interesting article on this subject, the general tone of which is echoed in all other discussions, is one by S. G. Strumilin.[28] In the cost-accounting instructions issued by the VSNKh in 1926, accountants were instructed to value joint products and byproducts "at their marginal utility," a formulation to which Strumilin objected on the basis of its "bourgeois Austrian" character. The instructions were drawn up by engineers, and Strumilin interpreted their error as the result of ignorance and the lack of guidance from the economic theoreticians. So he set out to resolve the problem in a way that would be consistent with Marxist theory. The essence of his suggestion was that the answer lay in substitutability. In poly-metallic mining and refining, the separate outputs could be valued in accord with the costs of the same metals produced in monometallic mines. Furnace slag is used as a fertilizer, and so it can be priced at its value as fertilizer and its value at this price subtracted from the cost of production of iron and steel. Different grades of coal could be priced in accordance with their technical common denominator — heat content. These are sensible proposals; the prices of joint products should be iden-tical with their marginal productivity in an optimum solution. But Strumilin was certainly misled in thinking that his proposal was any less Austrian than the VSNKh instruction. All the methods he suggests seem to differ from the words of the in-struction only by way of replacing the abstract formulation "at marginal utility" with operational definitions of the same con-cept or of the concept of marginal productivity. Moreover, Strumilin's suggestions are not fully worked out. For instance, distribution in proportion to technological equivalence of the separate outputs is impossible if the products are not techno-logically substitutable. On what grounds is one to say that not-so-good steel is worth 85 percent as much as high-quality steel, as Strumilin suggests? Even when there seems to be a more reasonable technological equivalence, his method is far too crude. Consider, for instance, the oil-extraction industry where joint costs are distributed between crude oil and well-head gas in proportion to their heat content.[29] It is true that both oil and gas are used to produce heat, but they are not merely identical outputs in different formats, so to speak. They can be used for technologically distinct ends (for one, it is not feasible to run locomotives on natural gas); and even when they serve the same general technological end, they still require a different structure of accompanying inputs in their transportation, stor-age, and utilization. So their value as derived from their marginal productivity as inputs is not necessarily proportional to their heat content. Indeed, if Strumilin's suggestions are carried to their logical conclusion, a host of other value problems will arise to plague the Marxist theorist of value in the form of the very capitalistic categories of rent, obsolescence, and market valuation. If the outputs of a heat and power combine are priced at the prices of electricity and heat from separate installations, what economic category will be represented in the profit of the efficient combine? Or if only the price *ratio* is used, so that the profit is eliminated, why should relative scarcities under the old technology dictate values under the new? Strumilin's suggestions raise more questions than they answer. Yet when one examines the actual instructions, one finds that these simple notions do indeed seem to be the only source of theoretical guidance underlying present-day practice.

The joint-product problem has arisen in many different contexts in the Soviet Union, and Russian accountants have shown a great deal of confusion in distinguishing joint-product cases and in elaborating rules for accounting for them. The topic is usually discussed as one aspect under the heading of "distribution," and the textbooks and other sources describe a number of different ways in which this pricing problem is handled.

First, for some joint-product cases no attempt is made to calculate the cost of production, and prices are set on some other basis. The allocation of costs among products is treated purely as a pricing problem. This is generally true in the traditional discriminating monopolies — the electric-power industry, railway and river transportation, and so on. In these branches a cost of production is calculated, but it is an average cost of production for all kinds and classes of service, rather than for individual kinds, and is calculated for control purposes. Thus in the cost accounting of the railroads all that is computed is the cost per passenger-kilometer, per ton-kilometer of freight, and per axle-kilometer of postal cars. The price decision in those cases may very well be based on some sort of marginal cost calculations, but these calculations are in the nature of special one-time investigations and are not made regularly as part of the accounting routine.

A similar case is that in which costs are distributed in proportion to output valued at existing prices. Here the cost accounting does determine a cost for the separate outputs, but obviously this distribution is predetermined by the pricing decision rather than vice versa. For instance, it is said that in polymetallic mining and refining the distribution among the component metals is made in proportion to value at "conventionally accepted prices." [30] In the case of nonferrous metals a conscious attempt is apparently made to take account of demand and productivity in setting prices, and the cost-accounting allocation is not a determinant of these prices.

In very many cases the Russians have interpreted joint-product cases as if they did not really involve joint products. In sovkhoz accounting, for instance, it is claimed that the separate costs of milk and of calves can be calculated on the basis of technical norms. It is estimated — the Russians alone know how — that the feed norm per tsentner of milk is so much and that the feed norm for the gestation of a calf is so much. The total cost of maintaining the milk herd and the bulls over the year is then distributed between milk and calves produced in proportion to the outputs valued in terms of these norms.[31] The same sort of an approach elaborated in an absurdly exact way is used in calculating the cost of production of various outputs in the classic case of sheep. One writer gives the followng list of "feed requirements" in sheepraising, which he considers to be a technical basis for distributing joint costs.[32] Even if Soviet agrobiology does surpass its bourgeois counterpart in knowing that exactly 38 percent of the feed intake of a ram goes for

Accounting group	Wool	Offspring	Growth of young animals	Milk
Sire rams	38	62	—	—
Grown dams	50	50	—	—
Grown dams milked	50	45	—	5
Lambs after weaning	25	—	75	—
Last year's young animals	37	—	63	—
Rams not used for breeding	100	—	—	—

growing wool and exactly 62 percent for producing offspring, this would still be no basis for distributing total costs.

An analogous case based on the same confusion of thought, but relating to the industrial sphere, is that of heat and power combines. In these combines steam is used at high temperatures and pressures for generating electricity and then is further used for various heating purposes. The accounting practice here is to separate out first those costs which benefit one or the other process exclusively and then to distribute the costs which benefit both in proportion to a theoretically calculated consumption of energy in the two processes.[33] Presumably in this case it is possible for such a determination to be made, but this is still no basis for calculating costs. It finds no support in the production function. As Soviet engineers themselves point out,[34] the laws of thermodynamics dictate that, whenever heat is converted into mechanical energy, some heat must be lost. The removal of the whole heating adjunct of the combine would not decrease the cost of producing steam for a given output of electricity. As long as electricity is to be produced, the heat literally costs nothing. So the technological distribution of energy consumption between the heat and the power processes is irrelevant to any economic calculation. If the accountants think that what they are computing is a cost of production, which from their Marxian point of view is the same as the value of the outputs and should regulate the prices, they are badly mistaken. A reductio ad absurdum of the same sort of thinking is the proposal by some oil-industry accountants that heat costs in refining should be distributed among the various distillation fractions in proportion to the heat content of each as it leaves the apparatus.

The oil industry reveals the joint-product problem in a clear-cut form. The variety of approaches the Russians have used here shows the absence of any theory of joint-product pricing. The problem in the extraction phase is the distribution of costs between gas and oil. As already mentioned, this distribution is made in proportion to the heat content of the two fuels. Actually what is done is to consider the output homogeneous, with gas converted to crude-oil equivalents on the basis of heat content. Then cost is figured per ton of this composite output. In the refining phase the system of allocation has a long and complex history. Under the first cost-accounting instructions issued in 1928, costs were distributed in the following way. (1) Distillation fractions going to fuel oil were written off the refinery account at a value-per-unit weight equal to that at which crude oil was taken on. (2) The remaining cost of crude oil was distributed among all other fractions in proportion to weight. (3) The cost of fuel used in refining was distributed on the same basis. (4) Distillation losses were distributed differently in different trusts — in some in proportion to conventional coefficients, in some in proportion to the specific gravity of the various fractions.[35]

This approach was apparently abandoned sometime after 1931 and was replaced with a centralized system of distribution coefficients.[36] The use of such coefficients greatly simplified cost accounting, especially since it was permitted to distribute nearly all expenses in proportion to the coefficients, even those which might have been distributable directly. Where the coefficients came from is not clear, though quite possibly they were determined on the same basis as those used for the distribution in individual plants. The coefficient method was succeeded by distribution of costs in proportion to prices and then, even more recently, by a somewhat more complicated formula in which raw-materials costs are distributed essentially in proportion to weight; processing costs are more carefully segregated by stages in the refining process and attributed to the outputs associated with those stages.[37] It is not certain whether the results are then to be taken as a basis for pricing, but this would seem to be suggested.

The method of distribution in proportion to coefficients seems to be very widely used. Industries mentioned as employing it are lumber milling,[38] meatpacking,[39] grain milling,[40] textiles,[41] paper and cellulose,[42] and ferrous metallurgy.[43] And other reports say that this is the general method used in any problem of grades and sorts.[44] Usually there is no explanation of the source of these coefficients, but it seems likely that most of them originate in some such spurious technological calculations as those used in the oil industry, or that they reflect relative values under the existing price system. For instance, one writer says that, in the calculations of the coefficients for the different grades (as in textiles, paper and cellulose, and lumber milling), a determination of the "real" underlying costs is used.[45] Some say that such coefficients are established in relation to wholesale prices.[46] On the other hand, Turetski, an eminent Soviet authority on costing and pricing, states that the determination of these coefficients is not scientifically grounded and is made in each case on an *ad hoc* basis and "by guess."[47]

A slightly different procedure is used in cases where the relative amounts of the outputs are greatly different. The relatively unimportant outputs are called byproducts (*otkhody* or *pobochnaya produktsiya*), and their value is subtracted from the total cost to obtain the cost attributable to the main product.

The procedure differs from that used for other joint products only in that the cost and price of the byproducts are taken to be identical and any profit or loss made on all products is attributed to the main products. As long as the magnitudes of possible error are small, this practice is probably justifiable on the grounds that it simplifies the cost accounting.[48] But it is claimed that sometimes under this method the value of byproducts exceeds all costs, leaving the main products with a negative cost.[49]

In general, it is unlikely that the formulas used in allocating costs among joint products mislead the Russians in their economic calculations. In many situations, the pricing decisions seem to be made more or less independently of the allocations among joint products which the cost accountants make. But if this is true, there is little point in making such distributions. If the prices are determined on rational grounds — that is, taking account of demand — one learns nothing by distributing the costs in proportion to value except that the profitability of all joint products is the same. If the costs are distributed by another formula, those who use the data conclude that profits on different products are different and they must surely recognize that this accounting result means nothing. Also, such distribution of costs among joint products cannot have any important control function. In such situations the accountants should concentrate on cost classifications that reveal areas of responsibility, costs of certain units and operations, and should forget about trying to estimate the costs of separate outputs. Altogether this seems to be, at best, an instance of the waste motion stemming from the Russians' preoccupation with a genetic conception of value; and to the extent that they take these costs seriously, as, in petroleum refining, they may well make errors in calculation.

ALLOCATION OF OUTLAYS

TO CENTRAL OVERHEAD

THE ALLOCATION problems discussed in the previous chapters have one thing in common: the outlays involved are always interpreted as costs of production, and the only point at issue is the assignment of these outlays to different kinds of output or separate accounting periods. This chapter takes up the question of dividing outlays between cost-of-production accounts and other kinds of accounts at the level of the enterprise. The question, a variant of the one posed in Chapter 2, is whether an outlay made by the enterprise should be charged as part of the cost of its output, or whether it should be written off through the overhead accounts in the head office to the cost of output of other enterprises. (I am concerned here only with outlays that benefit current output and shall ignore those which represent disposition of income by the enterprise on behalf of the head office.) These outlays may be divided into two categories: (1) enterprise outlays financed out of the state budget and (2) outlays written off directly to the profit and loss account. Is the Russian assignment of certain outlays to these overhead accounts justified? The objective in considering this question here is not so much to judge Soviet treatment as to discover the objectives underlying this treatment, to see how it is affected by the exigencies of controlling costs, and to clarify what constitutes a loss in the Soviet economy.

Enterprise Outlays Financed by the Budget

Although Soviet enterprises are generally operated on the principle of khozraschet, under which their outlays are supposed to be recouped by their revenues, some of the outlays are still written off at the expense of the budget. Most of the budget grants to enterprises are for investment purposes of one kind or another, and these are capitalized and later charged to production. But there are certain kinds of budget grants which are never so charged either in the current period or in subsequent periods. In enterprise accounting, budgetary grants for such purposes are called "financing for special purposes" (*tselevoe finansirovanie*) and are accounted for as follows. The approved amount is debited to the settlement account in the Gosbank and credited to the special-financing account. When the outlay is made, the amount is transferred from the settlement account in the Gosbank to an appropriate expenditure account, and at the end of the year the amount is simply erased from both sides of the balance sheet. It is credited to the expenditure account and debited to the special-financing account.

Under this procedure such outlays never affect either the cost accounts or the profit and loss account. Once made, they disappear from the balance sheet without a trace.[1] The correctness of this procedure from the point of view of accurate assignment of costs would seem to turn on whether the outlays are made in behalf of one plant or branch alone or whether the plant is acting only as an agent for the state in making expenditures which will result in some general benefit affecting a large area of the economy. As a matter of fact, these outlays are for a wide range of purposes, including many which seem to be for the exclusive benefit of the plant or at most for a limited portion of the economy. The most important of these are such investments as expenditures for developing new products, financing invention, and training workers.

One would think that such outlays should be charged to current production or, if their benefits are long delayed, capitalized to be charged against output later. Soviet economists and accountants themselves view the existing practice as undesirable. The economist Strumilin advocated that these expenditures be included in the cost of production,[2] and the same opinion was repeated in a 1947 source.[3] One factor that makes this treatment objectionable is that it is inconsistent with the treatment of other outlays similar in nature. All these expenditures may be alternatively financed from other sources, and then they are charged to the cost of production. The justification for their not being so charged when financed from the budget usually involves the overriding influence of administrative expediency on the cost concept. In the case of inventions, the present rules were probably introduced to remove funds from the control of enterprises and to put them under the budget in order to strengthen the control exercised over their use. Before 1940 inventions were financed out of the fund for assistance to inventions formed in each enterprise by a charge to general plant expenses.[4] Locally administered funds of this kind permitted plant management too much maneuverability in figuring the cost of production and the profit and loss result, however, and most of them were abandoned in the early forties. In the vocabulary of administration, enterprise management was divested of some of its authority, and administrative consistency then required that management no longer be held responsible for such expenditures. Since the cost report is the measure of an enterprise's performance in fulfilling its responsibilities for minimizing costs, these outlays were not to be included in it. This case illustrates one of the characteristic problems of Soviet administration. The present rules specify that it is only inventions of branch or economy-wide significance that are to be financed by the budget, and the cost of inventions with a purely enterprise significance are to be charged directly to the cost of production. It is said, however, that as these rules are interpreted nearly all the expenses of inventions are charged to the budget.[5] It turns out to be almost impossible to make authority and responsibility completely congruent. Enterprise managers have enough authority to incur expenses which the present accounting method enables them to escape responsibility for, but this output fails to get charged for some of the outlays that are made on its behalf.

Similar administrative considerations influence the present treatment of expenditures for the training of labor.[6] This is the kind of work that the enterprise is likely to neglect or to be reluctant to undertake. By having the enterprise list its training operations on the special-financing account, and omitting the outlays from cost, the state is better able to guarantee that the requisite amount will actually be spent on training. To enforce decisions taken at some higher level of the system, it is important that the performance norms for subordinates be defined so as not to tempt them to underfulfill the decision.

As for budget-financed outlays on developing new products, it is hard to imagine any truly expedient reason for omitting them from costs. These are true costs, usually specifically of the output of the plant which incurs them, and should be included in the cost figures. This particular omission is especially senseless because such expenses are always included in costs when they are financed out of working capital. If budget grants for financing such expenses were called an addition to working

129

capital instead of financing for special purposes, the expenses would then be capitalized and charged to production in the usual way. This is surely what is done in many cases. It is difficult to imagine what advantage the state sees in this divergent treatment. The managers have no incentive to improve their cost reports by foregoing such outlays, as they presumably do in the case of labor-training expenses. Nor is this policy dictated by any pricing or investment objective, since the state is free to set the price at any level and thus later to divest the enterprise of the funds spent for this purpose or to permit it to recoup them. The same inconsistency is found in the case of development work carried out by the branch "scientific research institutes." The maintenance of these institutes is sometimes included in costs of enterprises as "deductions for the support of higher organizations," but in some branches the institutes are supported by the budget.[7] Similarly, the extraordinary expenses of plants in the first period of operation (the so-called *puskovye raskhody*) are not treated uniformly. The official rule is that they must be assigned to the cost of production.[8] Other sources say that they may be capitalized[9] or written off to the budget or to the profit and loss account.[10] This divergence in treatment of a class of expenses which is homogeneous in its economic significance seems to be the result of accidents of bookkeeping formulation and of organizational structure; the mistake of omitting them from cost is not dictated by a competing expediency.

There are other miscellaneous expenses charged to the budget: in the coal industry, the costs of extinguishing underground fires; in the meat industry, the cost of sanitary inspection; in trade, certain expenses of haulage; in some construction organizations, the stumpage fee.[11] All of these are surely small in amount and whether they are included in costs or not will have only a negligible effect on costs. At the same time, they are true costs, and there is no reason why the Russians could not easily include them in their cost calculations. Hence, they are interesting for what they reveal about the Soviet concept of cost and about the kind of considerations that have influenced the construction of a cost-accounting system for the Soviet economy.

These examples make more concrete what was said earlier in Chapter 2 about the interrelation of the cost concept and the degree of administrative subtlety that can be mustered by so large a bureaucracy. Consider the losses from fires in coal mines as an example. The commentaries explain that these are treated as a head-office loss because no provision is made to cover them in cost and price planning. This implies, in turn, that the planners are unable to foresee them at the time they plan costs and, as a corollary, that mine management is given no explicit charge to minimize them. But obviously they are foreseeable and are subject to manipulation and economic choice. The device of insurance would be one way to improve administrative efficiency. An insurance premium charged against each mine would assign this cost to the coal-producing organization where it belongs, and if the insurance rates were made to vary with the degree of compliance to general protective measures, cost accounting in its control aspects would work to enlist management in the task of optimizing the amount of this loss. One may well suspect that the present accounting treatment simply recognizes the Soviet inability to achieve this kind of administrative subtlety, as their failure to allocate this cost down the hierarchy indicates. When mine fires occur, the controllers at higher levels must accept them as an unforeseeable loss visited upon them by a deus ex machina. Behind each of the other examples there lurks a similar tale, although it is not necessary to develop each of the arguments here.

Finally, a distinction should be made between the budget

financing described above and subsidies proper (*dotatsii*). Subsidies paid to cover a planned loss are fixed beforehand and are paid at an established rate per unit of output. In the accounting they are treated as revenue rather than as deductions from costs. Thus the cost reports of the subsidized plant show real costs. In subsequent accounting units, the costs are understated, of course, but this is a function of the pricing policy, not a result of understating costs in the accounting.

Assignments to the Profit and Loss Account

In Soviet enterprise accounting, a number of outlays are written off directly to the profit and loss account and are thus not counted as costs of the output of the plant. These outlays may still eventually be considered costs in subsequent units of the production system, if prices are set high enough so that the plant actually earns a profit to cover them. But this is a function of the markup-over-cost policy. In what follows I am concerned only with the independent effect of including or omitting these outlays from costs. The issue is whether they are true losses or true costs of production.[12] A long list of outlays is treated in this way in Soviet accounting, as is shown by the following items.

1. War losses
2. Last year's losses (or profits)
3. Losses on canceled orders
4. Losses on mastering the production of items which are never mass-produced
5. Losses from production risks not envisaged in the plan
6. Expenditures on fruitless experiments
7. Losses from stoppages
8. Costs of maintaining reserve enterprises
9. Loss or profit from writing off bad debts
10. Loss or profit from writing off claims on expiration of the settlement period

11. Fines, penalties and forfeits, excess of receipts
12. Loss (profits) of subsidiary enterprises
    (a) packing
    (b) subsidiary enterprises of construction entities which are on an independent balance sheet
    (c) housing
    (d) agricultural enterprises
    (e) realization on the side of materials and services
13. Losses from natural disasters
14. Revaluations of materials
15. Funds and reserves
    (a) director's fund
    (b) deductions to the guarantee reserve

The Russians generally rationalize the distinction between the items going to the cost of production and those going directly to the profit and loss account on the grounds that the latter are not connected with production or that they are not subject to the control of enterprise management. One Soviet authority, in discussing these losses, says:

In the process of the work of the enterprise there arise more or less significant losses . . . These losses are written off to the results account. Their inclusion in cost of production is inappropriate since, as was pointed out above, they are not connected with the production or realization of the goods being costed or are independent of the enterprise.[13]

The difficulty with this explanation is that examination of outlays treated in this way shows that most of them can be said to be unconnected with production only in a restricted sense. The crucial question is whether or not they are likely to vary with output, with various state policies, and so on, or whether they are completely fortuitous and therefore unpredictable and uncontrollable. If, when a given output program or industrial policy is being decided upon, expenses of the kind listed above can be predicted, then they are costs and not losses. It might

133

appear that in a centrally planned economy many types of losses familiar in a market economy ought to disappear. Losses arise in a market economy from failures of coordination; one firm undertakes projects on the basis of forecasts which the actions of others will invalidate. Although central planning implies more control over all actions, and we might expect more variables to be taken into account in every decision, the planners still have imperfect foresight and far less than perfect efficiency in administration. There will inevitably be unforeseen consequences to be accounted for as losses. Whether Soviet accounting treats some outlay as a cost or a loss is essentially a question of how effective the controllers in the head office consider their control over it. Let us consider each of the losses listed above in turn.

Certainly war losses are true losses and should never be counted as costs. The same is true of the second item, last year's losses (profits); they have nothing to do with production activity in the current year and this treatment of them is correct.

The next four items in the list all result from miscalculations in planning. Losses on canceled orders, outlays on fruitless experiments, and outlays for the mastering of goods which are never mass-produced are perfect prototypes of this kind of loss. When outlays represent pure waste, the best thing to do in the accounting is to write them off as a loss and forget about them.

At the present time losses from stoppages are actually included in the cost of production, and so, strictly speaking, their appearance in the above list is incorrect. It was thought worthwhile to consider them here, however, because of the interesting evolution in their treatment. They have been included in cost only since 1948.[14] Between 1941 and 1949, losses on stoppages of over fifteen days were written off to the profit and loss account, but stoppages of less than fifteen days were included in the cost of production. Before 1941 all stoppages of one day or more were written off directly to profit and loss.[15] The purpose of this change was to increase management's responsibility for and interest in avoiding stoppages. The earlier treatment implied that these outlays were outside the control of enterprise managers, while the present interpretation makes them their responsibility since failure to control them will result in a poor showing on the cost indicators. Also, as the definition of responsibility became sharper, the assignment of outlays to national overhead could also be replaced with assignment to a specific output. This case involves a different attitude toward precision in cost accounting from that observed in the treatment of coal-mine fires, for instance. Instead of accepting the clumsiness of the economic system as a rationale for vague cost accounting, here Soviet planners are hoping that a highly specific allocation will mobilize efforts to compensate for administrative awkwardness. One may have some doubts about the effectiveness of such specific allocation. Stoppages may be caused by equipment breakdowns, by supply failures, as a result of the poor quality of materials, all of which enterprise management is more or less powerless to affect. Earlier practice recognized these deficiencies as general costs of the system as a whole and charged them to national economic overhead, but the subsequent changes show a growing determination to pinpoint them in order to overcome them. This case suggests an important characteristic of Soviet cost accounting. The designers of the system will be more likely to make specific cost allocations when the problem is perceived as one of assigning responsibility to persons than when it is posed as one of assigning outlays to particular output. In the former situation, in fact, they are likely to show a bias in favor of overspecific allocation.

The refusal to charge outlays on the maintenance of reserve enterprises to the costs of current output is perfectly understandable. To interpret them as costs would make sense only if the reserve capacity was held specifically to meet peak loads of some sort. The fact seems to be, however, that the outlays referred to here are outlays on whole factories or shops that are more or less permanently shut down. Apparently expenses for the maintenance of seasonal and other peak facilities are reserved for assignment to the cost of production in the busy season.[16] In the absence of other sources of financing, then, it is understandable why these outlays are charged to the profit and loss account. However, this is a productive disposition of income and not a loss. Whether the excess capacity exists by intent or as the result of a planning mistake, the presumption is that the only reason for maintaining it is that these outlays are worth making — that the enterprise will be needed in the future. Therefore it would be best to capitalize them and charge them to the cost of production in some future period. The failure to do this is characteristic of Soviet accounting. I have mentioned several cases in which investment is left unrecorded. In this case, however, there is perhaps less justification for it than elsewhere, since there is no problem of specifying the assets in which this investment is made.

Items 9 and 10 on the list are essentially claim adjustments not connected in any way with the production activity of the enterprise. Bad debts written off represent only a failure to collect claims; this has no significance in assessing the production activity of the enterprise. The item "writing off claims on expiration of the settlement period" arises from the practice, introduced to strengthen khozraschet, of establishing a limited time within which a claim must be settled. If a debt is not collected within this period, it is canceled, thus representing a gain for the debtor and a loss for the creditor.[17]

Soviet enterprises pay and receive fines, penalties, and forfeits (*peni, shtrafi, neustoiki*) for various kinds of contract violations. The fines paid out are balanced against those received, and any excess of payments over receipts is charged to the cost of production by way of general plant expenses. If receipts exceed payments, the difference is credited directly to the profit and loss account.[18] The rationale for passing these payments and receipts through the cost of production accounts is that they represent an ex post judicial arbitration and adjustment of the prices at which goods and services have been transferred. They are subtracted from the costs of the recipient since supposedly they compensate him for the adverse influence on his production activity caused by the nonfulfillment of obligations by outside enterprises. And, conversely, they are added to the costs of the enterprise which pays them under the presumption that this organization has reduced its cost illegally by cutting quality, failing to meet contracts, or other illegal actions.

However, there is a certain asymmetry in the treatment: an excess of payments is added to the cost of production, while an excess of receipts goes directly to the profit and loss account. Moreover, it is often argued that receipts should never be subtracted from costs.[19] The grounds adduced for omitting the excess of receipts from the cost of production altogether are that in some enterprises the receipts are very large, exceeding in some cases general plant expenses, shop expenses, or even both of these together.[20] To subtract them would completely distort the meaningfulness of the cost reports. In effect this amounts to saying that, for individual cases at least, the system of fines and penalties is not carefully constructed enough to represent accurate compensations. This lack of correspondence is further acknowledged in the practice introduced in the last few years of taking directly into the budget the fines received by some enterprises. This has been done since 1947 in the river-transportation industry,[21] and apparently in transport and electric stations the state exacts a certain percentage of such receipts directly. If this much is admitted, then the case for including fines in costs is also hard to justify. However, no one suggests that these be written off directly as a loss. This is characteristic of Soviet administration. In assessing the work of an enterprise, it is always considered better to err on the side of strictness than on the side of leniency. In this area it is considered important to have the amount of managerial inefficiency included in the cost indicator as well as in the profit indicator.

Soviet accounting has a fairly uniform rule that losses of subsidiary enterprises are not included in the cost of production of the main activity. The line of reasoning is that the collection of diverse economic activities in a single enterprise is purely an accident of industrial organization and that there is no reason why the main activity should be burdened with the losses of the others. This is a reasonable enough proposition in the abstract, but analysis of the subsidiary activities shows that in general they are operated as a service to the main output; the only reason that they show losses is that their output or services have not been priced correctly.

Losses from operations involving packing materials (*ubytki po operatsiyam s taroi*) arise because of the fact that the Russians have conceptualized production and packing as distinct operations, performed by separate economic entities. For some items product and packing are billed separately on the invoice. Packing operations can make either a profit or a loss, depending on the price set for packing, but it is said that they usually make a loss. This loss is then written off to the profit and loss account. At the present time, "the majority of items" are billed without a special charge for packing.[22]

It is not exactly clear how the cost of packing materials is accounted for in this case, but apparently they still never appear in the cost of production. No textbook that I have seen shows this cost included in either overheads or in the "nonproduction expenses" which cover commercial costs. The amount of this loss is probably a fair-sized item, since expenses on packing materials for the economy as a whole now exceed 10 billion rubles.[23] This practice is a special case of a cost-price residual at a process boundary and as such has already been discussed, but it is mentioned again because this boundary seems a particularly sterile one. The services of the packing department are carried out wholly within the enterprise, and the unit of product that seems most meaningful is a tsentner of cement in a sack rather than a tsentner of cement lying in a hopper.

Something like 20 percent of the housing fund of the Soviet Union is owned and operated by production enterprises as a subsidiary activity.[24] Rental rates are fixed by the state at a level which does not cover costs, and so housing in general operates at a loss. Rents on housing operated by enterprises are permitted to exceed the regular rates by 25 percent, but still it is said that "only a small number" of enterprises do not make a loss on their housing operations.[25] These losses are in effect a form of additional payment to the workers and thus are as much a cost as any other form of wages. The point at issue is whether or not housing should be called a cost of production in the particular plant that happens to hold the unprofitable assets on its balance sheet. The existing practice may well be rationalized in the following way. Since the loss on housing not operated by individual plants is covered out of the budget and out of the profits of other communal enterprises, not treating losses on enterprise-owned housing as a cost of production might be judged correct on the grounds of consistency. Why should the housing subsidy be included in the cost of production of those plants which happen to house their own

139

workers while plants whose workers live elsewhere get no subsidy? Since plants have their own housing primarily because the usual agencies do not provide sufficient housing in that particular locality, the inclusion or exclusion of the housing subsidy in the outlays of a particular plant will be a geographical accident. But this rationalization is upset by the fact that in some cases, notably the coal industry,[26] the construction industry,[27] and the timber industry,[28] the losses on housing *are* included in the cost of production. It might be argued that in the case of the construction industry these losses are occasioned by the nature of the branch rather than by accident and that therefore to call them costs does not upset the rationalization proposed. The same cannot be said of the coal industry. The decision to omit or include the housing losses in individual cases seems to be purely arbitrary. They are treated as a cost in the coal industry so that there will be a systematic way of covering them.[29] However, although the textile industry is another branch where most workers live in enterprise housing and where the loss is presumably large,[30] the loss on housing is still not included in the cost of production.[31]

Losses from subsidiary agricultural operations represent another form of supplementary wages. These subsidiary enterprises supply food to the workers of the plant through the "worker-supply department" (*otdel rabochego snabzheniya*) or communal feeding operations of the plant. This output is transferred at official retail prices and turnover tax is paid on it. This means that the net price received by the producing subsidiary is the state procurement price, which will not cover costs when workers are paid regular wages. Therefore, although these operations show accounting losses, they are fictitious losses. The state collects turnover tax on this produce, even though it is a marginal form of production in which no corresponding

140

rent is earned.[32] Thus their exclusion from the cost calculations seems correct.

The exclusion from costs of the other item in this group, loss from realization on the side of materials and services, also seems correct. This is indeed a separate activity, and it would be arbitrary to assign it directly as a cost of the main activity.

The Russians divide losses from natural disasters into two categories, (1) losses of fixed assets and (2) "other," including losses of materials, expense connected with repairing damage, overhead during stoppages, and so on.[33] The first is written off to the charter fund and the other losses are written off to the profit and loss account. To evaluate the Soviet treatment of these items, it is necessary to explain the background. In the capitalist economy an individual producer usually covers these losses either by taking out insurance or, in the case of large enterprises, by the formation of self-insurance reserves. In Soviet industrial enterprises, as a rule, fixed assets are not insured, and it is prohibited for enterprises to form their own insurance reserves. Since the losses are written off, they are never reflected in costs. This peculiarity of Soviet accounting derives directly from Marxist theory. Marx considered that all losses from natural disasters were not costs of production, did not enter into value and had to be recouped out of surplus product. In the past, one school of thought led by Strumilin took the common-sense view that such losses were costs of production and should be charged to production either by insurance or by deductions into self-insurance reserves.[34] Other writers denounced this "amortization theory" as un-Marxist (as indeed it is), and in this particular case ideological purity won out over common sense.[35] If the amount of loss from fire, floods, and other disasters was completely independent of any actions taken by the planners, this procedure would be unobjectionable. Such losses would be an inflexible social overhead which

141

should be distributed on the same general basis as any other fixed overhead of the national economy. But losses from natural disasters obviously are not invariable costs. They vary first of all among different kinds of outputs and, as long as the planners have some discretion in the proportions among various kinds of outputs, such losses should be included in costs. Moreover, they vary in response to preventive measures. Particularly with respect to fire losses, the amount of loss will vary with the amount spent on protection (which, incidentally, is always considered a cost of production in Soviet accounting), with the production program selected (the percentage of fixed assets lost every year through fires and explosions surely varies between coal mines and explosives plants, on the one hand, and shoe factories, on the other), with the type of construction of buildings, and so on. Since it is a variable cost, it should always be considered when planning decisions are made and, in accordance with the general rule that accounting costs should embrace all planning costs, it would then be shown in the accounting. The case for including in costs the losses from other kinds of natural disaster is perhaps a little less clear, but again the amount of loss from earthquakes will vary with the kinds of construction used and with locational variants; the losses from floods will vary in response to antiflood measures and to locational decisions. Also it is interesting to note that in state-managed agriculture — the sovkhozes — where losses from natural disasters are much more important than in industry, the Russians do not make any such distinction, and such losses are included in the costs of whatever output is obtained.[36] All the outlays on a given crop are counted as costs even if natural disasters greatly reduce the crop. Unit cost is taken as the total outlays divided by the yield, even though much of the outlay may be a loss caused by adverse atmospheric conditions rather than by a "cost of production" in the Marxist sense.

The omission of an insurance charge is probably a minor point from the point of view of relative costs. It would be difficult to argue that the failure to include it in costs has any important distorting effect. But this is not the grounds on which the Russians reject it. They hold that such losses are not costs of production, and the concern here has been to point out that even in the Soviet economy this is not true.

By the same argument, other expenses connected with natural disasters, such as repair and loss of materials, are really costs of production, but the Russians write them off directly to the profit and loss account. Even if it is decided to treat them both as losses rather than as costs, it makes no sense to write off one to the charter fund and the other to profit and loss. The Russians seem to adhere to a notion that fixed-asset adjustments should be reflected only in the charter-fund account. It will be remembered that gains and losses on retirements of fixed assets are taken directly into the charter fund account. The writing off of losses on retirements to the charter fund rather than to the profit and loss account does have a certain rationale behind it. By this practice the Russians recognize that this is not really a cost or loss of the current period, but rather represents a belated recognition of a disinvestment that has been going on for the whole life of the asset.[37] By not showing this loss in the profit and loss account, the latter is left as a statement of the disinvestment or investment due to production activity in the current year. However, it seems pointless to extend this distinction to losses of fixed assets from natural disasters. These *are* losses of the current period and have to be replaced just as much as losses of working capital, if the enterprise is to be restored to the position from which it started the accounting period. The divergent treatment for the two kinds of losses from natural disasters deprives the profit and loss concept of a consistent meaning.

Losses and gains on revaluations are only outlays in a special sense, but they are included here because of the unique way in which Soviet accounting handles them. In a planned economy, prices are fixed and do not fluctuate in response to changing market conditions. Therefore, many of the inventory-valuation problems which are so important in capitalist accounting never arise in Soviet accounting. Nevertheless, there are occasional price changes, and this means that inventories must be revalued. The Russians handle this problem in a very interesting way. Inventory-revaluation gains and losses in some cases go into the capital fund; in some they are recompensed or exacted by the budget; in some they are taken up by an adjustment in the indebtedness to the Gosbank; and in other cases they are assigned to the profit and loss account. Let us consider the cases of a general change in wholesale prices and a change in retail prices.

The amount of working assets which the Soviet enterprise holds is determined on the basis of physical norms. The norms are originally determined on the basis of calculations of the number of days' supply of each item which should be held in stock in view of the location of the normal supplier, the size of shipments, and other factors. The enterprise is then assigned enough working capital to hold this planned stock (called the *normativ*). The fact of a price change does not affect in any way the amount of physical stocks which is considered appropriate for the enterprise to hold; when a price change occurs, the practice is to revalue the stocks and then to balance this change in value of assets with a corresponding adjustment of some account on the liabilities side of the balance sheet. This is done primarily by adjusting the charter fund by the amount of the gain or loss. In this way the goods are revalued, the balance sheet is still balanced, and the enterprise can still hold its assigned physical normativ. There are some exceptions to this procedure, however. The amount of stocks which the enterprise has on hand at any given time will not necessarily be equal to its assigned normativ. What the state wants to adjust on the liabilities side of the balance sheet is the ability to hold the normativ, not the actual stock which happens to be on hand at the time. An excess of stock may be financed by a bank loan or by other sources, such as a payables-receivables difference or an accumulated profit. The revaluation gain or loss on the stocks held on the basis of a bank loan is written off as an adjustment of the loan.[38] The gain or loss on the rest of the excess is taken into the profit and loss account. In contrast to the situation wherein an enterprise is holding excess stocks, some enterprises may be holding less than their assigned normativ. It is not always explained what is done in this event, but in the 1952 revaluation the adjustment on excess stocks in some enterprises was written off to the charter fund of other enterprises within the same ministry which had less than their assigned normativ. Only for the ministry as a whole was the revaluation of excess stocks written off to the profit and loss account.[39] These rules seem to be appropriate as far as cost accounting is concerned. The revaluation permits cost accounting to be translated immediately into the new prices.

This treatment of revaluation gains and losses is instructive concerning the meaning of the Soviet income concept. The Russians have been able to adopt this radical method for dealing with inventory-valuation changes because they attach to enterprise income a meaning that is different from the one held by accountants of capitalist firms. The adjustments for changes in inventory valuations can for the most part bypass the profit and loss account, since fewer issues turn on the determination of enterprise income. For example, there is no question of tax liability; nor does any argument arise over definitions of income between those who want it now and those who are willing to take it as capital gains. The Russians' approach implies that they see enterprise income as a measure of how much needs to be extracted or added to the enterprise to keep the amount of resources it holds unchanged. Any gain or loss on the revaluation of inventory within the assigned normativ is not reflected in income, for the one does not need to be extracted or the other recompensed if the enterprises are to be left in the same position at the end of the period as at the beginning. For stocks above the normativ, the situation is different. The presumption is that the firm should not have had these stocks in the first place. Hence, any gain from revaluation represents an augmentation of command over resources which it should not be allowed to retain. On the other hand, the profit and loss figure does not conform perfectly to this concept. To make it so, the treatment of losses on stocks above the normativ should go to the charter fund rather than to the profit and loss account; and some adjustment would have to be made for the capacity to maintain the normativ when it is more than actual stocks.

There is very little discussion in Soviet sources concerning the treatment of revaluation gains and losses when the retail prices of consumer goods are changed, but apparently they are handled somewhat differently from gains and losses on goods held by producing organizations. It is said that the revaluation loss on goods in trading organizations is covered by the budget. This is hard to believe, but all the sources I have seen agree on this point. It would mean an actual expansion of ability of trading enterprises to hold stocks (that is, an actual investment), and there appears to be no reason why a price change should warrant such investment. It is possible that these writers mean only that, since the price cut is effected through a cut in the turnover tax, the budget bears a loss; but this does not seem to be a reasonable interpretation since the tax on stocks held by retail organizations has already been paid. And the language seems to justify the interpretation that the loss is actually compensated. Gleik says that "as a rule, revaluation loss of goods by order of the government in the final analysis is written off at the expense of the budget," [40] and Penkov says that, when the revaluation losses are assigned to the budget, "they are written onto the account [called] Relationship with the Ministry of Finance." [41]

The last item on the list of outlays comprises various kinds of funds and reserves formed by charges against the profit and loss account. The most important of these are the various incentive funds such as the director's fund in industrial enterprises and the fund for economy of fuel. The items financed out of these funds fall into two categories: investment outlays and premium payments. To the extent that these funds are used for investment, this is just another allocation of profit for investment — they are capitalized and added to the charter fund and the fixed-asset account. The only difference in this case is that the direction the investment takes is left to the discretion of local administrators. So the formation of the fund is an allocation of income, not a cost.

The rationale for charging premiums to the profit and loss account through the director's fund and omitting them from the cost of production is as follows. In a world of perfect certainty and control, these should probably be considered costs. In setting up these funds, the state in effect offers a rate for extra effort. The premiums are a planning cost of production and accordingly might be handled in the accounting as a cost of production. But in the real world the controllers in the head office do not know whether this offer will be taken up. The various targets of the plan already express the best estimate which the central planners can make concerning input requirements and the attainable levels of output. Any addi-

147

tional economy of resources or any additional output is extra income. What the regime is after here is extra output, and one does not calculate the costs of windfalls.

Another such reserve is the guarantee reserve (*garantiinyi reserv*). It is found primarily in the enterprise accounts of heavy machinebuilding. In this branch contracts often include a guarantee on equipment, and the reserve is supposed to cover the expected expenses under such contracts. Obviously this is a cost, not a loss. Its inclusion in costs would also be desirable on the basis of khozraschet considerations, since the amount of expenses to fulfill guarantees will depend on the quality of the output. Such expenses are essentially the same as costs connected with "spoilage discovered by the customer" (*vneshnyi brak*), and the Russians do include the latter in costs. All costs connected with repairing or replacing such output must be included in the costs of the month in which it is discovered.[42]

The premium funds and the guarantee reserve are the only reserves permitted by the present accounting legislation. In the past, however, there have been several other funds and reserves — a reserve for bad debts (abolished in 1943), a reserve for possible price-change losses, a reserve for possible losses of materials, a self-insurance reserve, and more. The fate of these reserves gives us another indication of the forces shaping Soviet accounting practices. The existence of these accounts left too much freedom for local interpretations at the level of the enterprise. They were abolished to restrict the possibilities of upward or downward adjustments by the local bookkeeper.

Conclusion

In discussing the writing off of certain expenses to the budget or to the profit and loss account and their exclusion from costs, it has already been concluded that in some cases such treatment is incorrect from the point of view of real costs. This is understandable; there is no *a priori* reason to expect that the Russians would be guided by theoretically correct cost criteria. But the question remains as to the criterion which the Russians do consider relevant in assigning a given item. If the explanations given by the Russians for the exclusion of certain expenses from costs are reviewed briefly, it is obvious that this treatment defies rationalization in terms of any single criterion. The Russians' approach to this problem, as to the problem of pricing, is an eclectic one. There are, however, three explanatory principles that can be of help in understanding the various allocations.

First, some outlays are excluded on theoretical grounds of value or because of pricing considerations. Thus the explicit rationalization given for the exclusion of some of the investment outlays and for the exclusion of natural disasters in cost calculations is that these do not create value. And the omission of some of the other losses is based on the common-sense acknowledgment that they are in no way a cost of the actual output produced and so need not be covered by its price. This principle is ignored more often than it is invoked, however. Many "nonproductive" outlays, which in the interpretation of the theoreticians do not create value, are included in the costs. Examples are the cost of spoilage, shortages, and losses from lowered quality. Moreover, a large class of unrequited outlays which we would interpret as transfer outlays, and which the Russians characterize as "payments distributing and redistributing the national income," [43] are included in costs. I have in mind here such items as the stumpage fee, interest paid for the use of bank credit, fines and penalties, and local taxes and collections. Although the Russians deny that these outlays represent creation of value, they are still included in the costs. L. M. Kantor, one of the more thoughtful theoreticians of Soviet cost accounting, is right when he says that the concept of cost in Soviet accounting is not only quantitatively but also qualitatively different from the concept of value. It uses an idiom that is unconnected with the theory of value. The cost of production is simply "an objective economic category which is employed in the economic policy of the Soviet state" and "an indicator of the quality of the work of the industrial enterprise." [44]

It should be added that agreeing with Kantor does not require abandoning the earlier assertion that one of the main objectives of Soviet cost accounting is to determine value tags for all components of output. Kantor can draw the conclusion he does because he is comparing accounting practice with a mistaken theory of value; the inconsistency he sees is not necessarily there when practice is compared with a more comprehensive theory of value. For example, a penalty payment for delay in the unloading of freight cars would not represent to a Marxist theoretician a real cost or an element of value, but it certainly does to anyone whose theory of value involves the notion of scarcity.

Kantor's statement suggests a second allocation principle: the cost concept is designed to further the effectiveness of control. The concept should be such that it is a meaningful indicator of the efficiency of management. Therefore, in accordance with a well-known principle of scientific management, the cost measure of performance is defined to include all outlays for which the enterprise is held responsible. Most of the practices described in this chapter make sense in terms of this objective. It explains the inclusion of all the nonproductive outlays, the inclusion of transfer outlays, the general inclusion of losses from stoppages in the cost concept. It is true that the cost concept seems to imply an exaggerated notion of managerial responsibility. For instance, there is presumably no action an enterprise director can take to prevent a stoppage resulting from a failure of electric power. Hence losses from such a stoppage should not be included in the cost concept used to measure his fulfillment of responsibility. But it is characteristic of Soviet accounting procedures to interpret unusual situations in a way that works against enterprise management. The allocation of overheads, the valuation of unfinished production, and the treatment of fines and penalties all involve similar interpretations. It might also be objected that some of the outlays that *are* included in costs are not under the control of local management and that, therefore, the principle is not universal. The amount of the amortization charge, for instance, is entirely outside the ability of the manager to control. Its inclusion is justified, however, by the fact that it is fixed and that its amount per unit of output decreases with increased production. Thus the cost measure becomes a combined indicator reflecting to a certain extent the manager's responsibility for quantity as well as for cost of output.

Finally, some of the allocation decisions seem to reflect purely arbitrary accidents of bookkeeping formulation or peculiarities of planning procedure. The most notable example is the exclusion from costs of budget-financed outlays for development. There is nothing in the logic of double-entry bookkeeping requiring such outlays to be excluded from costs. Nor can the handling of housing losses be rationalized in any way; apparently the divergent treatment in different sectors of the economy is purely accidental. In both cases the Russians have simply failed to subordinate the mechanics of bookkeeping to the objectives it serves.

THE IMPACT OF ACCOUNTING DATA

ON DECISIONS: SOME ILLUSTRATIONS

SOVIET accounting practice has been reviewed thus far primarily in comparison with theoretically correct concepts of cost. The premise has been that errors here will affect price formation and, ultimately, economic decisions. In many cases, however, there is a direct interaction between accounting data and economic decisions without the intervening link of price. This chapter discusses several such cases. The collection of examples is not offered as an exhaustive list; it is intended to illustrate the general principle behind the interplay of accounting and economic decision making.

Obsolescence and Replacement

The first area of interaction involves the influence of depreciation accounting on a group of decisions having to do with obsolescence, repair, replacement, and modernization of assets. As will be seen, this is an area where ex ante calculation and ex post recording are confusingly intertwined. Hence, I shall have to include some explanation of the problem itself as well as the influence of accounting practices on decision making.

Basically the problem is that planners face a number of alternatives in the disposition of existing assets. The major alternatives are whether to keep assets in operation or to replace them. Generally speaking, there is no fixed service life for a productive asset (a building or a machine). The final abandonment of the asset can be postponed almost indefinitely by careful maintenance or by repair and reconstruction. But this is not necessarily desirable from the point of view of national economic efficiency. One factor which may make it desirable to scrap old assets is that the cost of repairing them becomes greater and greater as the assets get older. A more common reason, however, is that they become obsolete. As the techniques of production improve, there constantly appear new technical possibilities which are more productive than the forms embodied in old assets. By saying that they are more productive, I mean that they make it possible to produce a given output with a smaller expenditure of current inputs than is true with assets now in use. The different forms that obsolescence take are too heterogeneous to be catalogued here. But the essential point is that an asset becomes obsolescent when it wastes the inputs, such as labor, materials, or power, used in conjunction with it. Eventually there comes a point when old assets are wasting more resources than would be involved in scrapping and replacing them with more modern ones. Still another possibility is to modernize old productive equipment. By extensive rebuilding of an asset, it may be possible to make it nearly as efficient as its modern replacement rivals, at a cost less than actual replacement. The objective of economic rationality in this area is to modernize or scrap and replace old assets throughout the economy just at the optimum point. This is essentially what the problem of obsolescence consists of.

The Soviet attitude toward obsolescence has undergone a curious evolution over time, and its history is marked by in-

153

ternal contradictions and reversals of position. There are two accounting questions involved: how to value obsolete assets and how to determine whether depreciation rates should be set high enough to cover obsolescence. The Russians have apparently always accepted the common-sense idea that obsolete assets are not worth as much as technologically improved replacement rivals and that this loss of value should be reflected in the fixed-asset accounts. Marx is often quoted to this effect, and it is said explicitly that, when fixed assets were revalued in the past, obsolescence was one of the factors taken into account in determining the new values.[1] In practice, of course, revaluations of fixed assets have been extremely infrequent. But the resulting failure to show obsolete assets on the books at their real value is recognized as a concession to expediency rather than as a doctrinal imperative. On the other hand, the Soviet attitude toward inclusion of an allowance for obsolescence in depreciation rates has shifted markedly over time. The first official set of depreciation rates, those established by the VSNKh (the central administrative organ for the Soviet economy at the time) in 1923 were supposedly set high enough to include an allowance for obsolescence.[2] In the early period of the regime, Soviet economic theorists gave little attention to questions of accounting practice, and the rules and instructions were elaborated by practical accountants trained in the tsarist period, primarily along the lines of capitalist accounting theory and practice. By 1930, however, the Marxist theoreticians were attempting to reformulate accounting rules along more distinctively socialist lines, and, when the VSNKh drew up a set of depreciation norms in 1930, it was decided not to include any allowance for obsolescence. In the preliminary proposals for this set of norms, some groups had advocated the inclusion of a charge for obsolescence, but this proposal was rejected by the VSNKh authorities on the grounds that it was contradictory to

154

the conditions of a planned socialist economy.[3] Thus after 1930 there was an official position, taken throughout the accounting literature, that obsolescence was of so little importance in the Soviet economy that it was unnecessary to recognize it as a cost in accounting. Some writers went so far as to claim that obsolescence did not even exist in the Soviet economy.

In the past few years, the official line concerning obsolescence has been drastically revised. It is pointed out that it is one of the major problems that Soviet accounting must deal with. The change is neatly demarcated in two articles in the Soviet Great Encyclopedia, appearing before and after the change in doctrine. In the article on amortization in volume two, it is stated unequivocally that "the phenomenon of obsolescence . . . is inherent only in the capitalist economy." In a later volume, an article specifically on obsolescence still labels it a phenomenon of the capitalist economy but adds that in the Soviet Union technical progress means premature replacement of assets, with resulting losses. Soviet planners and economists are now engaged in a full-scale discussion on both the theoretical and practical levels of technical change, obsolescence, repair, replacement, and modernization. It would be far outside the scope of this study to discuss all the ramifications of Soviet theory and policy in the field of obsolescence and replacement, important though the question is. In many ways it represents a problem of planning and economic theory rather than one of accounting. My interest is directed primarily toward two narrower questions. What reflection should the fact of obsolescence find in accounting practice? How do Soviet accounting practices interact with the decisions concerning repair, replacement, and modernization posed for the planners by obsolescence?

Once it is recognized that obsolescence is bound to take place, then allowance for it should be included in depreciation rates. The point of depreciation accounting is to allocate the cost of assets in some reasonable way in relation to the output that comes from them. What is relevant here, of course, is the actual service life, rather than some notion of how long the assets might be made to serve. The Russians are often a bit confused about this question. Some economists assert that obsolescence is different from depreciation and should not be covered in depreciation charges. On the basis of some peculiar Marxist concepts and some Marxist distinctions between different kinds of obsolescence, they claim that absolescence must be covered from "accumulation" rather than charged to costs of production. But not all economists and accountants are of this opinion, and the opposite view seems recently to have predominated. The new depreciation rates which are to be adopted in 1963 have been set high enough to cover obsolescence.[4]

The other implication of obsolescence for accounting concerns the valuation of obsolete assets. In the general revaluation of fixed assets carried out as of January 1, 1960, a discount was made for obsolescence in figuring the present value of fixed assets. That is, the value of obsolete assets were marked down in comparison with similar but more modern assets. As was explained earlier, the approach used in the revaluation for estimating obsolescence was incorrect (see Chapter 3). The principle that obsolescence means a loss in value of assets, however, is fully accepted.

The other half of our problem is the interaction of accounting magnitudes with economic decisions concerning replacement. In order to make these interactions understandable, it is necessary first to explain the Soviet approach to making a replacement decision. Basically, Soviet planners treat it like any other investment decision — by reference to some payoff-period criterion. In a replacement decision, the question posed is whether the capital investment required to replace an old asset will save enough in current costs of operation to recoup the investment within a specified payoff period. This, of course, is perfectly sensible and reflects the proposition advanced in Chapter 3 that, from the national economic point of view, replacement investment is no different in principle from any other kind of investment. The Russian approach in practice, however, is mistaken in an important particular. It seems to be standard practice in any such decision to include the unamortized cost of the asset being replaced as one of the capital costs of the replacement project. This approach is erroneous in itself and will slow down the rate of replacement to less than the optimum. Any unamortized value shown on the books for existing assets should be ignored in the calculation. The decision the planners are making is one of capital allocation; they are trying to decide where to invest the available capital resources to get the biggest saving in current inputs. Resources already sunk in existing assets have no relevance to this problem. The Soviet method takes at face value an irrelevant value concept which grows out of the mechanics of accounting. Moreover (and this is the point of transition from errors in ex ante calculation to ex post records), this bias will be reinforced by the deficiencies of the accounting data employed in the calculation. Because the depreciation rates are too low, the accumulated depreciation shown on the books of an enterprise is less than real depreciation, and the unamortized value of its assets correspondingly is too great. The amount of depreciation is further understated because of the practice of financing capital repair from sources other than the amortization fund and then decreasing the depreciation account by the amount of such expenditures. One can well imagine that there are many instances where this exaggerated notion of the unamortized value of old assets will constitute another barrier to replacement. It will be remembered from the discussion in Chapter

4 that there are cases where very old assets are shown on the books as completely undepreciated. Such extremes are not typical, of course, but their existence suggests that instances of more moderate understatement of depreciation will be quite prevalent. As stated in Chapter 2, it was estimated in the 1960 revaluation of fixed assets that the depreciation shown on the books for *all* assets was only half the actual depreciation. Correction of the depreciation accounts as a result of the revaluation should eliminate this particular bias against replacement.

Another influence works by way of the financial constraints which the present system of depreciation involves. The funds designated for capital repair are left at the disposal of the enterprise, whereas the funds for replacement are withdrawn into the general pool of investment funds for larger units. In theory this need not prejudge the repair-replacement decision, if the decisions as between the two alternatives are always made rationally and funds are made available to implement the decisions. But there are indications that the financial mechanism is not neutral here. Apparently it is much easier to spend the repair funds, already at hand, for the purpose designated than to get funds from above for replacement or modernization. This is directly stated by some writers and is also indicated by the policies the Russians have established for financing modernization of assets. To stimulate the modernization of equipment, it was decided in 1954 that enterprises should be allowed to spend a portion of the capital-repair funds for this purpose. At the same time, the Gosbank was authorized to lend funds and, when the "enterprise fund" was established in 1955, half of this source was earmarked for purposes of modernization and technological improvements. There is an implication that the system of centralized capital planning and allocation is not well enough designed to approve and control these two types of investment, since they are usually fairly small in scale, and so tends to neglect them. If the enterprise is to make them, it must have its own funds earmarked for the purpose. Presumably the same problem arises with replacement investments. Soviet authorities assert that machines are frequently repaired at a cost exceeding the cost of replacing them with completely new machines.[5] Enterprises have funds for repair but find it impossible to get the funds for replacement.

It seems likely that this determination of the repair-replacement decision by the depreciation system is reinforced at another level. If individual decisions concerning replacement and repair are to be implemented, it is necessary that there be a corresponding reconciliation between the provision of replacement equipment and the provision of repair capacity. Apparently such a reconciliation is consciously made in aggregate terms in the plans drawn up at the center. For instance, many writers mention a "balance of equipment," which distinguishes between equipment for replacement purposes and for installation in newly constructed plants. Many writers have said that, despite the fact that much of the Soviet equipment is obsolete, it cannot be replaced at the present time "because the balance of equipment will not permit it." [6] Presumably these calculations at the center are based on such evidence as the service lives implied by the depreciation rates, the division of depreciation charges into repair and replacement allowances, and past experience with retirements.

At one level, the position that replacement must be decided by the balance of equipment is certainly valid. The amount of replacement decided on by planners at the local level must be reconciled with the aggregate amount of equipment available for that purpose. On the other hand, there is no reason to assume that a given plan for the balance of equipment necessarily provides the right amount of replacement equipment, particularly if it is based on the incorrect notions of the appropriate service lives for assets which are embodied in the existing depreciation rates. It may, therefore, be the balance of equipment that should be changed rather than the repair-replacement decisions of the local planners. If the decisions of the local planners are correct, then it should be possible to increase the production of replacements by a reallocation of resources from repair to the production of new machines. This would give a net saving of resources. In the short run, of course, the possibilities for such a shift may be limited — repair capacity and repair workers cannot simply be transformed into an expansion of the new-equipment industry. Nevertheless, the responsibilities of the Soviet planners include the making of such long-term strategic decisions, as well as the achievement of short-term equilibria. Thus the balance of equipment is not a datum, but is rather one of the variables to be decided upon in the general problem of replacement policy. Soviet writers are now beginning to treat it in this larger framework, although they emphasize the obstacles to converting the existing repair establishment into a new-equipment industry very quickly.[7]

Problems in Accounting for Overhead Cost

There are many kinds of decisions at the enterprise level which turn on a consideration of short-run differentials in costs. These are decisions which leave many of the fixed costs of the enterprise untouched. Hence, the relevant magnitude to be considered in the decision is marginal cost. The failure of Soviet accounting to distinguish fixed and variable costs may have an adverse influence here. As explained earlier, Soviet accountants accumulate a great variety of outlays under the heading of overhead costs and then distribute the totals by a very approximate method, generally on the basis of wages. There is also a tendency to treat these overheads as if they were fixed costs. One example of how this heterogeneity of the overhead category leads to difficulties is in the calculations for various kinds of technological improvements in an enterprise, such as the adoption of some rationalization proposal, the modernization of old equipment, or the introduction of an automatic process. In these cases it is necessary for the planner to estimate the cost savings to be expected from the innovation. An estimate is required both to decide whether the proposal is rational and in some cases to determine (because of the Soviet programs designed to encourage innovations) the payment due the person who proposed or effected it. The methodology for making decisions is essentially the same in all the different forms of this problem. The cost savings attributable to the innovation are compared with the capital investment required, if any, and if the project satisfies some payout-period criterion, and there are funds, it will be adopted. The power of Soviet accounting practice to distort these decisions comes from the difficulty of estimating changes in overhead costs when the innovation is adopted. In their routine ex post accounting, Soviet accountants have usually estimated overhead costs on the basis of an overhead rate of so many rubles per ruble of direct wages. The concept of special cost studies for particular decisions within the enterprise is not characteristic of Soviet accounting. The main function of the bookkeeping department of the enterprise is to generate the data and the reports called for in the system of reporting to higher organs. (This point will be elaborated in Chapter 8.) Hence what they are most likely to do is estimate overhead on the basis of wage costs for each variant. This implies that, if an innovation saves labor, it would also be blessed with proportionate savings in overhead. This treatment is seen in many of the formulas and calculations described in the literature.[8] But such an approach is grossly incorrect. The overhead category in Soviet accounting includes many items which by no means vary in accordance with wages,

161

and indeed many of them will vary inversely to wages when innovations are adopted. These innovations usually result in very large savings of labor, but at the same time there will be important increases in some items included in overhead, such as current maintenance, repair, depreciation, cost of fuel and energy, and so on. The practice of assuming that overhead will vary in proportion to wages will overlook these costs and thus exaggerate the effectiveness of the investment in the project. This is obvious enough and many Soviet economists have remarked on it. Many of them say that the distortions this approach involves are so serious that the bookkeepers' information should be ignored altogether and that direct estimates of all kinds of overhead costs should be made on the basis of engineering information.[9] But naturally this involves difficult computations. As an alternative it is sometimes suggested that overheads be ignored altogether in figuring cost savings. This may be an improvement but will involve errors in the other direction. The innovations under consideration frequently involve large increases in the productivity of a machine or plant. It is significant, for instance, that one of the indicators considered important in justifying the projects is the increase in output per square meter of floor space. Because of this increase in productivity there will be savings on many kinds of overhead expenses, and ignoring them will understate the cost savings to be expected from the project.

It is not that the Russian planners are unaware of the difference between variable and fixed costs, and its relation to various economic decisions. The writers on accounting and planning frequently introduce such concepts as variable costs, proportionally variable costs, semifixed costs, and fixed costs. Moreover, in many cases they show an obvious appreciation of the relevance of each of these costs to economic decision making. For instance, one author in analyzing a decision to buy or to make some part says that it is important to consider only the variable costs which this decision will affect, and to recognize that many costs will stay fixed regardless of the decision.[10] But such sophistication often founders on the intractability of the prescribed accounting classifications. It is important to remember in this connection that the enterprise has no choice in its system of accounting. The plan of accounts and the content of each is defined by instructions from above, and the existing cost classifications are not oriented to the distinction between fixed and variable costs. The books on cost accounting and on enterprise behavior never manage to reconcile the abstract concepts of fixed and variable costs with actual cost classifications used in accounting and reporting. In one book on planning and decision making, the author goes through the list of cost categories used in accounting in ferrous metallurgy and gives percentages for each category, indicating the relative shares of fixed and variable components.[11] But this is at best an awkward compromise, and it looks more like an *ad hoc* rule of thumb than the result of any careful investigation.

Evidently there has been little empirical study of the relation between output and the various items of overhead costs either in general or in individual kinds of plants. I have seen only one report of such a study, and it was made in 1954.[12] This particular investigation is very interesting in that it shows that the conventions usually followed by accountants in distinguishing fixed and variable costs in the plants involved in the study were not borne out empirically.

There are some areas of the economy for which the importance of the fixed-variable distinction is recognized, and here the accounting structure has been influenced by it. Probably the most important of these areas is the railroads. In the routine accounting of the railroads, all that is computed is the costs per ton-kilometer of freight haulage and per passenger-kilometer. But railroad transportation is an activity where the high share of overhead and fixed costs, varying intensity of utilization on the different parts of the network, and problems like the return of empty cars make the average cost per ton-kilometer of freight haulage a very poor index of the national economic sacrifice involved in a specific act of transportation. Both for tariff making and for calculations associated with specific locational decisions, it is necessary to have a more precise notion of the cost of different kinds of transportation. Such differentiated calculations are made not as part of the routine work of cost accounting, but periodically as special studies by the Economic Research Institute of the Ministry of Ways of Communication.[13] But the interesting point is that the need for these more detailed cost measures has apparently had an important influence on accounting concepts and classifications. The cost planners and analysts have tried to conceptualize certain intermediate outputs of the transportation process (or perhaps they could be thought of as dimensions of the final output), such as axle-kilometers and gross ton-kilometers, and to distinguish and classify outlays accordingly. Then the costs of specific transportation programs can be determined on the basis of their requirements in terms of the intermediate outputs.[14]

For administrative manageability, of course, the price of transportation (that is, the tariff schedule which they establish) cannot be differentiated to the same extent as the cost of individual acts of transportation can be. For one thing, the variation in costs between different parts of the rail network is about as great as the cost variation among commodities on the network as a whole. In 1950, for instance, the cost per ton-kilometer of freight haulage varied from 2.158 kopecks on the Omsk railroad to 10.361 on the Transcaucasian railroad.[15] This sort of regional variation, together with the complications introduced by disequilibria in directional movements, means that even a fairly differentiated tariff schedule will not give an accurate notion of the real marginal cost to the network of some proposed locational or supply variant. For example, the marginal cost of a given increment in traffic may be below average costs because of the existence of underutilized capacity, such as a flow of empty freight cars in the relevant part of the network. In other cases, increments in traffic may so tax existing capacity that expensive investments will be required. Apparently these decisions may sometimes be made on the basis of marginal-cost calculation, using the detailed cost procedures of the railroads, rather than on the basis of the prices shown in the tariff schedules.[16] The distinctive fact about the railroads is that the difference between their routine concepts of cost and the index relevant to some decisions is so obvious that they could not help recognizing it, and they have been forced in setting up their cost measures and expenditure classifications to give some attention to distinguishing the appropriate concepts.

The effort by planners to improve upon the accountant's routine computation of average cost is only one example of a very general phenomenon. Soviet planners in general display a strong distrust of the prices and the costs with which they are confronted in decision making and are very ingenious at devising ways to adjust or bypass them. It has been pointed out, for instance, that one of the distinctive features of the Soviet price system is the existence of a whole category of "planners' prices," distinct from the official transfer prices, created in order to improve economic calculation.[17] Let us look at some illustrative cases in which planners try to adjust the data of traditional cost accounting or ignore it in favor of other data more suitable for a given problem.

There is an interesting example in the electric-power industry. One problem faced by decision makers in this industry is the distribution of the load on an integrated power network among the different power plants and individual units of the system. The load is constantly fluctuating, and the cost of output produced by a given unit varies in a complicated way. This is true both of the boilers and the turbine, for instance, and even the variable costs per ton of steam or kilowatt-hour of electric power generated vary as the unit is loaded below or in excess of the capacity for which it was designed. Moreover, these cost functions differ as between units. In this situation the relevant magnitude for the load dispatcher to consider is the marginal cost of getting another unit of output by different distributions of the load among units. The Russians seem to have a perfectly clear understanding of the problem and analyze it in terms of marginal cost, though their term is "incremental cost." As we have seen, however, Soviet cost accounting is not organized to provide these relevant cost concepts. Not at all daunted by this, the planners have derived marginal-cost schedules for different units on the basis of engineering data, and they use these cost functions in distributing the load.

Some other interesting examples involve joint-product situations. Here decision makers often recognize that the usual cost-accounting distributions are irrelevant, and they try to manipulate cost data in ways to get the concepts they are interested in. One writer describes the following complicated problem in the petroleum-refining industry.[18] The petroleum refinery uses energy in the form of steam and electricity. Moreover, it is possible to run much of its equipment, such as pumps and compressors, either by steam engines or by electric motors. So it is necessary to decide whether to buy electricity, produce it in condensing stations, or, at another level of choice, to produce it jointly with steam in their own steam-byproduct turbines. It is also necessary to decide whether to use electric or steam engines to drive the equipment. Obviously the relative costs of steam and electric power are going to enter importantly in this

calculation, but again the prices figured by the usual accounting rules for such a situation are irrelevant. The author quotes
these bookkeeping costs for steam and electricity in different
variants, but apparently he ignores them in making the decision. The choice among variants is finally to be made in terms
of the common denominator of fuel input; this is the criterion
he uses in justifying his conclusion.

Another interesting joint-product problem arises in iron and
steel plants where planners have the alternatives of producing
the electric power they require with steam from regular boilers
or of using a heat-exchanger installation to convert waste heat
from the open-hearth furnaces into steam to run the turbines.[19]
At issue is the question whether to charge the power plant for
the waste heat and, if so, how much. This is supposedly necessary to determine what the cost of steam from the new installation will be. Apparently, if the planners follow the approach
usually used in such a situation and price the heat in terms of
its fuel equivalent, the cost of steam from this installation will
be higher than from regular boilers, since the heat exchanger
has a lower thermal efficiency and is also less efficient than a
regular boiler in terms of other current inputs and investment.
Essentially what the author of the article does is to make a
more refined calculation of the opportunity cost value of the
heat, discounting for some of the adverse characteristics of the
heat exchanger. For instance, he recognizes that the value of
heat in the form of a byproduct from the open-hearth furnace
is less than the value of heat in the form of coal, since choice
of the heat-exchanger alternative saddles the steam shop with
a lower thermal efficiency than could be had with conventional
boilers. Furthermore, he says that it would be wrong to charge
the steam shop a price per calorie equal to the price per calorie
in the fuel burned in the open hearth furnaces, since this is
higher than the price per calorie in the grades of fuel that can

1 6 7

be burned in conventional boilers. The author fails to make similar adjustments for all the adverse features of the heat-exchanger alternative and finally arrives at a price for steam from the heat exchanger which exceeds that for steam from regular boilers. Hence, he does not really end up with a true opportunity cost value for the heat. In the end, however, he redeems rationality by saying that the justification for the heat exchanger must be found in the overall fuel saving. He recommends that the heat be valued and priced at the cost he has figured, since this will give the personnel of the open-hearth shop an interest in getting the process adopted. But he states clearly enough that the decision on the economic rationality of the project should not be confused by the price set on the heat or by the way in which fuel costs will actually be distributed between steel and power in the ex post accounting.

In all three of these cases, the failure of cost accounting to deal with the relevant concepts does not mean that economic calculation must go astray. They illustrate the proposition stated in Chapter 2, that different kinds of decisions call for different concepts of cost and that decision makers may ignore cost figures produced by the accountant in favor of others. On the other hand, there are certain dangers in the alternative approaches used to avoid dependence on the regular cost information. In each of the three cases discussed, the decision turns essentially on minimizing a single input which has a preponderant influence on costs, and which is more or less homogeneous as measured by its heat content. But the real alternatives presented to the planner are usually more complex than this; even in such problems as these, where heat is a very important cost, the alternative variants may differ with respect to levels of other current inputs or in capital requirements. Minimizing heat expenditure alone, therefore, may give the wrong answer. And in other situations, such "engineering" criteria are

168

likely to be even less suitable than in heat problems, so that it will be much more difficult to ignore or bypass accounting data. In the end, the accounting department is the part of the plant that is in the best position to produce cost information, whatever concept of cost is involved, and it ought to be organized so that it can choose the concept most appropriate in a particular situation.

Conclusion

The examples of interaction between economic calculation and cost accounting described in this chapter suggest no simple conclusion. There seems to be good reason for believing that in some cases, at least, wrong cost data will trap decision makers into wrong conclusions. But it does not follow that bad accounting will always lead to bad decisions. The Russians often find a way around poor data. When one leaves the general economic literature of the Soviet Union, with its customary sterility in analysis, and goes to the specialized technical literature concerning individual branches of the economy, he is likely to be impressed by the sophistication of the economic analysis and calculation sometimes applied in practical planning problems. One should be wary of reading too much into these examples. They are useful antidotes to the usual Western presumption that Marxist economists cannot understand economic problems. Nevertheless, they are probably unrepresentative of the thinking of the mass of economic decision makers, particularly those at the level of the enterprise. The latter are undoubtedly vulnerable to the mistakes suggested by misleading cost data. Finally, in projecting any conclusions about the interaction of cost accounting and decision making into the future, we should be aware that the whole setting within which it takes place will probably change considerably. Among all the people concerned with economic planning in Soviet society, from those

169

primarily concerned with ritual expression in Marxist terminology to those at the actual operating level, there is a growing awareness of the importance of economic calculation and of its dependence on more suitable price and cost concepts. Any shift to a less centralized system of management, which places more decisions in the hands of people at the local level, cannot but direct closer attention to the need for better price and accounting data. As this happens, it is quite possible that an effort will be made to eliminate some of the present deficiencies in accounting.

ACCOUNTING FOR COST CONTROL

THE growing complexity of managerial structures in modern economies requires an increasing reliance on accounting as a tool of management. Effective management is sought through allocating responsibility unambiguously and then applying sanctions and conferring rewards in close accordance with the execution of responsibility. The effectiveness of control depends in large part on detailed reporting concerning the fulfillment of such goals, and the crucial role of accounting in this process is determined by the simple circumstance that responsibility is often specified in terms of accounting magnitudes.

In the Soviet Union, the consolidation of the entire economy under the direction of the state has confronted the Soviet economic administrators with the general problem of control in an acute form, and they have been strongly conscious of the necessity to strengthen the accounting tool. This and the following chapter will discuss two crucial areas of planning and management in which the regime depends heavily on accounting as an instrument of control.

One such area is the control of costs. The Russians have placed great emphasis on cost performance as a general index of operating efficiency, and they have elaborated a comprehensive system of cost accounting and reporting as an aid in controlling the manager-bureaucrats of their economic system. Accounting supplies merely an ex post record and so cannot in itself control anything. What it does, however, is to furnish information on performance so that performance can be checked against standards and appropriate action taken. Because of the oblique nature of this process, its effectiveness depends on two important conditions. First, there must be objective and detailed standards against which performance can be measured. If they are not objective, failure to comply with them means nothing; if they are not detailed, departures from them cannot be traced to their source. Second, the ex post reports on performance must be truthful and accurate. This is an especially important problem in the Soviet Union, where there exist strong incentives to falsify cost reports. The effectiveness of Soviet accounting for cost-control purposes should be considered against the background of these prerequisites.

In the Soviet system the primary motivation of management at the level of the enterprise is to fulfill the assigned plan rather than to earn the greatest possible profit. Because management at the lower levels has little incentive to minimize costs except to the extent that cost goals are embodied in the assigned plan, responsibility for controlling costs lies ultimately with some higher organ of administration (such as the ministry or the glavk). It will be useful, therefore, to discuss separately two levels of cost control in the Soviet system: (1) the level at which the higher agency sets and enforces cost goals for the enterprise (in the following discussion the glavk will be taken as the representative higher agency), and (2) the level at which enterprise management uses internal cost controls to meet the assigned goals.

Control from Above

The instrument used by the glavk to control costs in its subordinate enterprises is a set of cost plans similar to the budgets of American cost accounting. On the basis of planned prices and the input ratios underlying the plan, cost goals are set out both for finished output in general and for the most important kinds of output.[1] These cost indicators are taken as the principal measure of the firm's efficiency of operation. As one writer says, "The cost of production is the basic synthetic indicator characterizing the quality of the entire work of the enterprise."[2] In one sense, these cost goals are redundant, since they are only a recapitulation in value terms of many other goals assigned to the enterprise in physical terms. The use of cost accounting permits both the summarization of the multitude of partial indices of operating efficiency in an aggregate index and the inclusion of whatever detail is necessary for analysis. If the cost goals are met, the glavk can give premiums (bonuses) to enterprise management; if they are not, it uses the cost breakdowns to analyze the reason for the failure and then attempts to tell the manager what corrective action he should take.

Deficiencies in cost planning. Obviously, the effectiveness of this kind of control depends on the quality of the cost plans. If the cost goals which the enterprise director has to meet in order to receive a premium contain considerable reserves, then not enough pressure is being applied; or if the managers are deprived of premiums for failing to meet impossible goals, incentives are impaired.

Traditionally, the glavk has been in a very poor position to work out and assign technologically objective cost plans. It has neither the staff nor the mass of detailed information which is required to work out a cost plan by a process of aggregating

173

technological norms for all the processes involved in a given output program in individual plants. The establishment and use of such detailed standards is closely tied in with the day-to-day work of management and is therefore the responsibility of the enterprise rather than of the glavk. As might be expected in this situation, the job of working out the detailed cost plan has always been left to the planning section within the enterprise. The higher organs have controlled the cost planning only indirectly through the setting of certain "limits and directives" which the enterprise planners must incorporate in the final plan. These goals specify the cost plan implicitly, and so, if the glavk were in a position to set these summary determinants of the cost plan on an objective technological basis, then the enterprise would be forced to draw up an objective cost plan. But the glavk has usually had to rely on the record of past performance in setting the directives and limits. As Soviet writers are fond of pointing out, this in effect "legalizes" poor work on the part of the enterprise and does not permit the cost plan to be a directive for reducing costs.

Beginning with the 1947 plan, however, a full-fledged official campaign was begun to improve the cost planning and to base the cost plans more on technological standards and less on the standards of past performance. The Council of Ministers set a number of norms which were to be met or bettered in the plans of individual enterprises;[3] the ministries were instructed to work out aggregate "average-progressive"[4] norms for labor consumption, material consumption, and equipment utilization; the State Supply Administration (Gossnab) set up a large number of norms for material consumption for individual kinds of products and used these norms in making allocations of scarce materials. These measures were supplemented by the inclusion in the annual national economic plans of a general norm of cost reduction for industry as a whole which is differentiated and passed down to each individual enterprise. It appears that as a result of this campaign a great deal has been done to develop norms based on technological calculations and to encourage cost improvements by applying general pressure from above in the form of a cost-reduction assignment. On the other hand, it is also clear that the basic problem of the glavk — the inadequacy of the means at its disposal for determining objective cost plans — has not been solved. This problem is inherent in the Soviet system and cannot be overcome solely by decrees and campaigns.

Accuracy of reported costs. The second pillar on which the effectiveness of cost control rests is accuracy in the reporting of costs. One of the constant refrains of the literature is that the cost reports are drawn up inaccurately. There are distortions caused by the generally low quality of Soviet accounting and by outright falsification. A single example will suffice to illustrate the kind of distortion that is caused by the low quality of accounting, and I shall then go on to discuss in more detail the kind of bookkeeping falsifications which the Soviet enterprise is likely to engage in. These falsifications are extremely interesting not only in relation to the effectiveness of cost control, but also for the insight they provide into the kinds of pressures that are felt by the enterprise manager.

An illustration of the limitations which inaccuracies of accounting place on cost control in the Soviet economy is found in the widespread use of "simplified standard cost" or, as it is sometimes called, the "kettle method" of cost accounting. As explained in Chapter 5, under this method outlays are distributed on the basis of predetermined coefficients, and there is no real ex post cost calculation of individual kinds of output. Such practices deprive the cost reports of much of their usefulness for analysis because it is impossible to tell where overexpenditures have occurred. If the analyst asks why the wage

175

fund was overexpended, he finds that the planned amount of wages was exceeded by exactly the same percentage for every product. This continues on through all the items of the cost-accounting classification. It is possible to see whether the total cost plan was overexpended and what outlay items were over-expended, but the analyst is deprived of any possibility of finding out where these overexpenditures took place. Although the practice is often condemned, it appears to be fairly common.[5] It is a boon to the overworked bookkeeping staff, and, since the central agency is more likely to judge their work on the basis of speed rather than quality, there is great pressure to use it. This form of cost accounting is at its worst when, as often happens, the original cost plan is determined more or less arbitrarily.[6]

In addition to such more or less innocent errors engendered by the primitive technology of Soviet accounting, there is undoubtedly a great deal of falsification of cost reports. Under double-entry bookkeeping there are important limitations to the kinds of falsification that are possible. The cost reports of a Soviet enterprise are an integral part of its general accounting statement and must be reconcilable with such documents as the balance sheet and the profit and loss account. Nevertheless, there are some fairly easy ways of falsifying the cost reports, and under pressure to meet a cost goal the enterprise sometimes resorts to them.

The most important goal, the one which must be fulfilled in order to receive premiums, is the cost-reduction assignment. This goal covers the part of finished production which is "comparable," that is, the kinds of output which have been produced in previous years. Therefore, if outlays can be written off to any accounts other than this one, the cost report will be improved where it counts the most. There are, for instance, some accounts which are relatively difficult to inventory *in natura,* and so the Soviet plant managers are tempted to conceal part of the costs which are actually chargeable to the current period by inflating these sections of the balance sheet. The most important such account is unfinished production. Time and again in the literature there occur descriptions of instances in which the enterprise neglects to write off from unfinished production outlays properly chargeable to current output or to the profit and loss account.[7] These include spoilage, canceled orders, shortages of materials, and depreciation of tools and other small-value assets. The accounting authorities have tried to control this by a precise definition of the kind and extent of outlays that can be included in unfinished production. Before 1940 this was left to the discretion of the plant itself, but this provided too many possibilities for falsification, and since 1940 the Ministry of Finance has issued a series of successively more restrictive rules which leave the enterprise virtually no discretion in valuing its unfinished production. These rules have probably made it more difficult to understate costs by inflating unfinished production, but there continue to be complaints that enterprises conceal expenses in this account.[8]

Two other accounts to which expenses can be incorrectly assigned are "development expenditures" and "mining-preparatory expenditures." These expenses make up a fairly important part of costs in some branches. Sometimes these outlays are financed out of the budget, and in that case expense can thus be not only diverted from the cost of production in the current month but written off completely. It is virtually impossible to inventory these accounts, since they consist almost exclusively of intangibles. Moreover, it is often not feasible to establish a fixed budget for development expense because it is very difficult to predict in advance just what amount of financing will be necessary. These two circumstances have permitted Soviet enterprises to write off to these accounts many expenditures which should have been assigned elsewhere. Development expense, in particular, has been inflated by the costs of whole laboratories, capital investment, the purchase of experimental machines, and cost of production of the regular output of the enterprise.[9] When development work is carried out in part by the regular production shops, it is relatively easy to write off an excessively large share of their outlays to this account.

There is also a temptation to write off development expense to the cost of production at too slow a rate. Because these accounts are often kept only in very rough terms, with little detailed indication of the nature of the expense or the kinds of product or series for which outlays have been made, the enterprise can charge such expenses to the cost of production in a fairly arbitrary way. One writer cites as "characteristic examples" instances in which mining enterprises arbitrarily understated their cost by failing to write off the appropriate amount of expense.[10] Another source describes a situation in the Stalin diesel plant in Voronezh. Here all expenses of developing new products were kept in a single account without any indication of the particular series or orders involved. The development expense account grew until at last it reached 1.5 million rubles, at which time the glavk investigated. After reviewing the accounts, the glavk decided that 900,000 rubles of this amount should have been charged to production of earlier years and ordered that it be written off as a loss.[11]

In 1940, for the first time the Commissariat of Finance tried to deal with the problem by laying down in detail the kind of expense chargeable to development expense, but it left to the individual branches the task of establishing writeoff periods. After the war, when the Ministry of Finance made a special investigation of cost-accounting practices in Soviet enterprises, it was found that the handling of this expense was still unsatisfactory, especially in machinebuilding plants. As a result of this investigation, the ministry ordered that the accounting for development expenses be made more exact, and definite limits were set for the length of the writeoff period. The rules were made even more restrictive in 1952.

"Capital repair" and "capital construction" are other accounts to which expenses can be shifted.[12] Any expense shifted to these accounts will not appear in the cost of finished production. Capital repair is charged to the amortization fund rather than directly as a current outlay on production. The amortization fund is formed as the result of the amortization deductions, but the amount of these charges is fixed. Therefore, the more outlays that can be charged to capital repair, the lower the reported cost of production will be. (Such a practice may deplete the enterprise's funds for capital repair, but that is a separate problem.) The shift can be made by charging excessive overhead to capital repair or by accounting for current repair as capital repair.[13] An attempt has been made to prevent this distortion by setting up detailed lists in each ministry of what kinds of repair shall fall into the capital repair category and by setting limits on the amount of overhead that can be charged to capital repair.[14] If the enterprise is making capital investments, it may be possible to capitalize current costs by charging capital construction high prices for services and materials or by using the assets of the construction section for the purpose of the main activity.[15]

Another serious form of distortion is that in which shortages and inventory losses are omitted from the reported costs. Soviet accounting has traditionally emphasized the annual inventory, so that monthly and quarterly cost reports often do not take account of inventory shortages. There are frequently descriptions of cases where an enterprise has reported costs within the limits of the cost plan all during the year, but in the annual report, based on an inventory, has had to report failure to meet the plan.[16] The divergence between material consumption as shown in the documents and as shown in the inventory is likely to be unusually large in the Soviet economy because of poor warehouse management, under which materials are often issued without weighing or measuring and the documents filled in by guess.[17] Furthermore, poor bookkeeping control invites extensive pilfering, causing material shortages that show up only when an inventory is taken.[18] An attempt has been made to control this sort of falsification by requiring more frequent inventories. Presumably, the more frequent inventory will help to improve the cost accounting, but one wonders whether the monthly and quarterly inventories will actually be made. There are complaints that these intermediate inventories are likely to be mere formalities carried out by the lower-level personnel without participation of the bookkeeping department.[19]

Auditing. On the basis of what has been said so far, it is obvious that auditing has an important role to play in the Soviet system of control. The distortions described could be exposed and prevented if the books and reports were checked by trained auditors. In accordance with the multiplicity of control organs characteristic of Soviet administration, there are several separate auditing staffs which have the right to check the bookkeeping of the Soviet enterprise. The three main agencies which carry out audits are the Ministry of Finance, the Ministry of State Control, and the superior administrative body. Of these it is the latter which has the major responsibility for auditing the books of khozraschet enterprises. While both the Ministry of State Control and the Control and Audit Administration of the Ministry of Finance have auditing staffs and may inspect the books of enterprises, their work is limited in scope. The Control and Audit Administration is concerned primarily with auditing budgetary revenues and expenditures. In this connection it audits the books of all organizations financed by the budget and the whole structure of organs which collect and disburse state revenues. The Ministry of State Control audits all kinds of enterprises. Apparently it does not audit any great proportion of enterprises, however, and seems to operate only in the most important plants or in cases where fraud is suspected.[20]

The main responsibility for auditing the books of khozraschet enterprises is assigned to the superior agency on the basis of a 1936 decree.[21] This audit is supposed to be carried out not less often than once a year for all enterprises in the Soviet Union. This audit is initiated by the head of the superior agency and is carried out by the bookkeeping department of the agency through its staff of auditors (*revizory*). The tasks are to check the legality of the operations, to expose pilferage and wastage, to check the correctness of the bookkeeping practices, the quality of the documentation, and the accuracy of the bookkeeping entries, and to check on the handling of material accounting. There are three principal reasons why this auditing program is not fully effective.

First, the program of an annual audit for every enterprise is apparently never carried out fully. An investigation by the Ministry of Finance showed that the auditing organs of the twenty union commissariats had only 42 percent of their assigned staff in 1944. In that year they managed to audit only 45 percent of the enterprises under their jurisdiction. Some enterprises had not been audited for a period of several years. Because of the shortage of staff, many audits were carried out by outsiders, and in some instances these were either unqualified or interested parties.[22] There has been some improvement since the end of the war, but the coverage is said still to be incomplete. In 1952, and again in 1957, *Bukhgalterskii uchet* published a flurry of articles repeating these complaints — the auditing organs are understaffed, the available staff is assigned to work other than auditing, and many enterprises go un-audited. Incomplete coverage means that many enterprises go unaudited for long periods of time, and it is said that in these unaudited enterprises fraud occurs frequently.

Second, the audits are poorly performed. Auditors are over-worked, underpaid, poorly trained, and spend a great deal of time writing reports and documenting trivialities, but do little in the way of revealing weaknesses of the accounting arrange-ments of individual enterprises. This is the burden of recurring articles in *Sovetskie finansy*, *Finansy i kredit SSSR*, and *Bukh-galterskii uchet*. They are unable to detect frauds and cannot tell whether the books reflect the true position of the enterprise. One writer cites a case in which the auditor found an excess of 308,000 rubles worth of materials in one of the warehouses of the enterprise, but an "expert bookkeeper" working for the court found that there was a shortage of 42,000 rubles.[23] It is frequently pointed out that the pay scales for auditors are be-low those of chief bookkeepers, so that it is impossible to attract competent people. The auditors are less skillful at detecting fraud than enterprise bookkeepers are at concealing it.

Third, as a general rule, the Soviet auditors are concerned with problems other than checking the accuracy of book-keeping reports. It is clear from the decree outlining their func-tions and from the discussions of their work in the literature that they are preoccupied with what an American accountant would describe as "internal audit." The principal task of the auditor is to uncover fraud, pilferage, and illegal actions of one kind or another. Since in the Soviet system there is considerable pressure on the enterprise director to permit illegal actions and to overexpend the wage fund, and a temptation to overlook or participate in pilferage, the superior organization has had to assume considerable responsibility for what would be a purely internal function in a capitalist enterprise. In view of this preoccupation with problems of internal audit, Soviet auditors do nothing comparable to the certification of accounting statements which plays so important a role in the work of auditing in the United States. The objective of auditing in the United States is to ascertain whether the income statement and balance sheet of a firm accurately represent the result of its operations and its current position. The statement attached to a firm's accounting statement by a certified public accountant states a judgment on this matter for the information of interested outsiders. The judgment is based on a detailed examination of the accounting documents and on a consideration of whether the accounting interpretations follow accepted conventions, but the ultimate end is to certify the report to people outside the firm rather than to uncover violations of the law or fraud for purposes of managerial control within the firm.

Control Inside the Plant

However precise the cost planning, however accurate the cost reporting, the control which the superior administrative agency exercises over costs can never be anything but indirect. The glavk can set cost goals and can confer rewards and apply sanctions in accordance with their fulfillment, but the actual control is inevitably in the hands of the managers within the enterprise, the men who are in control of the day-to-day operations of the firm. Their ability to control costs depends on a system of accounting which provides them with frequent and detailed reports on the performance of the units under their jurisdiction.

Soviet accounting has traditionally been weak in what is called in the United States "managerial accounting." The energies of the bookkeeping department have been concentrated mostly on the compilation of the system of reports described in the previous section. It is expected that these reports

183

will also be used by the management of the enterprise to analyze the work of the firm and to serve as a basis for cost control, but actually they are not well adapted for this purpose. It will be recalled that the focus of interest in the reports to the higher agency is the operation of the plant as a whole or the costs of individual kinds of output. For the purpose of internal control, however, it is necessary to look at the operations of the enterprise in terms of individual processes, operations, and administrative units. If the supervisors at the various levels of management are to control costs, they must be able to fix responsibility for overexpenditures in terms of persons rather than in terms of products or gross categories of outlay. Since the bookkeeping department has been so absorbed in working out the reports to the outside, it has neglected to develop a system of internal reporting. This tradition is explainable primarily in terms of two factors: (1) the role of the chief bookkeeper of an enterprise in the Soviet system of industrial administration, and (2) the primitive technology of Soviet accounting.

The chief bookkeeper of the Soviet enterprise has traditionally been the servant of the higher agency rather than of the enterprise director.[24] Because of the strategic position which he occupies with regard to the operations of the enterprise, he has been given the responsibility of serving as the "eye of the state" within the enterprise and of checking on the legality of the actions of the director and other officials. Although the chief bookkeeper is subordinated to the director in an administrative sense, he is subordinated directly to the bookkeeping department of the superior agency as far as accounting procedure is concerned. He has the right to appeal to the higher group if the orders of the director are illegal, and his loyalty is further ensured by making his appointment or removal subject to the approval of the glavk, and by the fact that his premiums are granted directly by the superior agency rather than by the firm's director. Thus the outside organ has first claim on the services of the chief bookkeeper, and compliance with its demands often leaves him little time for acting as an adviser to the enterprise director.

Because of a low level of mechanization, the bookkeeping department of the Soviet firm does not have the computational capacity to prepare the detailed system of reports which is necessary for effective cost control. In a large enterprise, the task of collecting data in a breakdown by individual units and processes within the plant, and the preparation of reports in the same detail, becomes a formidable problem of data processing. In most Soviet enterprises this computational work is all done with pen and ink, with no mechanical aids other than the schety, the Russian abacus. Given the first priority of reporting to the superior agency, the bookkeeping department is simply unable to take on this additional job.

Because of these two factors, Soviet cost accounting has characteristically been carried out only in very aggregative terms. Cost centers are not distinguished and materials are not charged to specific operations or units, but only to the production account of the shop or enterprise as a whole. Moreover, the costs of subsidiary shops, such as the power station or the repair shop, have not usually been allocated among the users of their services. The bookkeeping department may not even document the movement of semifabricates, tools, or materials through the various processes, but simply let outlays accumulate in a single production account for the plant as a whole and then write them off to finished production at the end of the accounting period on the basis of an inventory.[25] It is said that even in such an important plant as the Chelyabinsk tractor plant, up through 1948 the material accounting was such that it was impossible to know what units of the plant were responsible for the consumption of various metals, or even to

185

know in what part of the tractor these metals were being employed.[26]

Since the war there has been a considerable effort made to improve the techniques of cost control within the plant, primarily through the method of "intraplant khozraschet," which may be translated as intraplant accountability. The essence of this method is the disaggregation of the general plan into individual assignments, including cost assignments, for individual units within the enterprise. There is usually also some sort of incentive offered for performance, such as premiums or sharing of the economies achieved with the workers. As these plans are described in the literature, they seem to be essentially the same as the cost-control methods used in American enterprises.[27]

From literature that has grown up around the postwar campaign for intraplant accountability, it is obvious that even in many of the largest and most important enterprises such schemes were not used before about 1948. One wonders how widely it has been adopted even now. According to G. Bocharov, a high official of the central bookkeeping department of the Ministry of Machinebuilding, intraplant accountability had been introduced into most of the largest machinebuilding plants by 1951, but not in medium-sized or small plants.[28] Further evidence that the smaller plants have been little affected is given in the report of a conference sponsored by the Institute of Economics of the Academy of Sciences of the Latvian SSR. It was reported that in 1952, of 107 enterprises of the Latvian ministries of local industry, food industry, and building-materials industry, only in 21 had shop khozraschet been introduced; in the other ministries scarcely any start had been made.[29] As both Soviet and American writers point out, these techniques require a great deal of preparatory work by way of setting objective norms for all processes, defining responsibilities, and improving internal planning, and there is no reason to expect the Russians to be able to "implant" this account-ability very rapidly. Despite the emphasis on norms in the Soviet economy, there is a great deal of evidence that carefully worked-out norms of material consumption, labor consumption, and equipment utilization simply do not exist for the operations of many plants. The absence of measuring devices necessary to charge the costs of service shops to consuming sections has already been mentioned. For other service shops, such as the tool and die shop or the repair shop, there may be no measure of output on the basis of which costs could be planned or dis-tributed among the users. Indeed, as one authority says, almost all that is covered in any of the Soviet applications of intra-plant khozraschet is wages and materials in the main production shops.[30]

In connection with what was said earlier about the role of the bookkeeper in the enterprise, it is interesting to find consider-able evidence that the bookkeeping department has been an unwilling participant in the effort to strengthen internal cost control. The official position is that accounting for the fulfill-ment of intraplant cost goals should be integrated with the reg-ular system of cost accounting in the enterprise. Apparently, however, the bookkeeping departments in many firms have re-fused to cooperate in remodeling their accounting procedures to make it possible to account for fulfillment of the intraplant cost assignments. There are many complaints that the book-keepers stand aside from the problem of intraplant accountabil-ity,[31] and one writer cites an interesting case in which the book-keeping department of the superior agency held that the duties of the bookkeepers in the enterprise did not include handling the accounting for fulfillment of internal cost goals.[32] Failure of the bookkeeping department to remodel its accounting pro-cedures to suit the needs of intraplant khozraschet may make it virtually impossible to check on the fulfillment of intraplant cost goals. For instance, it is reported that in some enterprises the bookkeeping department handles its material accounting on an actual cost basis, rather than on a planned cost basis; as a result, individual production units may appear to fail to fulfill the cost goals, whereas it is really the fault of the supply department. The same problem arises with regard to the costs of the services of such subsidiary shops as the power station.[33]

Conclusion

In reading the Soviet literature on the control functions of cost accounting, one is struck by its similarity to the American literature on the subject. The Russians use essentially the same general techniques as are used in American enterprises. Such devices as the technical-industrial-financial plan, normed accounting, and intraplant khozraschet, for all their Soviet flavor, have virtually identical counterparts in American managerial practice. The similarity is not surprising. The objective problem of controlling costs in large, complicated firms is the same in both the capitalist and the planned economy. Moreover, there is considerable evidence that the Russians have been directly influenced by American ideas.[34] But there are some distinctive features of the Soviet situation which interfere with the effective use of these techniques. The total effect of these peculiarities on Soviet cost accounting can be summarized in two generalizations. First, the cost-accounting system has been biased too much toward the needs of outside control agencies. Second, and probably as a corollary, there is an overemphasis on the unit of production as the costing unit.

As was said earlier, expenses are usually classified in Soviet cost reports by general economic category and by product rather than by center of responsibility or by individual operations and processes. From the point of view of the superior agency this makes sense. First of all, unit-cost data are needed for the purpose of price setting. In the second place, this sort of cost plan and cost report presents the generalized indicators of fulfillment which are necessary for its main task of control. Such breakdowns as are given, though superfluous to any judgment about the fulfillment of the cost plan, permit the glavk to make useful comparisons between product costs in different plants and thus reveal "reserves" for lowering production costs.

It is expected that these same reports will be analyzed and used by enterprise management for controlling costs, but in fact they are ill suited to this purpose. It is much more useful for the purposes of cost control to plan and report expenses not in terms of final products, but in terms of individual operations, processes, and administrative units. These breakdowns assist in revealing where expenditures or savings occur and thus make it possible to assign responsibility for them. Similarly, the breakdowns permit the revelation of poor performance more quickly after it occurs — if overexpenditures are revealed only when finished products have been assembled and their cost computed, it is then too late for management to take the necessary corrective action. It would be possible, of course, to perform both kinds of cost accounting, and in the postwar period an attempt has been made to this end. As might be expected, the attempt to carry on both forms of cost accounting puts a severe strain on the bookkeeping department and leads to an inflation of bookkeeping staffs. In the most recent period, the reaction of the regime to this growth in the bookkeeping labor force has been to demand a rationalization and simplification of accounting and a reduction in the volume of reporting. So far the emphasis has been primarily on the volume of reports that the enterprise sends to higher organs. The number of indicators that the reports must contain has been considerably decreased since 1954, and for some of the remaining indicators there has been a reduction in the number of times they must be figured

189

and reported each year. As one author says, since 1955 the Ministry of Finance has been revising accounting laws and instructions to "simplify and curtail recordkeeping and cost calculation by means of consolidating the costing units, unifying the methods of distributing indirect expenses, lengthening the duration of the cost accounting period, and transferring the center of gravity in cost control to the revelation of variances from existing norms and budgets." [35] It might be expected that this reduction in reporting would free the bookkeeping department to give more attention to providing data to enterprise management for internal control, but any such shift has probably not been great. As some Soviet accountants point out, the actual filling out of the reports is the least of their worries, and many of the indicators now omitted from the reports still have to be figured as intermediate steps in the process of writing the reports.[36] In other words, the work of the accounting department is still basically structured by the objective of reporting to higher agencies. There has apparently been some exploratory thought about reducing the planning and control of cost by outside organs still further so that the only indicator of cost that would be planned and reported would be the percentage reduction in cost over the previous year, or the cost per thousand rubles of output. The glavk would then no longer be involved in drawing up the detailed cost plans which require information it does not have, and the bookkeeping department of the enterprise would be left to devote their efforts to aiding enterprise management. But it is doubtful that the system of cost control can ever be changed so radically. Such general indicators would be too sensitive to factors other than actual cost reductions, and so those in the superior agency feel that they need more detailed data to understand the cost performance of enterprises or territorial groups of enterprises. Thus there is little prospect that, even with the present trend toward decentralization, the bookkeeping department will cease to serve two masters. Nevertheless, there will surely be a gradual improvement in "managerial accounting." Prospective shifts toward the mechanization of accounting will make it possible for the bookkeeping department to handle the burden of more detailed accounting for the needs of enterprise management, while continuing to carry on fairly detailed cost reporting for the outside control agencies.

INVENTORY CONTROL

INVENTORY behavior is a second aspect of enterprise performance in which accounting data play a very important role in the control process. Inventories of materials, work in process, and finished goods arise because of specialization in the process of production and because of the gap in space and time between the production and consumption of goods. Thus inventories are a necessary prerequisite of the production process, and one half of the inventory problem is to ensure that adequate stocks are always available so that production can proceed without interruption. On the other hand, there is the problem of preventing excessive accumulation of resources in the form of inventory, since this would represent a wasteful tying up of resources that might otherwise be used to increase output. The objective of an economical inventory policy could be described as keeping inventories to the minimum amount that is consistent with assuring uninterrupted production.

In a market economy, the regulation of inventories is the responsibility of individual firms. Given demand forecasts, production schedules, and the length of the period required to replenish supplies, the management of a capitalist firm tries to keep inventories at the minimum necessary amount. In order to survive, the capitalist firm must do moderately well at handling the dual objective described above. It must be able to fill orders without unreasonable delays, and it must avoid failures of supply that might halt the production process. But it cannot afford to have excessive amounts tied up in inventory because of the heavy costs of carrying inventories, such as storage and handling, insurance, explicit or implicit interest costs, and the risks of deterioration, devaluation, and obsolescence. In addition, there is always the problem of financial stringency. If the firm holds too much of its assets in the relatively illiquid form of inventories, there is the danger that it will be unable to pay its bills on time.

When firms become very large, the problem of inventory control increases greatly in complexity. The number of individual items that must be carried and the number of interactions among persons making decisions that affect inventories increase greatly. The present-day firm must arrange its managerial structure in such a way that control of inventories is made the explicit responsibility of some unit within the firm, and the accounting procedures must be designed to provide the data necessary for control. Almost any book on management or accounting in the American economy devotes considerable attention to inventory control, and there is a growing specialized literature on the subject.

In the Soviet economy, the inventory-control problem appears in a very different institutional environment. In some ways, the problem is simpler than in the United States. Two major issues facing the capitalist firm, the need to forecast demand and the necessity of considering price fluctuations, are completely absent. The primary difference is in the locus of authority and responsibility for inventories. The Soviet manager works in a setting wherein it is sensible for him to maintain the largest inventories that he can. From the point of view of national economic efficiency, of course, the prevention of excessive inventory holdings is just as important for the planned economy as it is for the market economy. Thus, someone somewhere in the administrative hierarchy should be concerned with the size of inventory holdings. Given the nature of the Soviet managerial structure, it cannot be the management of the firm, and the control of inventories is entrusted to a large extent to outside control agencies.

There are strong indications that the Soviet approach to inventory control does not work as effectively as it might. Altogether, it appears that Soviet enterprises hold much larger stocks of inventories than they really need. This conclusion is based on comparisons of the rate of turnover of inventories in Soviet industry with the rates of turnover in the United States. (The same general conclusion applies to trade as well.[1]) Because of differences in industrial structure and other noncomparabilities between the two economies, valid comparisons of inventory-turnover rates involve complicated statistical manipulations. It would be inappropriate to go through all the details of my calculations here: in general they indicate that in 1956 the rate of turnover of inventories in Soviet industry was in the range of four or five times a year, whereas it was about seven times a year in the United States. It is not at all certain that the American rate of inventory turnover is a valid criterion for evaluating the Soviet system. There may be certain features of the Soviet situation, such as slowness of transportation, geographic dispersion, and differences in the scale of plants, which make it rational for them to hold larger amounts of inventories. Moreover, their performance might not compare so badly with countries other than the United States. But the contrast with the American rate of turnover is striking enough to suggest the existence of an appreciable reserve of resources immobilized in inventories that might conceivably be freed by improved inventory control. If, in 1956, the Russian rate of turnover could have been speeded up to the American level, some 60–90 billion rubles of inventories would have been freed. This is nearly equal to the total investment in industry in 1956, and so the magnitudes involved would clearly justify an intensive effort toward improving the techniques of control over inventories.

In addition to having generally excessive inventories, the Soviet system also seems to be plagued by a maldistribution of inventories among individual units. Some enterprises manage to accumulate inventories considerably in excess of the planned inventory levels, whereas others are chronically short of inventories. It is stated, for example, that on October 1, 1955, some Soviet enterprises held 10.2 billion rubles worth of inventories above their normally planned levels; other enterprises had holdings of 6.8 billion rubles below planned levels.[2] It seems likely that these inventory shortages interfere significantly with production. There is no simple statistical measure of this effect, but we do know that total loss of work time from stoppages in industry in 1954 was 18 million man-days, equivalent to a loss of output of about 5 billion rubles.[3] Only part of these stoppages would be caused by supply interruptions, but surely the losses in this area must be appreciable.

When one begins to study the Russians' approach to inventory control, it soon becomes clear that their difficulties are not primarily attributable to deficiencies in the accounting practice of individual firms. The ineffectiveness of inventory control in the Soviet economy is not only a problem of information but also one of administrative structure, delegation of authority, and the specification of responsibility on a national scale. In other words, given the setting of this particular economic system, inventory control becomes a problem not so much of enterprise accounting as one of accounting in an extended structure, characterized by several levels of authority, an

institutional separation of financial authority, and multiple channels of communication. Analysis of the reasons for poor inventory control will take us some way into accounting on the
grand scale, where common accounting concepts may look unfamiliar because the supercorporation whose operations are
being described contains within itself all the units and articula-
tions of a national economy.

The first step is to describe the general system of inventory
control. Once this is done, the problem can be considered more
carefully from the point of view of management at the enterprise level and from the point of view of outside control
agencies.

General View of the Inventory-Control System

The main features of the Soviet system for controlling inventories can be outlined briefly in the following way. The
foundation of the system of inventory control is the normativ,
which can be described as an upper limit, expressed in number
of days' supply, for individual components of inventory. Since
the credit reform in 1931, the plans of Soviet enterprises have
specified normativs for the main inventory balance-sheet accounts, such as raw materials, auxiliary materials, purchased
semifabricates, fuel, unfinished production, and so on. These
normativs are set each year in the process of drawing up the
tekhpromfinplan. They may remain the same for a long period
of time or may be changed from year to year or even at shorter
intervals as the enterprise grows or as it changes its production
program.

A firm's holdings of inventories are inevitably subject to short-
run fluctuations. They rise and fall as shipments are received
and as transfers are made to production and, even if they
remain fairly stable in the aggregate, their composition is constantly changing. It would be an impossible job to try to plan

and check in detail the physical stocks themselves both in time profile and in structural classification. Rather, the approach is to confine an enterprise to the planned normativ by controlling the amount of resources available to it for financing inventory holdings. Generally speaking, the normativ for inventories is to be covered by what is called "own working capital." The best way to explain this concept is in terms of the balance sheet of an enterprise. A simplified version of a Soviet balance sheet, with illustrative data, is shown below. On the equities side of the balance sheet, there are a number of accounts representing the permanent assignment of resources to the enterprise, such items as the charter fund, retained profits, and a few others. (These are essentially the same as the capital and surplus of a capitalist firm.) If the more or less permanently illiquid assets of the firm, such as fixed assets or funds tied up in capital construction (shown in the simple balance sheet as Fixed Assets and Immobilized Resources) are subtracted from this total, the difference represents the amount of its own resources which the enterprise has free to invest in inventory assets.

Yet another source for financing inventories is a miscellany of short-term obligations. These are the "stable liabilities" shown on the equities side of the illustrative balance sheet. In actual practice the amount of stable liabilities counted as working capital is some normal expected amount rather than the actual amount on the balance sheet. This planned amount is shown in a separate column on the equities side. These include claims against the enterprise by the budget or superior organ, claims for fines, disputed claims, and some small obligations vis à vis individuals. To a large extent, these resources are offset by similar claims against other units, but in some cases they may finance real inventories. The sum of these two resources, figured essentially as the difference between the two halves of part A of the balance sheet (except that planned rather than actual

197

BALANCE SHEET FOR A TYPICAL SOVIET FIRM
(thousand rubles)

AKTIV (ASSETS)			PASSIV (LIABILITIES)		
A. Fixed Assets and Immobilized Resources			A. Sources of Own and Equivalent Resources		
1. Fixed assets		65,294	1. Charter Fund		94,531
2. Profits paid to state on account		393	2. Depreciation of fixed assets		14,656
3. Funds paid to bank to finance capital construction		2,040	3. Profit Previous years		—
4. Deductions in special incentive funds		867	Present year		4,602
5. Losses		—	4. Stable liabilities *Included in working capital*		
			Due social ins. fund ⎤ Due workers ⎦	780	1,531
			Deferred expense	390	342

Availability of own and equivalent working capital 46,365

AKTIV (ASSETS)			PASSIV (LIABILITIES)		
B. Normed Resources	*Normativ*		B. Short-Term Bank Credit Borrowed on Normed Inventories		
1. Materials	16,670	16,470	1. On materials		9,539
2. Unfinished production	18,880	19,312	2. On unfinished production		180
3. Tools	13,950	13,709	3. On finished goods		3,650
4. Finished goods	4,350	10,005			
5. Prepaid expense	2,750	3,306			
C. Resources in Settlement and Other Assets			C. Miscellaneous Bank Credit, Claims, and Other Liabilities		
1. Money		377	1. Gosbank credit		4,333
2. Goods shipped		5,918	2. Due other firms		6,690
3. Due from other firms		1,795	3. Special financing		11
4. Capital repair		434			
5. Other		169			
Balance		140,089			140,089

Source. Adapted from S. A. Shchenkov, *Otchetnost promyshlennykh predpriyatii* (Moscow, 1952), pp. 166–176, 200–205.

stable liabilities are used on the equities side), is called "own and equivalent working capital." Comparison of own working capital with the normativ indicates whether the enterprise has a shortage or an excess of own working capital and, when the financial plan is being drawn up, provision is usually made for adjusting the working capital by transfer of funds to bring working capital into line with the planned normativ.

In addition to own working capital, however, the enterprise also has access to bank credit to cover some of its inventory holdings. If an enterprise finds that it must acquire inventories beyond the normativ for certain well-defined reasons, such as the necessity to accumulate seasonal stocks, it may obtain additional financing in the form of a loan from the Gosbank. Furthermore, there are some kinds of inventories for which a normativ is not specified, such as goods shipped but not paid for, and it is intended that these will be covered by the extension of bank credit. In trade, the Gosbank also provides a large share of the resources for holding even the normal volume of normed inventories, and in recent years there has been some experimentation with extending this system to other sectors. It should be obvious from a glance at the balance sheet that the accounting documentation has been greatly influenced by the objective of facilitating this system of control. For instance, the balance sheet is drawn up to show not only the actual inventory holdings but also the normativs. Moreover, the balance-sheet accounts are classified so as to make it easy to figure own working capital, and in fact the amount of own and equivalent working capital is figured and entered on a separate line, as in the balance sheet shown here. Further, Gosbank credit is shown separately for the amount loaned against normed assets and for that against other kinds of assets. Indeed, examination of Soviet books on the analysis of enterprise activity suggests that the main purpose for which the balance sheet is used by outside control agencies is to analyze the inventory position and performance of the enterprise.

The picture presented above is a somewhat idealized version of how the system of control is supposed to work. We are now ready to examine the factors that interfere with its effectiveness in practice. First let us examine the environment with which the inventory behavior of enterprise management must cope, and management's reaction to it.

Inventory Control at the Level of the Enterprise

From the point of view of enterprise management, the inventory problem is almost exclusively one of making certain that there are adequate stocks of inventories, and there is very little motivation at this level to minimize inventories. This approach to the problem is the inevitable result of several elements of the setting. The first of these is the rigidity of the supply system. Because of the importance attached to fulfillment of the output plan as a measure of success, it is very important for management to avoid stoppages, but this must be done in the face of a somewhat erratic and inflexible supply system.

The ineffective functioning of the supply system is a feature of the Soviet economy which is well known and, since it has been admirably discussed elsewhere, there is no need to go into it fully here.[4] Rather I want only to show the impact of the system on the inventory attitudes of enterprise management. The heart of the problem is that the manager has only a limited autonomy in regard to actions that affect his holdings of inventories. For instance, he does not have authority to purchase or decline to purchase most of the important material inputs at will, since most of the important materials are subject to central planning and allocation. Materials in the Soviet economy are divided into three main categories, known as funded, centrally planned, and local.[5] Of these, only the local materials can be bought by anyone who wants them at any time. The distribution of the others is planned in advance, and an enterprise can get them only if an allocation has been planned and it has received authorization to procure them. At the time that the plan is being drawn up for the coming year, enterprises send in requisitions (called *zayavki*) for their estimated requirements of rationed materials. The requisitions are channeled through the glavks and the ministry (or now in most cases the sovnarkhoz), checked along the way, and finally submitted to the material planners in the Gosplan who attempt to reconcile them with the planned output of the material in question. Of course this is a process in which people at the lower levels are likely to ask for more materials than they absolutely need, and those at higher levels must cut authorizations below requests, perhaps in an arbitrary way. When the allocations have been finally determined at the center, they are passed back down the administrative hierarchy, with contracts being drawn up along the way, until finally the enterprise holds an authorization to procure certain materials and a contract with some supplier who will provide them. These contracts specify the total amount of such materials, frequency and size of shipment, and various other details.

In addition to the general danger that enterprises will request and succeed in obtaining unnecessary materials and thus have excessive inventories, there are some more or less institutionalized deficiencies in the procedure. For instance, the timing of the various steps in the process is out of phase. The enterprise must submit its request for materials considerably in advance of the beginning of the planned period, but at this point in time it does not yet have an actual production program assigned to it. Consequently, it must draw up its requisitions for materials without knowing precisely what its material requirements will be. It makes the best guesses it can, but inevitably many enterprises will end up with contracts and authorizations for materials which they do not need.[6] Other enterprises will find that they do not have authorization to procure the materials they need to fulfill their production program. Unfortunately, once the planning machinery has ground out the contracts and authorizations, it is very difficult to change supply plans. The system lacks short-term flexibility. The producing organs, of course, do not want their sales plans or shipment plans upset, and so they are unwilling to cancel orders. Apparently the shippers have the upper hand in such a conflict. In a "sellers' market" consumers do not want to antagonize their suppliers, and apparently it is generally impossible for a buyer to decline to accept materials in such a situation even by legal action. When the purchaser *is* able to refuse materials, the problem is simply shifted to the supplier. He will have excessive inventories of finished goods because his plan does not specify what must be done with the unsold output.[7]

Another problem is that in the Soviet economy it is often impossible to order less than a specifically sized lot. For most of the centrally allocated materials, there are established "order lots" and "shipment lots." The producing organization will not accept an order for less than a certain amount, and the railroads will not accept shipment of less than certain amounts. If an enterprise needs less, it will probably still send in a requisition and hope to get an authorization for an amount equal to one of the minimum sizes. Even if its annual requirement coincides with the specified lot, it will still need a large average inventory of the commodity since it will have to buy a year's supply at once. It is envisaged that in such situations the procurement organization of the ministry (now the sovnarkhoz) will buy in large lots and then supply enterprises within the ministry with small lots. But the procurement organizations in ministries never did work very satisfactorily, and the director of an enterprise frequently preferred to take his chance on getting a shipment directly from the producer. Presumably the abolition of ministries and the shift to regional economic councils has improved this situation — at any rate that was one of the important objectives of the reorganization.

There are even occasions when Soviet enterprises are forced to take materials which they have not ordered and have absolutely no need for. Such a result may come about through a complete breakdown of the supply system or because a superior administrative organ, which has hoarding motivations of its own, may direct that a shipment be sent to one of the enterprises under its jurisdiction. The glavk wants to hold the goods for possible future use and so must put them in the warehouse of some enterprise.[8]

Even when the material-planning system works perfectly, so that an enterprise receives an allocation for just the amount it needs and has a contract with a supplier, there still may be difficulties. There is often great variability in sizes of shipments and in shipment intervals. Contracts frequently fail to stipulate delivery dates, but, even when they do, they are often violated. For instance, an editorial in the Gosbank journal mentions an investigation which showed that, in 46 percent of the cases studied, suppliers had failed to comply with dates of shipment or sizes of shipment stipulated in the contracts.[9] As a result, shipments may come too soon or too late. In the one case, the enterprise will have excessive inventories and, in the other, the management will soon learn the desirability of hoarding materials. And there is always the danger that the supplier may fail to fulfill his output plan or supply contract. One author even claims that there have been cases where goods were shipped and invoices sent and accepted by the buyer but, while the goods were in transit, the shipper had the goods sent to another buyer en route without notifying the original customer.[10]

Errors in supply are aggravated by the difficulties in disposing of surplus inventories. Even when local management would be willing to reduce its inventories, it is unable to do so because there are inadequate channels through which to unburden itself of unwanted stocks. For a long time the laws were very restrictive on this score. The regime was afraid of black-market activity and so was reluctant to give managers the right to dispose of excessive inventories at their own discretion. In recent years there has been some easing of these restrictions. A change in the laws in 1955 made it possible for managers to sell off excessive inventories, and in the last few years there have been campaigns to have enterprises turn in lists of unwanted commodities to the supply organs of their sovnarkhozes. These lists are then circulated so that other enterprises can shop from them. But, to judge from the reports of these operations appearing in Soviet publications, one doubts that they have done much to stimulate inventory liquidation. The problem is that management is reluctant to get rid of anything that it might possibly need at some time, and it does not put on the lists anything that other plants would want.[11] There are Soviet data which permit a comparison of the breakdown of Soviet industrial inventories by kind with that in the United States; they show that the Soviet structure is characterized by a very low share for unfinished production. I suspect that the low share of unfinished production is related to the strong pressure for output which leads the manager to deplete unfinished production to the limit, particularly as of the end of the month, which is of course the date to which the inventory figures refer. One of the characteristic features of Soviet production is *shturmovshchina,* or "storming," which means a frantic effort in the last week or ten days of the month to push as much output as possible over the line into finished output in order to fulfill the monthly output plan. On the other hand, a surprisingly large share of the total inventories is in the form of materials and supplies. This disproportion between materials and unfinished production suggests that a bottleneck of sorts exists between these two stages of production, and one is tempted to deduce that a large part of the materials and supplies are surplus items unsuitable for current production needs.

Finally, one of the important differences between the Soviet and the market setting is the attitude toward liquidity. The capitalist firm for good reasons wants to maintain liquidity, and this is one of the motivations for careful control over inventory. For a Soviet firm, however, liquidity has largely a negative value. This is partly a general effect of the sellers' market but is more directly caused by the fact that the plant lacks financial autonomy. The glavks and ministries always had the explicit right to extract part of the working capital of an enterprise. The glavk could take away up to 10 percent of the working capital of one of its enterprises and hand it over to another one. It was supposed to do this only if the plant temporarily had no need of the funds; it had to return them within a specified time and was supposed to make such transfers only at specific intervals. In practice, however, the glavks never conformed to these limitations and, in any case, could justify whatever shifts of working capital they cared to make by arbitrary changes in the normativs of enterprises. These are some of the sins for which the now defunct ministries were long berated, but essentially the same rights were given to the sovnarkhozes, and it is unlikely that their practices will be radically different.[12] In this situation the enterprise is not master of its own working capital as long as it is in money form. The glavk can simply send a note to the Gosbank and the money is gone. The enterprise must recognize that money is not only liquid but also highly volatile. Physical stocks are much harder to remove, however, and so the enterprise strongly prefers goods to money.

Inventory control at the level of the enterprise is also hampered by some more strictly mechanical deficiencies in accounting. Just as in the case of cost accounting, the speed and rhythm of accounting for movements that affect inventories is much influenced by the demands of outside control organs and by low computational capacity. There are supposed to be great delays in accounting for receipts and consumption of materials, for instance. Documents for receipts of goods are drawn up far behind the actual arrival of materials, and there are similar delays in recording issues. Moreover, the bookkeeping department does not post these documents to the books as they are generated, but lets them accumulate over the entire accounting period of a month. At the end of the month, they are sorted and summarized in special registers, and totals are then posted to the separate inventory accounts. But this process is not completed before the tenth or twelfth day of the following month. Current inventory developments must appear rather vague to the management, and the one clear statement of the inventory position as of the end of the month must arrive ten days or so after the fact.[13]

Some might argue that the aberrations described are exceptional and uncharacteristic examples. In many cases procurement of inputs and disposal of outputs proceeds routinely enough. But the reader of Soviet literature on the supply system, the financial system, and inventories finds that there is no end to these examples. The best rule for an enterprise manager to follow in his inventory behavior seems to be to accumulate whatever he can get his hands on. He has limited autonomy with respect to inventory, but, to the extent that he can exercise control, he should react in only one direction and store as much inventory as possible.

Control by Outside Agencies

Given the nature of the economic setting, it seems more or less inevitable that the responsibility for preventing excessive accumulation of inventories must rest with outside agencies, and this is, in fact, where it has been placed. Do the accounting standards and accounting reports of the system provide an adequate tool with which outside agencies can actually control inventory holdings? What I am asking here is not merely whether the reported information is accurate but also whether it is useful, whether it is designed to meet the needs of those for whom it is intended, whether it is aggregated to the right extent.

As explained earlier, the normativs constitute the foundation of outside control. They play the same crucial role in inventory control that the cost budgets do in cost control. If the superior administrative organs could set them correctly, the battle for inventory control would be half won. But the general consensus of Soviet writers on working capital is that the normativs set by the higher agencies are not correct and that this is one of the difficulties in the inventory-control process. This, of course, is easy to believe. It would be extremely difficult for the outside control agencies to set these standards on any technically determined basis or to check on their accuracy when calculated by the enterprise. In line with the general procedures of Soviet planning, the setting of normativs proceeds more or less in the following way. Enterprises first propose normativs for the coming year. The glavks aggregate them and pass them on up to the ministries. The ministries again aggregate them and propose the combined normativs to the Gosplan. But these estimates proposed from below must be reconciled with the amount of funds available for financing working capital which Gosplan has worked out in the aggregate economic plan. The proposals from below meet limits from above, and at the end of the process the ministry passes down a finally reconciled limit to the glavk which then passes down final normativs to its enterprises.

From what has been said earlier, it seems clear enough that an enterprise will always try to have its inventory limits set as high as possible. Its motivations naturally prompt it to do this, and the discussions concerning working capital are full of statements that enterprises do indeed behave thus. There is of course a very extensive literature on recommended procedures for planning normativs at the level of the enterprise. The interesting thing about this literature is that it betrays an extremely cautious attitude toward inventory needs. The writers place great emphasis on allowing for seasonal fluctuations, transportation bottlenecks, for possible nonfulfillment of supply plans. The general attitude is illustrated by the argument over whether the normativ for materials should be calculated as equal to the total shipment size or to one half that amount. In the normal work of a plant, the average stock of a given material fluctuates widely. Suppose that shipments of some material arrive once a month; the supply will fall nearly to zero just before the next shipment arrives. If consumption proceeds uniformly over the period, the average stock will be one half the size of a shipment. The same will be true for every material used. If there are many different kinds of materials, the peaks and low points of different materials should overlap so that the total stock of all materials on hand at any given time should be just one half the total of the shipment sizes. But this simple idea has been disputed by some Soviet writers, on the grounds that the peaks might coincide, and for other reasons, and that therefore the normativ should be more than half the shipment size.[14] The same attitude shows up in discussion of the "reserve stock" that is held to take care of interruptions in supply. Normally this should be figured on the basis of data about the actual probabilities of shipment delays. Very often the writers suggest that the reserve stock should be large enough to cover the longest delay on record, and one writer felt it necessary to point out to his more cautious colleagues that in any case the reserve stock should not exceed the normal shipment size. His argument is that this will be adequate even if one shipment gets lost entirely.[15] Frequently it is said that making these calculations is too complicated, and thus the reserve stock is set at about half the normal stock.[16] Probably most efforts at determining normativs are not dignified by any such explicit calculations as these textbook discussions imply. But they are interesting as an attempt to legitimatize the precautionary proclivities of enterprise management.

By and large, however, the enterprise plays a subordinate role in determination of the normativs. The writers seem to be agreed that for the most part they are worked out by the superior agency (usually the glavk) and simply assigned to the enterprise. The difficulty is that the glavk is in a poor position to calculate and propose accurate or economical normativs. There is a problem here analogous to the planned cost calculations. Economically rational normativs obviously must be calculated in a very detailed way. The required stocks of raw materials will depend upon such factors as shipping distance, variation in delivery date, shipment size, average interval between shipments, and so on. Correct normativs for fairly aggregated balance-sheet accounts, such as raw materials, should obviously begin with detailed calculation of normativs for individual kinds of material, for individual sizes, for different grades. In any moderately large enterprise there are literally thousands of separate components of inventory for which such normativs would have to be calculated. Moreover, there would have to be frequent changes as conditions within the plant change. In the nature of the case, the superior organ is simply incapable of carrying out such detailed calculations and must confine itself to interpretation and manipulation of rather general information. Some of the pitfalls involved in interpreting and using this data are outlined in an interesting article by a writer who is concerned with the problem of aggregative inventory planning in the coal industry.[17] He says that the content and comparability of reported inventories are unclear because the instructions on the classification of materials are ambiguous and impossible to interpret consistently. One mine may list certain items as basic materials, another may put them in auxiliary materials, still another in repair parts. Another ambiguous borderline is between fixed assets and working capital. The criteria are value (five hundred rubles per unit) and length of life (one year). In practice it is not certain whether an item will last more or less than a year, and it may be treated differently by the accountants of different mines. Moreover, the price may be different in different parts of the country, and in any case the price of an important item may change, shifting it from one category to the other. These differences in meaning may make the amount of reported stocks so different as between mines or years that a planner in the glavk who tries to use them as guides in setting the normativ may be hopelessly misled. In this industry, at least, Soviet inventory control fails to conform to one of the common dicta of American authorities, that "the basis of all good inventory control lies in the setting of proper classifications and in the assignment of each commodity to its proper class."[18] But this article is all the more interesting for being unique. The same sort of classification problem undoubtedly arises in other branches of industry, and the failure to mention it indicates the lack of concern for accuracy or precision in the setting of normativs.

Essentially what the superior agency does is to project forward the normativs established or achieved in previous years. The first normativs expressed in terms of days' supply were established in 1931 by examination of the turnover rate for individual inventory components for the 1930–31 economic year. The idea was to select the lowest quarterly turnover rate, and then perhaps make some adjustment in it on the basis of the special conditions in individual plants. Many writers claim that the normativs have not been systematically reviewed since, though some say that since the thirties the superior administrative agencies have reduced somewhat the normativs expressed in days. The total value of the normativs in terms of rubles has grown greatly as new plants were added, and as the value of a day's outlay has increased, but the original figures in terms of days have never been thoroughly overhauled. The following statement by a financial worker familiar with the situation in the lumber industry is typical. "The norms for stocks worked out in 1931 on the basis of the stocks of unfinished production actually in existence at that time have not undergone any serious changes since, even though the conditions of production have changed in a radical way, and the length of the production process has decreased significantly."[19] It is also asserted that the normativs for new enterprises and such changes as have been made in the normativs for existing enterprises have frequently not been based on any actual calculations of inventory needs. For instance, the writer just cited also says that "there are not a few cases where the normativs for individual lumbering enterprises have been established on the basis of average ministry norms, or on the basis of norms for aggregative combinations, and are not founded on any calculations at all."[20] Another writer cites the wide variations among the normativs established for essentially similar enterprises in Leningrad and goes on to explain them:

Such a divergence in the size of own working capital is not accidental, but is the result of the practice of ministries and glavks over many years. Instead of setting norms for working capital on the basis of actual calculations, which would involve defending their estimates before the Ministry of Finance, they have preferred to take the easier route of maneuvering with the increments of working capital assigned to them by the budget. These increments . . . are determined each year long before the production plans by type of output are drawn up. In these conditions the need for own working capital is based on such aggregative indicators as the expected increase in output, the actual stocks of normed assets, and the desired reductions in these stocks, that is, the "willed" assignment for the speeding up of working capital.[21]

The arbitrariness of the normativs has been aggravated by careless financial planning at the level of the glavk. The normativs have not always been made consistent with other elements of the plans which have been drawn up for enterprises. For instance, one common-sense requirement is that, if the enterprise plan specifies a growth in unfinished production as one component of gross output, there should also be specified an increase in the normativ for unfinished production by the same amount. But this is not necessarily done. One man mentions the case where the glavk planned an increase in unfinished production of 26.2 million rubles while at the same time, in the financial plan, it specified a reduction in the normativ for unfinished production of 1.2 million rubles.[22] The normativ expressed in days' supply and in rubles are frequently inconsistent. For instance, the established normativ for materials in a given jurisdiction might be a supply big enough to last 25 days. What should normally be done then is to look at the cost budget to get the total outlay of materials of the year, divide the figure by 360 to get the daily expenditure, and then multiply by 25 to get the value of a 25-day supply. But even this simple kind of consistency is not necessarily achieved.[23]

Other examples of poor coordination involve the plan for increases in own working capital and the increase in the normativ. Suppose, for instance, that a certain increase in the normativ is planned. The intention may be to finance this by retaining some of the profit earned during the current year. The planned increase in output together with an estimated cost reduction implies a certain profit, and this may be the source of the new own working capital to cover the increase in the normativ. But the planning of profit is often very careless and may not really be consistent with the planned cost reduction and planned increase in output. As a result, it may happen that the profit that is supposed to cover additions to inventory never materializes or is excessive. This mutual inconsistency of interrelated indicators is apparently one of the chronic diseases of planning at the level of the glavk.

To summarize, the normativs are very poor standards against which to measure the actual inventory holdings of an enterprise. They have not been worked out from below through detailed calculations and, as the Soviet administrative structure has changed, as plants have shifted from jurisdiction to jurisdiction, as new plants have been added, the normativs have become very heterogeneous. For some enterprises they are extremely tight; for others they allow excessive room for maneuver. A plant may not have a normativ to cover a constant and absolutely necessary inventory. One writer cites the case of a cognac factory in which the normal conditions of production require it to have 3–4 million rubles of unfinished production and semifabricates but in which there is no normativ for unfinished production.[24] And one can find many references to enterprises that have such generous normativs, as in the lumber industry, that they can

213

handle even extreme seasonal inventory peaks without resort to bank credit.[25] In connection with the industrial reorganization of 1957, much attention has been given to examining the working-capital position of enterprises. The new economic councils find themselves with a collection of enterprises that have come from many different ministries and have discovered extreme diversity in the normativs for different plants. For instance, the enterprises taken over by the Leningrad economic council from the ministries included essentially comparable machinebuilding plants among which the normativs for raw materials ranged from 10 to 260 days.[26]

As Soviet authors frequently point out, the inaccuracy of planned normativs stultifies "control by the ruble." If these standards are inaccurate, how can the outside controllers expect any improvement from the application of sanctions? Such sanctions only penalize an enterprise fruitlessly and make it even harder for the enterprise to work successfully. On the other hand, sanctions may fail to be applied where needed because overgenerous normativs permit an enterprise to be wasteful of inventories without attracting attention.[27]

The next peculiar feature of the control system which should be noted is that responsibility for enforcing adherence to normativs is divided between two lines of authority. These are the superior organs of the enterprise and the state bank. Responsibility has not been left with the higher agency alone for two important reasons. In the first place, there is too great a lag between enterprise inventory actions and the reports made to the superior agency. Even if the superior agency did faithfully compare inventory performance with inventory standards and then attempt to chastise enterprises which performed poorly, it would be relatively unsuccessful. During the year, the enterprise could still acquire excessive inventories and, at the end of the year, the superior organ would be faced with a fait accompli.

A second reason for dividing responsibility is that the glavks have some of the same hoarding tendencies as enterprises. There are many instances given in the literature of glavks which hoard materials by sending them to enterprises under their jurisdiction. Materials are sometimes acquired by enterprises not because they have requested them but because the superior agencies have assigned them. Moreover, as has often been pointed out, financial considerations and financial measures of success play a subordinate role in the system of incentives in the industrial administrative hierarchy. Failure to stay within the assigned normativs and the resultant insolvency and financial difficulties which an enterprise suffers are likely not to be counted against it by the minister or the chief of the glavk. The system of control must therefore be implemented by some more current restraints. The ex post sanctions are not real or strong enough to be effective, and the enterprise can be controlled only by the pulling of financial strings during the year. The ideal organization to exercise such control is the Gosbank. Since all the receipts and payments of an enterprise flow through its settlement account in the Gosbank, the latter has an intimate day-to-day picture of the buying and selling operations of the enterprise. And it is these operations that determine its inventory holdings. Consequently, much of the responsibility for enforcing inventory control is handed to the Gosbank, and there is probably more discussion of inventory problems in the books and journals that emanate from this sector than in the entire literature of general economics and planning.

The main difficulty which the Gosbank faces in trying to discharge its responsibility is that it lacks accurate standards against which to measure enterprise performance. The principal evidence which suggests to the bank that an enterprise is accumulating excess inventories is illiquidity, as indicated by a failure to pay its bills on time. If the enterprise accumulates excessive inventories, it cannot meet its payments on time and falls in debt to suppliers and other claimants. But since the normativ is not an accurate measure of "correct" inventory holdings, the bank cannot rely on the payment position as a valid indicator of performance. These standards are not a sufficiently accurate measure for the Gosbank to use in deciding to exert financial sanctions. In an organization of the size of the Gosbank, there must be general rules set up to guide people at lower levels. If the Gosbank is to exert financial pressure to affect an enterprise's holdings of inventories, it must set up criteria for taking such action. Inevitably these criteria and rules must be expressed in terms of "appropriate" levels of inventories for an enterprise, and it is the normativs that are supposed to express them. Since these are in many cases poor standards, their application may cause the Gosbank to do the wrong thing. Suppose, for instance, that the Gosbank rule is that credit cannot be extended to cover holdings of inventories above the normativs except for certain special reasons, such as seasonal accumulations or delay in shipping finished goods because of transportation bottlenecks. Remember also that in a bureaucratic system these rules have to be spelled out in precise detail. Now suppose that an enterprise which has received a normativ far too small to cover its real need for some inventory component asks the bank for a loan to cover the difference. According to the rule, the bank cannot extend credit. Conversely, if the superior organ assigns an excessively generous normativ to an enterprise, the Gosbank will have no way of influencing the enterprise. It can accumulate and hold very large stocks of materials, pay its bills on time, and never have occasion to seek credit from the bank.

A second complication which dilutes the bank's power to control enterprise inventory behavior is that it controls only one of the pursestrings. Apparently the bank often goes behind the assigned normativ and makes serious investigations of the inventory requirements and holdings of an enterprise. But it still lacks power to impose effective financial sanctions. Again an illustration will make the point clear. An enterprise which has excessive inventories is illiquid and constantly in debt to other enterprises and organizations. The Gosbank analyzes the inventory situation of this firm conscientiously and in detail, finds that the assigned normativ is perfectly adequate, and so concludes that the firm is indeed hoarding resources. On paper the bank has sufficient power to force the liquidation of the excessive holdings. In accordance with the decree of August 21, 1954, it can refuse to extend credit to the enterprise and can impound all resources that come into the enterprise's bank account to be applied on overdue claims. It can notify the firm's suppliers that, since there are no funds in the enterprise's bank account, the Gosbank will not accept any invoices for goods shipped to the enterprise. But all these sanctions can be invalidated by actions of the superior agency. The glavk may simply increase the normativ of the enterprise and transfer working capital to it from some other enterprise. Moreover, one writer cites cases where glavks have ordered enterprises under their jurisdiction to continue shipments to the bankrupt enterprise despite the absence of any legal way to exact payment.[28]

So far we have been talking about the aggregate normativ for all types of inventories. The superior organ specifies for an enterprise not only a single aggregate normativ for inventories but also more detailed ones for separate inventory balance-sheet accounts. These detailed standards are probably more arbitrary, but one of the Gosbank's rules is that it can extend credit for seasonal accumulations above the norm for an individual kind of material. It may be that the normativ for one material is far too low and the normativs for other materials far too high. But the enterprise can hoard the other materials up to the extent of the normativ and, in order to cover its real needs for the material which has a small normativ, it can get bank credit. Thus it is still able to get extra credit and thereby accumulate excessive inventories.[29]

The bank must maintain a delicate balance. If it limits itself to a formalistic application of sanctions on the basis of the normativs as standards, it runs the risk of aggravating already bad situations. There are many complaints of such a formalistic approach.[30] If, on the other hand, taking advantage of its closeness to the enterprise and its intimate knowledge of the enterprise's affairs, it tries to exercise some initiative, it may find its efforts frustrated by the superior agency. From the other direction, the bank's control over one of the financial constraints can interfere with control by the superior agency. The books on analysis of enterprise behavior, a function carried out by the superior agency, always imply that they are not interested in inventories financed by bank credit. They assume that these are justified and they deduct them from the stocks they consider in evaluating inventory performance.[31]

To restate in more familiar terms what has been said above, control from outside based on the normativs involves too much centralization. The attempt to specify too much detail in the plans handed down from above makes them inaccurate, with the result that comparison of performance with standards is inconclusive. At the same time, it induces lower levels of authority to abandon the attempt to work out these details themselves and reinforces the bias in favor of excessive inventories. Overly detailed control is thus, in effect, no control at all. Many planners undoubtedly hold essentially the same conclusions, and there have been two revealing periods of experimentation with accounting for inventory control. The first involved the experimental introduction of a new indicator of inventory performance beginning in 1949, and the second comprises the changes that have accompanied the reorganization of industry since 1957.

Dissatisfaction with inventory control seems to have come to a head in the late forties. Enterprises were criticized for excessive inventory holdings, and a campaign to accelerate the turnover of working capital was set in motion. Beginning in 1949, there were some experimental modifications in the system of control. The most publicized step was the attempt to supplement or perhaps supplant normativs as the main standards for inventory performance in industry with a new indicator called the "rate of turnover of working capital." This is essentially the flow of output divided by the average stock of inventories during a given period. This change can probably best be interpreted as an attempt to achieve a more appropriate balance of detail and generality. In the explanations for the introduction of the new indicator, much was said about the poor planning of the normativs, their arbitrariness, and their ineffectiveness as control instruments. The heart of the problem was that they were assigned by the superior organ and were often grossly inaccurate. This interfered with their usefulness for measuring enterprise performance and meant, moreover, that they stultified inventory planning at the enterprise level. Since the standards were not worked out by people in the enterprise, they were not integrated concretely with the purchasing plans, the production schedules, the marketing plan, and so on. Thus there was no detailed plan which bridged and reconciled the normativs assigned from above and the day-to-day actions which took place in the enterprise and actually determined inventory results.[32] Since the enterprise had to accept the normativs assigned from above, there was no incentive for it to try to integrate the two. Moreover, there is a problem analogous to the one described in cost accounting. The work of the accountants, planners, and statisticians in the enterprise is strongly structured by what they have to do for the superior agency, and they do their thinking in terms of what the higher group wants. The shift to the turnover concept was supposed to give more maneuverability to management and confine the control to an appropriate level of generality. Also this would be simpler, more nearly compatible with the glavk's power to discriminate among phenomena, and more useful for intertemporal and interfirm comparisons.

In 1949, for the first time this indicator was included in the plan of enterprises, and goals were assigned for increasing the rate of turnover over the previous year's performance. This planned increase was apparently also used by the planners at the center in defining the aggregate need for new inventory investment. But the new indicator was far from satisfactory as a measure of enterprise performance. The problems involved were discussed at length in a very illuminating series of articles and comments in *Voprosy ekonomiki* in 1950, after a year's experience with the new indicator. One of the difficulties was in finding a concept for measuring the flow of output that would not make the rate of turnover misleading or have adverse repercussions on other aspects of enterprise behavior. Neither cost of output nor value of output is free from difficulties. If cost is used as the measure of the flow, then failure to stay within cost budgets raises the numerator of the ratio and gives a turnover rate that is too high. Poor cost performance might thus mask poor inventory performance. Alternatively, an enterprise in trying to meet the cost plan may fail to write off to costs of current output such items as spoilage and losses. This inflates the unfinished-production account, understates the cost figure, and makes inventory performance appear worse than it really is. Finally, if cost is used, cost reduction achieved by savings in labor makes it appear incorrectly that inventory performance has deteriorated. Labor is a smaller fraction of inventories than of outlays on production, and so the

220

labor savings would reduce cost more than they reduced inventories. Actually this is only a special case of a more general difficulty — that both the elements involved in the turnover ratio are heterogeneous composites, which makes the ratio sensitive to changes in the composition of either. There were also some arguments against the use of value of output as the numerator, one being that this would make it difficult to compare the indicators for plants with different rates of profit. But none of these objections is insurmountable, and many of the participants in the discussion pointed out how they could be avoided. Probably more important in the planners' evaluation of the usefulness of this indicator were some bookkeeping falsifications that enterprises used to show good performance. According to the instructions for computing the ratio, only the stocks of normed assets were to be included in the denominator. Enterprises could thus improve the reported indicator by shifting normed inventory items, such as finished output, to nonnormed categories, such as goods shipped. They would write up, and record as shipped, goods which had not in fact left the factory or ship goods ahead of the dates specified in contracts. As one of the commentators remarked, "It is no accident that in the balance sheets of the majority of these enterprises there is a big discrepancy between the amount of goods shipped and the credit from the bank covering documents in transit." [33] (When goods are shipped the invoices and bill of lading are normally handed to the Gosbank as security for a loan until the payment is made by the buyer. Enterprise directors apparently felt that they could get by with the shifts in the balance sheet, but they were not willing to ask for credit from the bank on the basis of false invoices.) Another complication arose because of the splitting of the inventory-control function between the superior organ and the Gosbank. It is necessary to have a planned rate of turnover against which the reported achievement can be compared. Since the stocks held by enterprises on the basis of Gosbank credit are not planned in advance, they had to be "planned" and included in the planned stock ex post. Under the instruction for computing the turnover indicator, Gosbank credit actually granted was included as part of the planned inventory stock.[34] The rationale of this decision was that the Gosbank would not extend a loan unless the accumulation above the normativ was justified by some good reason not envisaged when it was first set. But one writer says that in his experience it often happened that enterprises managed to obtain loans for spurious "seasonal accumulations." This was facilitated by the peculiar circumstance, mentioned earlier, that the Gosbank can give loans for seasonal accumulations above the normativ for individual items, even if the total normativ for the enterprise as a whole was not exhausted. By getting extra credit from the Gosbank, the plant could manipulate its "planned" stock upward and make the rate-of-turnover target easier to fulfill.[35]

This sort of maneuver is an old story, of course. Whenever an indicator is given a dramatic buildup and great weight in measuring success in the Soviet economy, there is likely to be an attempt to improve reported performance by outright falsification or subtle manipulations. These difficulties in evaluating inventory performance are probably not inescapable, but they presented enough of an obstacle so that the rate of turnover seems to have been unobtrusively dropped. It is mentioned in analyses of enterprise activity as a general approach to checking on inventory performance, but it is apparently no longer an important indicator of plan fulfillment.

Nevertheless, the striving for control instruments more general than the detailed normativs is echoed in the changes in inventory control that have been made since the reorganization of industry in 1957. The reorganization was accompanied by renewed criticism of the deficiencies of the normativs, and there have been many suggestions that such detailed specifications be replaced by some more general indicator. Under the reorganization the normativs have indeed been made more general, having been aggregated to only three categories, and some authors recommend that these be replaced by a single limit for all normed working capital or, what comes to essentially the same thing, a single goal for inventories per ruble's worth of output.[36] The interesting point about this episode is that it shows clearly the dangers of leaving too much inventory control at lower levels of management. So far, at least, putting inventory supervision closer to the enterprise seems to have effected no acceleration of the rate of turnover. There have been numerous reports of the excessive inventories that have been unearthed by local initiative and reports of rather more limited amounts that have been disgorged and liquidated. But at the same time local inspection has disclosed that some enterprises have inadequate inventories and must be given more. It is suggestive that the reports of excessive accumulations involve *millions* of rubles, and one author says that there is needed an increment of working capital in unfinished production alone of 2.5 to 3 *billion* rubles.[37] Another indication of the unwillingness of the sovnarkhozes to exert strong pressure on their enterprises to reduce inventories is their attitude toward "reserve funds." The sovnarkhozes have been given the right, also formerly accorded the ministries, of keeping under their control a reserve of up to 3 percent of the total working capital of all enterprises under their jurisdiction to cover unforeseen inventory needs. But it is said that by January 1, 1958, the sovnarkhozes had handed over virtually all of this to enterprises.[38] There seems to be a bias here — plant management, sovnarkhoz officials, and local branches of the Gosbank seem more interested in filling in the holes left by the maldistribution of inventories in the past than in reducing the aggregate holdings of inventories. The few statistics available suggest that the rate of turnover of inventories in industry has slowed down rather than speeded up since the reorganization. Own working capital has certainly grown faster than industrial output, and this does not seem to have been offset by a decline in bank credit.[39] This should not come as a totally unexpected surprise. Some Soviet authorities on inventories have predicted as much. One has warned that making the normativ more general will only result in a tendency to hoard the scarcest kinds of materials, and others have said that there is little to be gained from having better inventory planning from above unless the plans are enforced by effective sanctions in the form of premiums for fulfilling the goals.[40] The experience with reorganization seems to underline the fact that there is no simple way to speed up the rate of turnover in the Soviet economy. Moving responsibility for inventory control closer to enterprise management will in itself do little to free the mass of resources frozen in inventories. The marketing and procurement system is an intractable underlying obstacle that will hamper any acceleration of inventory turnover, unless the system of managerial motivations is reconstructed somehow to make inventory minimization a high-priority goal.

THE MECHANIZATION

OF ACCOUNTING

ONE of the greatest impediments to the effectiveness of Soviet accounting is its primitive technology. The discussion in previous chapters of the effectiveness with which Soviet accounting performs its various functions has emphasized the importance of being able to handle information in great detail with little delay. Because the Russians have been so slow in introducing modern accounting machinery, the ability of bookkeeping staffs to achieve speed and detail is very limited. Throughout the Soviet economy, with only rare exceptions, the bookkeeper has traditionally done his work with pen and ink, with no mechanical aids other than the schety and an occasional arithmometer.[1] One writer has said that, of the 2.3 million people engaged in computational work in the Soviet economy in 1947, no more than 3 or 4 percent did their work with the aid of electrical computing machinery.[2] The situation has improved somewhat since then, but not much. The total stock of machines used in accounting is now about 8 for every 100 persons engaged in computational work.[3] Moreover, almost half of this stock of machines consists of simple adding-listing machines, and an appreciable fraction of it is used for statistical and planning work rather than strictly accounting work.

This dependence on outmoded technology has two very important effects. (1) The number of people required to carry on even the rudiments of bookkeeping, cost accounting, and reporting is very large, and (2) the quality of the accounting is extremely low. The depth, detail, and accuracy of accounting possible under Soviet conditions of limited computational capacity is inadequate for purposes of analyzing and checking on the work of the enterprise, and the slowness with which information is gathered and processed greatly reduces its usefulness for day-to-day control. The purpose of the present chapter is to describe Soviet efforts in the field of accounting mechanization and the implications of the low level achieved for the quality of the accounting job and the size of the accounting labor force.

Production and Stocks of Accounting Machinery

The prewar period. The Russians made a very late start in mechanizing their accounting. The earliest Soviet efforts at mechanization go back only as far as the late 1920s, and it was only in 1931 that the urgent need to improve the efficiency of accounting was officially recognized and measures taken for beginning the mechanization of accounting work. The first experiments with accounting machinery were carried out by the All-Ukrainian Institute of Labor in Kharkov and the Institute of Management Technique of the Workers' and Peasants' Inspection. These organizations supervised experimental operations with punched-card and other machines in several state plants, did research on the feasibility of producing accounting machinery in the Soviet Union, and through their publications (the periodical *Tekhnika upravleniya* [Management Technique] and a long series of monographs) attempted to popularize the use of office machinery in management. *Tekhnika upravleniya*, in particular, contains many articles on experiments with punched-card routines, reports on foreign machines and exhibitions, and reviews of the foreign literature on mechanized accounting.

These experiments had been part of a general program sponsored by the Communist Party to rationalize administrative work, and the Fifteenth Party Congress in 1927 passed a resolution instructing the government to "continue the work on the creation of accounting and a system of reporting that is concise, cheap, clear, and corresponds to the tasks of planning and administration; in particular, to extend experimentation with the mechanization of office and computational work."[4] In 1929, at the Sixteenth Conference, the party again directed its attention to the problem of mechanizing accounting and enacted a decree which said in part:

We must guarantee the fastest possible mastering by our administrators of the achievements in the field of management technique and the extension of mechanized accounting in the next few years to all the largest business establishments. (The experience of carrying out such mechanization in transport, in the First Wool Trust, in the VTS, in the plants of the State Electrical Trust, and so on has already given positive results.)[5]

The decree also included instructions for the Institute of Management Technique to draw up a plan for actually achieving this program of mechanization.

In 1930 the institute presented its report, outlining its recommendations for the next steps to be taken.[6] The report noted the backward condition of accounting in the Soviet Union, explained the great savings and other advantages to be gained from mechanization, and recommended that a stock of machines be acquired by import and domestic production with the aim of raising the level of mechanization above that in America and Western Europe. Concrete steps were taken to implement these proposals in a decree, enacted by the Council of People's Commissars in 1931, entitled "To Guarantee the Full Mechanization of Accounting." [7] This decree is said by all the Soviet writers in the field to be the most important step in the mechanization of accounting in the Soviet Union. It said in part:

The creation of a system of unified socialist accounting is hindered by the backward, craftlike technology of accounting and the extreme shortage of workers in this field. Socialist accounting must be organized on the basis of the widest application of mechanical means. In its present state, the production of calculating machines in the country does not guarantee the rapid technological re-equipment of all accounting. In connection with this, the Council of People's Commissars has approved a decree obliging the Supreme Council of the National Economy to begin immediately the organization of a new branch of machinebuilding, the production of calculating machines. Beginning next year, the mass output of these kinds of machines and apparatus must be mastered and such rates of output developed as will guarantee the full technical re-equipment of all accounting within five years. [8]

It then went on to outline a number of specific steps to be taken. All in all, the decree gives the impression that the government considered the mechanization of accounting to be a matter of the highest importance. Despite the urgent tone of the decree and the obvious importance which the regime assigned to the program, however, actual achievements fell far short of a "full technical re-equipment of all accounting." It was several years before any new accounting machinery was produced at all and, except for the arithmometer, the actual level of output achieved in the prewar period was very low.

The available data on Soviet production of accounting machinery in the prewar period is summarized in Table 6. Soviet production of accounting machinery was characterized both by a limited variety of types and by a small volume of output. The

TABLE 6. PRODUCTION OF ACCOUNTING MACHINERY IN THE SOVIET UNION (PHYSICAL UNITS)

| Year | Arithmom-eters | Calcu-lators (KSM) | Ten-key adding ma-chines (DSM) | Punched-card machinery | | | |
				Punches	Veri-fiers	Sorters	Tabu-lators
1927–28	5,809						
1928–29	8,001						
1929–30	12,826						
1931	30,137						
1932	41,363		17				
1933	54,534		472				
1934	64,584		1,667			126	8
1935	59,802	34	2,660	31	544		10
1936	58,000	3,000	1,237	792	209	250	48
1937	(64,000)[a]	(4,000)	(1,500)	(400)	(500)	(275)	(75)
1938	Approx.						
1939	40,000	2,500					
1940	per yr.						
1941	(15,000)	(250)	(1,400)				(85)

[a] All figures in parentheses are planned figures.

Sources. *Arithmometers:* 1927–28 through1935 — *Sotsialisticheskoe stroitelstvo,* 1936, p. 168; 1936 and 1937 — Gosplan SSSR, *Narodno-khozyaystvennyi plan Soiuza SSR na 1937 god* (Moscow, 1937), pp. 86–87 (hereafter cited *1937 Plan*); 1938 through 1940 — V. A. Ginodman, *Mekhanizatsiya ucheta i vychislitelnykh rabot* (Moscow, 1950), p. 104; 1941 — *Gosudarstvennyi plan razvitiya narodnogo khozyaystva SSSR na 1941 god* (Moscow, 1941), p. 50 (hereafter cited *1941 Plan*). *KSM:* 1935 through 1937 — *1937 Plan;* pp. 86–87; 1939 — this is an estimate based on a statement that the planned output for March 1939 was 175 units and that this goal was overfulfilled (*Mashinostroenie,* April 14, 1939); 1941 — *1941 Plan,* p. 50. *DSM:* 1932 through 1935 — Central Administration of Economic and Social Statistics of the State Planning Commission of the USSR, *Socialist Construction in the USSR* (Moscow, 1936), p. 83; 1936 and 1937 — *1937 Plan,* pp. 86–87; 1941 — *1941 Plan,* p. 50. *Punchers:* 1935 through 1937 — *1937 Plan,* pp. 86–87; some punchers were produced before 1935, but figures on the number of these are not available. *Verifiers:* 1935 through 1937 — *1937 Plan,* pp. 86–87. *Sorters:* 1934 — A. Popov, "Za sovershenuyu technicheskuyu bazu ucheta," *Planovoe khozyaystvo,* no. 3, 1935, pp. 120–121; 1935 through 1937 — *1937 Plan,* pp. 86–87. *Tabulators:* 1934 — Popov, p. 120; 1935 through 1937 — *1937 Plan,* pp. 86–87; 1941 — *1941 Plan,* p. 50.

only machine produced in large numbers was the arith-mometer, put out by the Dzherzhinski plant in Moscow. It was already being produced at the time of the 1931 decree, and its output was expanded fairly rapidly. This was still basically the same machine as that invented by Odner and produced in Russia since the mid-1870s. Even in 1929 it was considered obsolete, and one authority recommended that it be dropped from production,[9] but the Russians continued to produce it. It is not a very efficient instrument, especially for addition and subtraction, and so has limited usefulness in book-keeping. The DSM is a ten-key adding-listing machine pro-duced in several models. The original machine was a one-regis-ter, hand-operated model, but in 1934 a model with electric drive was added.[10] A model with additional registers and a movable carriage was designed in 1940,[11] but apparently was never produced in quantity. The KSM is a full-keyboard cal-culator, copied from the Monroe calculator.[12] The punched-card machinery was copied from the Hollerith electromagnetic machines. The Russians had experimented with both the Pow-ers mechanical type and the Hollerith electromagnetic type and decided on the latter. They began copying machines fairly early, starting with the simple ones and working up to the more complicated ones. They began with the perforator and verifier as early as 1929,[13] and in 1934 produced their first lot of sorting machines and six experimental tabulators.[14] All the Russian punched-card equipment of the prewar period was of the forty-five-column type.

Comparison with American production shows how insignifi-cant the Soviet level of output was. In 1937, for instance, the United States produced for domestic use 172,789 units of cal-culating, adding, adding-list, bookkeeping, and billing ma-chinery, whereas the Russians planned to produce 5,500 com-parable machines and 64,000 arithmometers.[15] It is impossible to make an exact comparison of punched-card machinery, but in this case, also, Soviet output was insignificant in comparison with American output. It is unfortunate that fuller data for the years 1938–1940 are not available. One might expect that in these years production of the new machines would finally have been mastered and large-scale production achieved. Although the planned outputs for 1941 are quite small, these figures probably reflect a changeover to war production and may not be a good indication of output in the immediately preceding years. To judge from occasional references in the newspaper *Mashinostroenie*, however, production did not grow much in the years 1938–1940, and it is probably safe to assume that the 1937 planned figures may be representative of the several years before the war.[16]

Table 7 shows that domestic production was not significantly augmented by imports. Soviet imports consisted almost exclusively of American and German machines. Addition of American exports of calculating, adding, adding-listing, bookkeeping, and billing machines to the German exports brings the total for the whole period 1937–39 to only about 3,000 units, whereas production for domestic use in the United States was well over 100,000 units per year. The number of punched-card machines imported was also quite small, something like 1,500 units. Moreover, these were leased rather than purchased, and after 1936 most of them were returned.[17]

In terms of stocks, which is the magnitude we are most interested in, the lag behind the United States was even greater than in production. In the United States a high rate of production had extended back for more than two decades, while the flow to stocks was only beginning in the USSR. Moreover, much of the Russian output soon became inactive either because the machines were defective or because it was impossible to get them repaired. The literature is full of complaints that

231

TABLE 7. SOVIET IMPORTS OF ACCOUNTING MACHINERY

Year	German export figure (units)	U.S. export figure (units)		Soviet import figure (thousand rubles)
		Adding, billing, calculating, etc.	Punched-card machines	
1927	448	142	143	180
1928	204	184	172	800
1929	57	571	119	802
1930	81	172	82	241
1931	77	54	73	340
1932	74	24	40	289
1933	9	16	—	94
1934	—	1	9	96
1935	19	75	166	317
1936	526	38	44	6,131
1937	101	4	1	1,748
1938	—	6	—	66

Sources and notes. The German export figure is from Statistiches reichsamt, *Monatliche Nachweise uber den auswartigen Handel Deutschlands,* for the respective years. The figures for U.S. exports are from the United States Department of Commerce, Bureau of Foreign and Domestic Commerce. *Foreign Commerce and Navigation of the United States,* for the respective years. The figures on Soviet imports are from the following sources. For 1927–28 — *Soviet Union Year Book,* 1928, p. 297; 1930 — *ibid.,* p. 335, and A. N. Voznesenski and A. A. Volozhinski, *Vneshniaya torgovlia SSSR za pervuyu piatiletku* (Moscow-Leningrad, 1933), pp. 322–23. The figure for 1928 is derived by adding the October–December figure from Voznesenski to three quarters of the 1927–28 figure, and the 1927 figure is derived by taking one quarter of the 1927–28 figure and three quarters of the 1926–27 figure. For 1929 through 1933, the source is Voznesenski, pp. 322–23. For 1934 through 1938, the source is the periodical *Statistika vneshnei torgovli,* for the respective years. The figures as given in the source are not actually comparable over time because in 1936 the Gosbank reduced the dollar-ruble exchange rate, and it is on the basis of this official rate that imports are valued in ruble terms.

The U.S. and German export figures have been included in the table to provide an indication of the number of units involved. There are no Soviet figures on this basis except after 1934, and then they include other office machienry as well. It seems likely that nearly all Soviet imports of accounting machinery came from the U.S. and Germany, since the Soviet sources speak almost exclusively of U.S. and German machines.

the machines are defective and that repair is poorly organized. In 1930 some organizations found that half the arithmometers they received would not operate; whole series were found to be defective. When the defective machines were returned to the plant, they were simply shipped without repair to other buyers.[18] The savings banks in 1938 had a stock of 960 DSM machines, of which 521, or more than half, were not being used because they were out of order.[19] One writer complains that the special plant which was to handle the repair of accounting machinery was able to fill only 15 to 20 percent of its orders, so that computing machines often had to be repaired in general repair shops by unqualified persons.[20] Another source states that in 1939 the Moscow SAM plant (for punched-card machines) filled its orders for spare parts by only 37.5 percent and that some of these parts were defective and should have been scrapped.[21]

The few figures available confirm that stocks were very small. In 1935 the entire stock of computing machines in the Soviet Union consisted of 85 complexes of American punched-card machinery, 1,065 bookkeeping, billing, adding, and calculating machines, and slightly less than 200,000 arithmometers.[22] The addition of all the production and imports of the next six years would not bring the stock at the end of 1940 to above 35,000 units of all kinds except arithmometers, the stock of which might then have been somewhere above 300,000, depending on how rapidly the old ones were discarded.

It is difficult to conceive what a primitive level of technology these figures imply, but a few examples will help to dramatize the situation. In 1938, in such an important industrial center as Leningrad, only four plants had their accounting mechanized.[23] In the State Bank, which had always had a priority in the mechanization drive, in 1940 there were only 160 branches which had mechanized their accounting, and the remaining 3,340 branches did all their accounting work by hand.[24] When a stock of 35,000 machines at the most is contrasted with a bookkeeping labor force of 1,700,000 persons in 1939, it is obvious that the Russians were trying to do the accounting work of a twentieth-century economy on the basis of a centuries-old technology.

The postwar period. At the end of the war, mechanized accounting in the Soviet Union was completely disorganized. No machines had been produced during the war, and, in addition to normal wear and tear, the stock had been further depleted by looting and war damage. No spare parts had been produced, and the impossibility of repairing machines had reduced the usable stock still further.[25] The slight start which had been made on the mechanization of accounting in the 1930s was nearly wiped out, and the process had to be started all over again.

Of the several decrees on accounting mechanization issued since the war, that of April 6, 1949, appears to have been the most important.[26] This decree ordered the investment of "tens of millions of rubles" in accounting-machinery plants with the aim of "widening the production base so that within a period of four to six years the equipment of workers doing computational work will be increased by fifteen times." This decree also introduced a system of centrally approved plans for the mechanization of accounting, and in 1949 for the first time such plans were worked out for eighteen ministries and departments.[27] At the same time, a Research Institute for Punched Card and Mathematical Machines was set up, and this organization, together with the Institute of Precision Mechanics and Computational Technique of the Academy of Sciences, was to provide a scientific center for the design of computing machinery.[28]

The Russian production program of the postwar period has

been more ambitious than that of the 1930s. The number of plants has been expanded to five as against two in the prewar period. The prewar models have been dropped or modernized; some new varieties of punched-card machinery, such as a totaling punch and a reproducer have been designed; the production of eighty-column machines has been started; and some completely new types of machine, such as a billing and bookkeeping machine, have been projected. But there has been a great deal of difficulty in mastering this production program.

The plan has been badly underfulfilled enough to suggest that it occupied a very low ranking on the priority scale. Output of accounting machinery for those postwar years for which information is available is shown in Table 8. This should be considered an unimpressive effort. Note first the very late start in organizing the output of accounting machinery. As early as May 1945, there was a decree ordering the resumption of the production of accounting machinery, but none was actually produced until 1948. Moreover, in both 1948 and 1949 the number of machines produced was so small that it should be described as experimental production. In the United States the output of accounting machinery, interrupted by the war, was already larger by 1947 than it had been in the prewar period. Although by 1955 Soviet output had been raised to several times that of the prewar level, it was still insignificant in relation to the kind of flows attained by the accounting-machinery industry in other countries. The peak output of a little less than 19,000 machines in 1955 is only a tiny fraction of the annual flows to stocks attained in the United States. In 1958, according to the Census of Manufactures, 304,361 adding machines, 96,971 calculating machines, and 39,033 bookkeeping and accounting machines were produced, worth all together about 196 million dollars. In addition, there was produced 194 million dollars worth of punched-card machinery and cash

TABLE 8. SOVIET ACQUISITIONS OF ACCOUNTING MACHINERY IN THE POSTWAR PERIOD

Machinery	1949	1950	1951	1952	1953	1954	1955	1956	1957
Domestic production	437	2,065	5,857	9,413	13,405	15,775	18,497	1,457	7,858
Punched-card machines	408	1,492	2,473	2,473	2,730	2,254	2,357	—	1,824
45-column tabulators	136	247	321	315	268	291	290	—	276 }
80-column tabulators	1	3	15	25	37	40	62	—	189
Sorters	78	248	292	325	336	315	350	—	770
Punches	23	404	1,048	1,170	987	927	956	—	278
Totaling punches	15	101	115	216	232	256	275	—	311
Verifiers	155	489	682	679	527	425	424	—	
Adding-listing machines	29	569	3,384	6,243	10,730	11,069	10,000	—	5,000
Ten-key calculators (VK-2)	—	3	—	440	288	2,452	7,000	—	1,034
Other acquisitions	9,872	14,697	6,666	6,626	9,342	7,479	4,046	5,964	8,669
Total	10,309	16,762	12,523	16,039	22,747	23,254	22,543	7,421	16,527

Source. Moskovski Ekonomiko-statisticheskii Institut, *Voprosy statistiki i ucheta* (Vol. 2, Moscow, 1959), pp. 10–11. (The figures for 1955 do not add up to the total shown, but are as shown in the source.) Full descriptions of these machines can be found in any Soviet book on the mechanization of accounting, such as V. A. Ginodman, *Mekhanizatsiya ucheta i vychislitelnykh rabot* (Moscow, 1950), or V. N. Riazankin, et al., *Vychislitelnye mashiny* (Moscow, 1957).

registers. There were some exports, but these were nearly balanced by imports, so that the figures cited closely approximate the flow for domestic use. Nor is it necessary to take the United States as the opposite pole in the comparison. The Russian output in 1955 was only a few percent of the output achieved in such small countries as Italy and Sweden.[29]

Accounting-machinery production was also insignificant in relation to the Russians' own concept of their requirements, and the plans for output were seriously underfulfilled. For instance, the 1949 decree on the mechanization of accounting set a target of 15 to 20 accounting machines per 100 accounting workers for the end of the Fifth Five Year Plan (by 1955). By 1957, two years beyond the target date, the stock had reached an actual level of only 7 accounting machines per 100 accounting workers.

The postwar production history is also unimpressive in its qualitative aspects. The Russians never succeeded in producing the full range of machines that they wanted and planned. Most of the models planned for the postwar program were to have been mastered and put into production by 1950, but only a few of them actually were. The T-5 tabulator, for instance, supposed to be mastered in 1950, was not actually produced until 1953.[30] The bookkeeping-billing machine on which the designers had been working for years was still not produced by the early 1960s, and only a few of the full-keyboard machines had been produced by then.[31] The Russians themselves characterize the machines which were put into production as poorly designed and deficient in quality. In recent years a common theme in the economic literature of the USSR has been that Soviet machinery output contains too many machines which are obsolete as compared with foreign models. Accounting machinery is one of the favorite illustrations — it is described as obsolete in design before the machines are put into production.

The virtual cessation of production in 1956 and the slow recovery in 1957 are not explained by any of the Soviet writers. One wonders whether it represents a decision to abandon production completely because of the low quality of equipment, with a plan subsequently to create new models. But when production started again in 1957, the machines turned out were still the same models as before.

The Russian effort to mechanize accounting in the postwar period was greatly aided by Soviet control over East Germany at the end of the war. The Russians not only collected as war booty and took to the Soviet Union all the accounting machinery they could find, but they also claimed as reparations every important plant in East Germany which produced such machinery. Some of these were dismantled and shipped to the Soviet Union; others were left in operation in East Germany as Soviet property and under Soviet administrative control. The plants left in operation in Germany were included in one of the Soviet holding companies, the Sowjetische Aktiengesellschaft Totschmash. They were subsequently turned back to the Germans but continued to supply a considerable number of machines to the Russians.[32] As is shown in Table 8, the number of machines acquired from abroad was about equal to domestic production over the period shown in the table. Imports shown for the early years probably include large amounts of confiscated machines, but after about 1951 they represent current production from the East German plants. After 1957 accounting machinery imports expanded considerably. In 1958, 16,600 units were imported and in 1959, 16,700. Virtually all of these were from East Germany.[33] Dependence on imports is especially great for certain kinds of machines. As mentioned earlier, the Russians have never managed to produce billing and bookkeeping machines or full-keyboard calculators, obtaining these machines solely through import.

The stock of accounting machinery on January 1, 1959, consisted of 184,436 machines distributed by types as follows.[34]

Punched-card machines	21,254
Adding machines	81,746
Ten-key computing machines	13,021
Calculators	59,275
Billing machines	6,288
Bookkeeping machines	2,852

With an accounting labor force of about 1.8 million, this stock means about 10 machines per 100 workers, which is still far below the goal of 15 to 20 machines per 100 workers set a decade earlier in the 1949 decree. Moreover, these stock figures are somewhat deceptive. Many of the machines included in the total are out of operation either because they have not been assigned to an organization which can use them or because they are awaiting repair. In 1954 about 20 percent of the total stock of machines was out of operation for these two reasons and, although there has been some improvement since, the unutilized part of the total stock is said to be still almost 10 percent.[35]

It should also be emphasized that many of the machines are not used strictly for accounting. Many of them are concentrated at relatively centralized levels in the administrative structure, and many of them work in what should be described as statistical rather than accounting functions. The Gosbank has about 25,000 of the total, the Central Statistical Administration has some 10,000, and the railroads use a large number in their statistical work. With a stock so small, and with this kind of allocation, only a very small fraction of even the large important enterprises have their accounting mechanized. It is said that in 1959, of the 29,000 enterprises subordinated to the economic councils, only 2,200 or 8 percent had achieved mechanized accounting.[36]

One wonders why the results have fallen so far behind the plans. The production of accounting machinery is a very complicated branch of machinebuilding, and it might be argued that the Russians have simply been unable to master the production problems involved. This interpretation finds some support in the long delay in getting the new models of machines into production. But a nation that can produce space rockets surely has the capability of producing accounting machinery, and it seems more reasonable to interpret their underfulfillment as a matter of the low priority assigned to accounting machinery.

Orders of priority can change, however, and it appears that the regime has now been sufficiently impressed with the disadvantages of relying on unmechanized accounting. The Seven Year Plan envisages a great expansion of output. There are to be six new plants built (more than the number now in existence); output is to rise by 4.5 to 4.7 times; and there is to be a large importation of accounting machinery from East Germany. A special decree in 1959 (made on the initiative of Khrushchev himself, according to one writer) has established the detailed program. This decree does not seem to have been published, but its main outlines are available in the commentaries on it.[37] The new plants are to have a capacity of 100,000 calculating machines, 100,000 adding machines, and 15,000 bookkeeping and billing machines. As a result of these large flows, the stock of accounting machinery is to reach 40 per 100 accounting workers by the end of the Seven Year Plan. The exhortations, the explanation of the urgency of this program, and the output goals all sound familiar enough from the past and may only lead to the familiar disappointments of the past. If this program is assigned sufficient priority, however, a real revolution in bookkeeping technology will at last have been effected.

Effects of Undermechanization

Failure to achieve any high degree of accounting mechanization up to the present time has greatly hampered the effectiveness of the Soviet accounting system in its role as a control instrument. In the first place, low computational capacity greatly reduces the fineness of detail with which the accounting can be carried on. Soviet accounting reports have perforce been limited to fairly gross analyses of data, and this makes it exceedingly difficult to fix responsibility for failures in performance. Second, reliance on hand operations rather than on machines greatly slows down the speed and frequency with which the system can generate reports. The usefulness of accounting data for control purposes depends to a large extent on the speed with which it is gathered, processed, and made available to management. If the lag between performance and the report on performance is too long, the possibilities of corrective action are diminished.

Lack of detail. It is always emphasized in the Soviet accounting literature that the primary function of accounting is to serve as an instrument for the control of plan fulfillment.[38] The accounting statement is one of the most important parts of the report submitted periodically by every enterprise to its superior administrative organ and to other outside control agencies, and it is one of the principal sources used in evaluating and controlling the work of the enterprise. Because of this high priority, accounting operations in the enterprise have always been strongly oriented toward the task of preparing these reports for outside control agencies and have tended to neglect the task of processing data for internal use. As one bookkeeper says:

> The aim of bookkeeping and operational reporting is to provide the necessary minimum of indicators for analysis and operational direction of the work of the enterprise. At the present time, reporting is so inflated that it has been transformed into an aim in itself. If the establishment draws up and turns in all the reports on time, then it is considered that it is working well. At the same time, the reports are not analyzed and are little used for operational guidance, since there is no time left for that.[39]

In theory it is expected that this same set of reports will also be used by management as a basis for internal control of the enterprise. But as the discussions in Chapters 7 and 8 make clear, the reports are inadequate for that purpose. The various levels of management within the enterprise need data very different from what is appropriate for the purposes of the glavk; they need more detail and, for their purposes, it should often be organized in a different way.

The dilemma which the regime faces here is reflected in the history of the postwar campaign for "intraplant khozraschet." The exact nature of intraplant accountability varies in individual cases, but the general principle is one of disaggregating the total plan for the enterprise into goals for the subordinate units within the plant and then restructuring the accounting to permit a check on their fulfillment. In other words, it is an effort to introduce into planning and reporting the detail needed by management at the enterprise level. But it is clear that this campaign has been greatly hampered by the fundamental problem of the low degree of mechanization of accounting work. It involves a great deal of extra work. In many plants, the bookkeeping departments have found it impossible to take on this additional time-consuming task, and accounting has retained its aggregative character. There are many indications in the sources that the chief bookkeepers in enterprises are reluctant to become involved in the additional burden. There are constant complaints that they stand aside from the task of intraplant accountability, and in one interesting case the reluctance of the chief bookkeeper was backed up by his superiors in the glavk.[40] It is the glavk, not the plant management, which has first call on the services of the bookkeeping department. Many of the descriptions of specific plants state that the accounting for intraplant accountability is done outside the regular system of accounts.[41] Since the accounting system is geared to the needs of outside agencies, accounting would have to be completely restructured to fit the needs of the firm. Therefore, the results often have to be computed by supervisory personnel or by a new contingent of clerks outside the bookkeeping department. When intraplant accountability has been introduced and made the responsibility of the accounting department, it has required an increase in the bookkeeping force.

In Soviet conditions of low mechanization, any such attempt to increase the degree of disaggregation in accounting simply requires too much manpower, and in 1954 and 1955 there was a countercampaign to get rid of accounting personnel. This was part of an effort to reduce the number of administrative workers generally, but much of the blame was put on bookkeeping departments. In the reports describing how individual enterprises managed to reduce the number of bookkeepers, it was usually claimed that the reduction was accomplished by organizational rationalization or by mechanization. But in many cases reductions in staff were undoubtedly made at the expense of detail in cost reporting. It seems significant, for instance, that editorials in the accounting journal *Bukhgalterskii uchet* blamed the inflation of staffs partly on the documentation and reporting which some enterprises used in accounting for fulfillment of intraplant accountability, implying that this was no longer justifiable.[42] Indeed, one chief bookkeeper states that the way in which he was able to reduce his bookkeeping staff was by reducing the detail in intraplant reporting. Previously the bookkeeping department sent daily cost reports to the shop chiefs and foremen, but these were dropped.[43] The earlier attempts to introduce more detail into accounting required more persons than the regime felt it could afford under the growing tightness of the labor supply in the Soviet economy. This dilemma will continue to exist until a much higher degree of mechanization is achieved.

Slowness in reporting. Working with little or no machinery, the bookkeeping department of the Soviet enterprise is usually far behind the actual operations for which it is accounting. According to one writer, the chief bookkeeper and his staff spend a large part of every month closing the books and working out the reports for the previous month; the documents on the operations of the current month accumulate unprocessed and unheeded.[44] The slowness with which the Soviet accounting apparatus works is indicated by the official dates for the presentation of balance sheets and reports. Under the 1936 "Statute Concerning the Balance Sheet," enterprises were supposed to have their monthly and quarterly balance sheets and reports drawn up and presented to the superior organ not later than the twentieth day of the following month, and the annual reports were supposed to be in by February 5 of the following year. The corresponding dates for the glavks and trusts were the twenty-seventh of the following month and March 1 of the following year. Under a 1952 statute these dates were shortened, although not greatly. The enterprise is now supposed to present its monthly and quarterly statements by the fifteenth of the following month and its annual report by January 25 of the following year. These official dates are somewhat misleading, however, since it is said that they are regularly violated.

One interesting study of lateness in reporting found that the proportion of late enterprises was as high as 80 percent in some glavks and that the reports were often as much as a month late.[45] The situation has probably improved since the war period to which this source refers, but complaints continue that reports are presented long past the official deadlines.[46]

The effect of slowness in reporting is to deprive management of the information which it needs for effective control. The problem does not lie in the fact that the superior organ receives the reports so long after the event, since their control is very indirect in any case. But the manager, who does have the ability to control, gets the information no sooner than the higher agency does. Until the monthly balance sheet and cost reports are worked out for presentation to the superior organ, even the manager and the chief bookkeeper have a limited idea of how the work of the plant is progressing. One Soviet writer says that reports which are so late are more or less useless for purposes of control, and the huge expense of preparing them is mostly wasted.[47]

Labor productivity in accounting. A second important result of the low level of accounting mechanization is that labor productivity is extremely low and a very large number of people must be employed in the accounting function. To get some notion of the great number of people required for bookkeeping in the Soviet economy, some comparisons can be made with the United States, where accounting has been brought to a high level of efficiency through several decades of emphasis on scientific management and through the unflagging efforts of business-machinery salesmen. The amount of information which the Russians have published on accounting employment is not great, but there are available some census figures on the total number of bookkeepers at work in the entire economy and some sample data for the 1930s on the number of bookkeepers at work in different industries. These figures are inadequate to permit any precise measurement of relative productivity levels, but they do make it possible to demonstrate the generally low level of Soviet accounting productivity.

The census figures make possible a few global comparisons with the United States. The total number of bookkeepers in each country, together with some assumptions about the respective accounting outputs, will provide a rough notion of general accounting efficiency. The concept of the accounting labor force is a fairly concrete and manageable one, although there is a difficult problem in delimiting the accounting function and of deciding what classes of workers belong in the accounting labor force. One faces such questions as whether accounting includes the work of auditing and statistical reporting, whether the work of the cashier and the timekeeper are part of the accounting function, and so on.

The coverage of the Russian figures as explained in the census is not perfectly clear, but the Soviet definition seems to be a fairly narrow one, excluding such auxiliary accounting workers as auditors, cashiers, timekeepers, and so on. The coverage of the American figures is stated explicitly in the census, but there is a problem involved in adjusting the figures to a coverage comparable with the Soviet figures. The figures as they appear in the census have three principal defects as far as our purposes are concerned. First, two nonaccounting groups are included, cashiers and operators of office machinery. Second, the figures include auditors and public accountants, while on the basis of the 1926 census, at least, the Soviet data exclude persons performing similar functions. Third, for 1920 and 1930 the concept is "gainful workers," which includes both employed and unemployed. Thus the figure for 1930, especially, ought to be adjusted downward. After adjustment for these factors, the American accounting labor force was 742,000 persons in 1930,

1,103,000 in 1940, and 1,114,000 in 1950. The corresponding Soviet figures were 340,000 in 1926, 1,769,000 in 1939, 1,500,000 in 1947, and 1,817,000 in 1959.[48]

If the figures on the relative size of the bookkeeping labor force are to mean anything about relative productivity, they must be related to the size of the accounting output. The question of the relative magnitude of the output in the two countries is a far more formidable problem than that of determining the accounting labor force, since the aggregate output of the accounting function defies measurement or even conceptualization. It might be assumed that most of the accounting work in any economy is related to the output of goods and services by some sort of technological ratio at a given stage of development. For instance, it seems reasonable that the amount of payroll work might be roughly the same per worker no matter what economy is under discussion. Similarly, we might expect that the number of invoices to be handled in a wholesale trade organization would be the same for comparable physical flows in either the Soviet or the American economy. Even with such bold assumptions, however, the comparison of accounting output in the two economies is still difficult because the composition of each differs so greatly. For example, in the United States, something like one fourth of the bookkeeping labor force is engaged in wholesale and retail trade.[49] The smaller importance of consumption in the Soviet Union requires a much smaller proportion of all bookkeepers; the Soviet Census of Trade in 1935 shows that trade accounted for only about 7 percent of the total number of bookkeepers.[50] Furthermore, American accounting embraces a number of activities which are absent in the Soviet economy, such as the accounting involved in installment buying and in the use of personal checking accounts. On the other hand, in the Soviet economy a complicated state-prescribed system of accounting embraces all units down

247

to the least significant; in the United States, much economic activity is never accounted for in any formal way, as in most of agriculture and in many other small establishments.[51] The list of differences could be extended to a point where comparison might seem meaningless. Perhaps, however, we can salvage at least a very unquantified statement that the volume of accounting work of the Soviet Union is much smaller than in the American economy. This is on the assumption that the functions present in one and absent in the other will tend to offset one another and that the much smaller national product of the Soviet economy must imply a smaller output required of the accounting function. On the basis of this assumption and of the figures on the number of bookkeepers quoted earlier, it is obvious that the productivity of bookkeeping operations in the Soviet Union is very low compared with that in the United States.

These conclusions on the basis of global comparisons are supported by the few statistics available on the number of bookkeepers in specific industries. The Russians have apparently never published comprehensive statistics on the number of accounting personnel working in individual industries, but one of the labor-statistic handbooks does give for small samples of plants in several individual industries a breakdown of supervisory workers and white-collar workers, in which bookkeepers are distinguished as a separate class. On the assumption that the ratio of bookkeepers to supervisory personnel and white-collar workers in the sample plants is representative for the branch as a whole, some estimates of the total number of bookkeepers in each industry can be made and the ratio of bookkeepers to total employment in each industry determined. When these ratios are compared with similar ones for the United States, we arrive at an oblique indication of the relative productivity of Soviet bookkeepers. Some estimates of this kind are presented in Table 9.

TABLE 9. BOOKKEEPERS AS A PERCENTAGE OF TOTAL EMPLOYMENT IN SELECTED INDUSTRIES

Soviet Union			United States
Electric-power stations	6.0	4.8	Electric and electric-gas utilities
Petroleum extraction	6.3	2.6	Crude-petroleum and natural-gas extraction
Iron mining	3.4	6.5	Metal mining
Cement	9.8	1.9	Cement and concrete, gypsum, plaster products
Ferrous metallurgy	3.0	1.2	Blast furnaces, steel works, rolling mills and other primary steel
Machinebuilding and metalworking	6.8	2.2	Fabricated-metal industries, machinery, transportation equipment
Lumber milling	5.6	1.2	Sawmills, planing mills, mill work
Paper	5.5	2.0	Paper and allied products
Printing and publishing	3.5	3.1	Printing, publishing, allied industries
Cotton, linen, and wool textiles	4.4	.9	Textile-mill products
Fur and leather	5.7	1.7	Leather (tanned, curried, finished)
Sewing	4.2	1.5	Apparel and other fabricated textile products
Shoes	5.0	1.1	Footwear (except rubber)

Sources and notes. This table is based on TsUNKhU, *Trud v SSSR* (Moscow, 1936), and *U.S. Census of Population, 1950:* "Occupation by Industry."

The nature of the Soviet figures is as follows. The source gives for the respective branches of large-scale industry the total employment broken down by the Soviet categories of workers, apprentices, engineering-technical personnel, white-collar workers, and service personnel, and then for a sample of plants within each branch a further breakdown of the engineering-technical and white-collar workers category which shows separately "bookkeepers and assistants to book-

TABLE 9 (*continued*)

keepers" and "ledger clerks." The exact coverage of these classes is not explained, but it obviously does not include statisticians (given separately) and probably does not include the chief bookkeeper, since there is a separate class for "chiefs o sections." The size of the sample is quite small, consisting in most cases of about ten enterprises, and no explanation is given of how the sample was selected.

It would be desirable to have U.S. figures for some year earlier than 1950, but the only industry-by-occupation tabulation which was made in the 1940 census and earlier censuses was based on the intermediate occupational classification, in which bookkeepers, accountants, and ticket agents are all grouped together. In view of the fact that the growth of productivity of Soviet accounting since 1935 has probably not been very great, I thought it would be more useful to use the 1950 data for the United States than to make some guesswork adjustment of the 1940 census data. The U.S. figures include accountants and auditors, bookkeepers, and office machine operators, which is probably a somewhat broader class than the Soviet one. Thus the divergence between the Soviet and United States percentages is, if anything, understated.

There are some unexpected exceptions in the table, in the case of electric-power stations, iron mining, and the printing industry. The explanation in the case of the power stations might lie in the lighter load of billing work in the Soviet Union, because of the fact that a much higher proportion of Soviet output goes to industrial users. There appears to be no obvious explanation of the mining and printing industry figures; it is possible that they are the result of sampling variations.

It is obvious from the explanation of these figures given in the notes to Table 9 that they cannot be treated as conclusive. Their patent implication, however, is that even by general Russian standards labor productivity in accounting was very low, and even lower still by American standards. It is unfortunate that the comparison must be made between 1950 data for the United States and 1935 data for the Soviet Union, but this difference in no way invalidates the general conclusion. The productivity of Soviet bookkeeping has risen some since 1935, but probably not much.

It seems legitimate to infer from what has been said above that the Soviet regime has made a mistake in failing to mechanize accounting more rapidly. It would, of course, be incorrect to base such a conclusion solely on the fact that the Russians have mechanized their accounting to a smaller degree than the

United States has. After all, capital is still scarce in the Soviet economy, and computing machinery, requiring great precision in its manufacture, has proved expensive and difficult for the Russians to produce. Nevertheless, even in terms of relative resource costs in the Soviet economy, there is a strong presumption that the Russians have made an economic miscalculation in not having made greater efforts to mechanize accounting. One authority has said that the payoff period for investment in the smaller accounting machines is often as short as one year — that is, the investment in the accounting machinery is recouped by the cost savings in one year.[52] The Soviet government has not hesitated to invest billions of rubles in less productive uses of capital elsewhere. The savings on punched-card machinery are presumably also very large. A full complex of such machines costs about 100,000 rubles,[53] with an annual depreciation charge of about 12,000 to 15,000 rubles.[54] Cards cost 20 kopecks each,[55] so a year's consumption of 200,000 would cost 40,000 rubles. Such a complex should release ten or fifteen workers,[56] with a corresponding annual savings in wages of perhaps 100,000 rubles. The total savings would thus be on the order of several tens of thousands of rubles, which is again a high rate of return on capital. It appears that the costs of mechanization could have been paid out of the labor savings alone; the putative increases in output resulting from a qualitative improvement of accounting would have been an absolute gain.

ACCOUNTING IN THE SOVIET
ECONOMY: CONCLUSIONS

THE problem originally posed for consideration in this book was the effectiveness of Soviet accounting as a tool of planning and administration. How well does it perform its many functions in this area? Does it do as well as it might in giving Soviet planners and managers the information they need to administer the economy? Some aspects of this question have been explored in detail in the preceding chapters, but in concluding it will be useful to attempt a more general evaluation of Soviet accounting. The purpose is not so much to summarize what has already been said as to remedy a few omissions, to reflect on the place of accounting in the Soviet economic system, and to state some of the generalizations which seem to be implied in the discussion.

My central conclusion has been that Soviet accounting has important failings for both the major functions which it is supposed to perform. Its concepts generate cost data that are often inappropriate for economic decision making, and such features as its slowness, its aggregative character, and its lack of objective standards diminish its effectiveness for control purposes. It should also be added here that the preceding description of its weaknesses has probably concentrated too much on the rules and procedures themselves and has failed to stress sufficiently the gap between textbook descriptions and actual practices. Such basic errors as failing to follow explicit rules in allocating costs or valuing balance-sheet items, ignoring the official criteria for assigning items to various accounts, neglecting to document transactions and post them to the accounts, and even committing arithmetic errors are probably more characteristic of Soviet accounting than of accounting in other countries. For instance, in making plans for the revaluation of fixed assets, the Ministry of Finance made a survey of fixed-asset accounting in a sample of enterprises, finding that many of them held significant amounts of fixed assets not shown on their books and that bookkeepers failed to follow the completely unequivocal rules on division of items between fixed assets and working capital. Regularly once a year, the Ministry of Finance holds a conference at which the bookkeepers of enterprises and higher administrative organs are taken to task for their errors in day-to-day application of the specified rules for accounting and reporting. These harangues characteristically include the following criticisms. Items shown in the balance sheet are not checked against a physical inventory; the detailed accounts are not reconciled with the more aggregative balance-sheet accounts; profits have been calculated in a manner that violates the rules. These deficiencies are partly the result of the pressure of time and the limited computational capacity already discussed. But they also reflect the low level of skill and education of Soviet accountants. The few statistics available suggest that most Soviet accounting personnel have had some training but that the bookkeeping labor force is notably deficient in people with higher education or even specialized secondary education in accounting. Accounting is alleged to be a relatively unattractive occupation, and it is often complained that it is difficult to persuade competent people to specialize in accounting in higher education. Moreover, the training which accounting personnel get, emphasizing a mechanical familiarity with the given rules and routines, tends to create a narrow outlook and a conservatism toward change. Thus the usefulness and dependability of Soviet accounting in practice is hampered not only by the peculiarities of the concepts which the accounting authorities have built into the rules but also by the failure of the practitioners to perform their jobs adequately within the limits of authority assigned to them.

But even if the textbook ideal were met, most of the failings we have noted would still exist. One of the important reasons for them is that accounting often lacks a single, clearly defined purpose. The accountants do not have a clear sense of what they are trying to achieve. Accounting has been burdened with a multitude of criteria to satisfy and accordingly does not meet any of them perfectly. It is being pulled this way and that and thereby fails to serve any one of its objectives as well as it might. Among the different functions it is supposed to perform, pride of place is assigned to plan fulfillment. This is the objective to which most of its practices and rules have been tailored. In the process, concepts of cost and value are often distorted. A system that tried to determine correct measures of sacrifice to be used in economic calculation would not necessarily be useful for control purposes. Chapter 6 described some examples of this conflict arising in the decision to assign outlays to cost of production or to other accounts. The rigidity in the rules required by centralization also frequently sacrifices accuracy and subtlety to the objective of simplicity and ease of definition.

The inappropriateness of accounting information for economic decision making cannot always be explained by concessions to a higher-priority objective, however. The errors in depreciation accounting, for instance, seem to have come more from a fundamental carelessness. Depreciation accounting in the past has interfered with all conceivable objectives, except perhaps that of simplicity. It distorted the cost of output, interfered with accounting's role in the channeling of funds, and permitted some aspects of enterprise performance to go unechoed in any khozraschet indicator. Apparently the Russians simply neglected to consider what they expected from depreciation accounting and to structure the rules accordingly. But they are bewilderingly inconsistent in their carelessness, and it would be difficult to support the proposition that there is anything inevitable about it. Now that it has been acknowledged that previous depreciation practice was inadequate, they have taken vigorous action to analyze what errors were made and to institute major reforms.

The objectives of effective cost accounting are sometimes sacrificed to the competing demands of Marxist orthodoxy. The incorporation of Marxist notions in accounting practice may interfere both with the calculation of economically relevant cost magnitudes and with effectiveness in control. The most serious instances of such conflicts involve accounting in the national economic context discussed in Chapter 2. The Marxist prejudice that value is created only by labor, and that cost and value can be determined by a summation of labor expenditure ex post, is the source of the trouble. This outlook makes difficult the creation of institutional devices for determining opportunity costs in a national economic context, to be passed on for inclusion in enterprise cost accounting. The Marxist attitude concerning insurance similarly prevents the establishment of institutions or administrative procedures within the whole Soviet production establishment that would allocate this head-office "overhead" appropriately among the accounts of individual firms. Marxist

255

concepts may also seep down to the level of enterprise cost accounting and confuse an important issue, as in the case of the joint-product costing problem.

On the whole, however, I would judge that the impact of Marxist economic theory on accounting per se, on the formulation of accounting practice at the level of the enterprise, has probably been rather slight. Many Marxist ideas are either ignored or contradicted in the process of establishing the actual rules. For instance, Marx makes a distinction between fixed and circulating capital on the basis of whether the items are the "instruments" or the "objects" of labor. Probably every Soviet accounting book ever written explains this distinction in introducing the subject of working capital and fixed assets. But, in drawing the line between these two kinds of assets in accounting practice, doctrinal precision has been abandoned in favor of a distinction that can more easily be specified for control purposes. (The distinction is drawn in terms of value — five hundred rubles — or in length of service life — one year.) Although the scholars always try to describe accounting concepts in terms of Marxist categories, it is not the categories that have determined the concepts. For instance, all discussions of inventory holdings emphasize the distinction between working capital in the sphere of production and working capital in the sphere of circulation. But this distinction is virtually ignored in the delineation of balance-sheet accounts for inventory items. The accounting classifications are usually determined on the basis of control objectives, and only then are they reconciled at least superficially with Marxist terminology.

Probably the most pervasive conflict in the whole structure is that between emphasis on the use of accounting for control of plan fulfillment by the central authorities and its potential but neglected usefulness as a managerial tool at the level of the enterprise. Many aspects of this conflict have been noted in the preceding chapters but these form only a partial list, and examples could be multiplied. For instance, one of the consequences of emphasizing the control functions of Soviet accounting is excessive uniformity and too little tailoring of accounting categories or rules to meet the needs of particular enterprises. There are constant complaints that the definitions and accounting instructions are irrelevant or are not concrete enough to solve the actual problems of individual firms. This general principle can be illustrated by an example involving material accounting in the coal industry. Here, as in most cases, the ministry has established a plan of accounts and laid down general criteria for assigning materials to one or another of the accounts. The classification scheme may be logical enough at the level of description in which the glavk or ministry is interested and may meet its planning needs well enough, but it does not necessarily meet the varying needs of individual enterprises. First, the rules do not fully cover all the concrete problems of classification which will confront the enterprise accountant and so general rules from above do not necessarily insure consistency. Ambiguous cases will be handled differently by different accountants. At the same time, they have the adverse effect of preventing the local bookkeeper from exercising his own initiative. One coal-industry accountant familiar with the situation argues that the ability of enterprise management to control inventories would be much enhanced if the chief bookkeeper were allowed to classify materials not on the basis of some general economic concepts which might occur to someone in the ministry but on the basis of their relative importance in use. The plan of accounts should segregate and show separately the few items that bulk large in enterprise inventories and consumption, so that enterprise management could concentrate its attention on these important items. The rest could be considered together in broad categories apart from any abstract scheme of material classification. By concentrating attention on the most important items, such an approach would make possible better control. Very often, when abstract distinctions or classifications are introduced for the purpose of consistency at some higher level, they serve no real purpose in enterprise accounting.

At the bottom of this conflict is the hybrid nature of the Soviet system — it is neither fully decentralized nor fully centralized. There is a large element of control from the center, and this means that a framework of accounting rules and definitions must be imposed by the controllers. At the same time, the centralization is far from complete; execution by local management of commands issued from above requires much more information than is passed on up the channels of central reporting. One could hypothesize a fully centralized economy characterized by what might be called "perfect administration." Such a system might be run by issuance of commands in very detailed physical terms, as was suggested in Chapter 2. Alternatively, it might be administered in a value idiom. Once the planners possessed full knowledge of the possibilities of the system (production functions, resource availabilities, behavior characteristics of the actors) and had decided on what they wanted produced, they could attach value indices to all the ingredients of economic activity and specify rules of behavior (such as "maximize profits"). This kind of model is familiar from the literature of the 1930s regarding the economics of socialism. But to achieve "perfect administration" under either alternative, the planners at the center would have to use all of the information that existed. There would no longer be any room for a distinction in type or degree of detail in the information needed for drawing up a plan and that needed for executing a plan. It is their inability to attain such total centralization that generates the conflict between the information

258

the central controllers ask for and the information that enterprise management needs in order to operate. The system was designed by the outside controllers and the result has been dominated by the amount of detail, classificatory complexity, and a conceptual subtlety limited to the degree of centralization they have managed to achieve. They have slighted the informational base underlying the area of decision making and control that is relegated to enterprise management. As was pointed out in Chapter 10, however, this conflict is related to the low level of accounting mechanization. It is a conflict only in the face of the impossibility of doing two jobs at once. As the discussion of intraplant accountability indicated, accounting for both internal control and reporting purposes can probably be handled when mechanization reaches a decent level.

In evaluating Soviet accounting, it should also be remembered that accounting is interrelated with the planning and organizational features of the Soviet system. Many of the weaknesses that Soviet accountants are criticized for are actually more in the nature of organizational problems, not the result of imperfections in accounting methods. For instance, one of the constant complaints from bookkeepers is that accounting for wages is extremely complicated and that perhaps half of all Soviet accounting work is devoted to payroll accounting. But this is not so much the fault of cumbersome accounting methods as it is the natural result of the very complex wage system with which the Russians have saddled themselves. When so many workers are on the piecework system and when the piecework rates are figured by such complicated formulas, payroll accounting must inevitably involve a great deal of work. Also, the failure of accounting to meet reasonable standards of effectiveness in checking on performance comes from the fact that certain prerequisites in planning and organization have not been fulfilled. Standards are totally lacking or are unobjective;

measuring and weighing devices are absent, so that there are difficulties of following the flow of input; authority and responsibility may not be clearly defined. I have not even mentioned many of the problems to which Soviet accounting literature devotes much attention just because they are problems essentially beyond accounting. For example, the journals are full of admonitions to chief bookkeepers about their responsibilities for keeping wage expenditures within planned amounts and for preventing waste in investment outlays. In fact, however, there is relatively little the bookkeeper can do about these problems — they are the responsibility of management, not of the "figure man," and indeed overexpenditure often involves less a failure of enterprise management than it does of central planning. Until planning and organization are improved, enterprises will overspend the wage fund, investment funds will be squandered, and it will continue to be pointless to heap blame on the accountant for letting this happen.

One general question that has not been treated very explicitly is the use to which this system of accounting information is put. The vision of a veritable flood of accounting statements handed up the Soviet administrative hierarchy once each month, each quarter, and at the end of every year prompts one to wonder how much use is made of it. The accounting report of a Soviet enterprise is a document of impressive size. One writer mentions the annual report of a sugar-beet-procurement base, not, after all, a very complicated kind of enterprise, which amounted to 328 pages. The Soviet economy has committed a large amount of resources to this reporting system, and one cannot help but wonder whether the results are worth the effort. How extensively are the results utilized, and do people in authority act on the basis of them? The digesting and utilization of such information is called *analiz khozyaystvennoi deyatelnosti predpriyatii,* which may be translated "analysis of the economic performance of enterprises." *Khozyaystvennyi* also has the connotation of "managerial." This is distinguished as a special course of study in economic education; many books are written bearing such a title and specialists are trained in this field. The authorities envisage that this analysis will be performed at several levels. Each superior agency is supposed to analyze the work of the enterprises under its jurisdiction, on the basis of the quarterly and annual reports, and to write up these analyses in an official document as part of the process of approving the reports. Apparently only informal analyses of the monthly reports are made. The Ministry of Finance and the State Bank are also supposed to analyze those parts of the reports closely concerned with their areas of interest. The State Bank, for instance, is interested in financial behavior and in working-capital performance, and the Ministry of Finance analyzes the report in order to check on the fulfillment of cost and profit plans. In addition, an analysis is also supposed to be made within the enterprise either by the planning department or by the bookkeeping department. This is supposed to be written up as a formal document, which can serve as the basis for managerial action within the firm.

There is no very concrete evidence on the nature of the typical analysis, and we must rely for an impression of its effectiveness on general evaluations made by Soviet economists and accountants themselves. A survey of the literature suggests that this stage in the use of accounting reports has serious shortcomings. The analyses may never get made at all or are made in a superficial way. At the level of the enterprise, where such reports would be most useful, those responsible may not have the time to devote to wading through the bookkeepers' analyses. One Soviet writer well acquainted with both American and Soviet accounting practices suggests that the typical analysis made in the Soviet enterprise is likely to be too long, too detailed, or too trivial to merit the attention of busy managerial officials. He recommends a recasting of these reports into a more abridged form, directed precisely at the questions in which the enterprise director is interested. Soviet plant directors are often pictured as disdaining so dull a task as poring over these masses of figures. Finally, to judge from the books describing the procedures of analysis, the main objective usually seems to be a mechanical reconciliation of performance with the plan. If the wage fund was exceeded, the analyst tries to determine how much of the overexpenditure was caused by too high an average wage and how much by an excessive number of workers. He looks to see how much of the cost reduction can be explained as the result of overfulfilling the output plan, thereby saving overhead. This kind of analysis is certainly useful as far as it goes, but obviously it is crucially dependent on the plan as an objective standard of performance. As has been pointed out in the chapters on cost control and inventory control, the plans are often inadequate for this purpose.

One implication emerging from the study is that an understanding of Soviet accounting is a valuable aid in interpreting and evaluating Soviet statistics. I have not given a great deal of attention to this, but it is obvious that many economic statistics are strongly influenced by the accounting rules and practices at the level of the firm. The discussions of inventories, depreciation, fixed assets, and costs, for example, have illustrated the interconnection between accounting practices and the meaning of the published economic statistics in these areas. The same principle applies to many other kinds of statistics. Fortunately, there is enough detail in the extensive Soviet literature on accounting practices to cast light on the meaning of certain pertinent statistics. Investigation of accounting practices that affect economic statistics should be an ingredient of most studies of the Soviet economy.

Something should also be said about the likely future development of Soviet accounting. Several influences at work in the Soviet economy may well have a big impact on accounting and result in great improvement. The first of these is the increasing mechanization of accounting. As suggested earlier, this will make it possible to speed up accounting and provide more detail, but, more important, it may stimulate a remodeling of the whole accounting process. It is a commonplace in American accounting literature that the transition to more mechanized routines often calls for a complete overhaul of the documentation, the procedures, the system of reports, and indeed almost every aspect of accounting work. Such revisions have probably not yet occurred in the Soviet Union. Only selected aspects of the work are mechanized, and the machines merely take over the preparation of given documents or the performance of certain calculations previously done by hand. Soviet accountants are generally not prepared either by education or experience to take the broader view, and they are frequently criticized in the Soviet journals for their conservatism in changing accounting methods. They accept the machines only so long as they do not upset the established process of accounting. But this partial mechanization creates a certain tension. It frequently means that machines are underutilized, and there is an obvious imbalance between the parts of the work done by machines and the parts that are still done by hand. This tension may eventually stimulate a rethinking of the whole approach to accounting — a remodeling of the original documentation, a reconsideration of what the objective of accounting is, and a determination of what kind of information is useful.

In the second place, Soviet accounting has been subjected in the past few years to an unprecedented amount of stimulation from foreign sources. The general line now proclaimed by the regime, that Russians should try in any field of endeavor to learn what they can from the outside world, is duly repeated by accounting authorities, and one feels that Soviet accountants have indeed been eager to look for new ideas in foreign practice. One of the most interesting examples is the Soviet interest in the report of the productivity team sponsored by the Organization for European Economic Cooperation, which surveyed American accounting. Various groups of European specialists toured American plants to study management methods, and one of the teams reported its impressions in a booklet, "Management Accounting in the U.S." This report was read and reviewed in a Soviet journal and has now been translated and published in a large edition in the Soviet Union. The English specialists were much impressed by the idea of management accounting, with its emphasis on speed and the conscious bending of accounting to the needs of management, and with the notion of controllership. The Russian reviewers have also been obviously impressed by these conceptions and, despite some tendentious remarks about the book, imply that this is an approach they would do well to cultivate. There have been many hortatory articles in the economic journals on the theme that all the management men in the enterprise should appreciate accounting and understand the ways in which it can be helpful to them, and this point was also emphasized to me in talks with Soviet accounting officials.

Finally, the declaration of intent to make accounting more useful as a tool of management at lower levels may find a more propitious environment in the future than it has in the past. The future of accounting (in the sense of the data of bukhgalterskii uchet) will inevitably reflect the evolution of Soviet economic organization and, as one aspect of that evolution, the nature of the informational system that it develops. There seems to be a strong feeling, both among Soviet economists and among those abroad who comment on their work, that the Soviet economy has arrived at an important crossroad with regard to its organizational characteristics. It is too early to state with much assurance what the nature of the crossroad is, much less to forecast what path Soviet organizational change will actually follow. Nevertheless, two rather different possibilities seem obvious. Neither implies any diminution of central control over the economy. On the contrary, it is likely that the operation of the economy will be made ever more responsive to the wishes of the leaders and more effective in the service of the objectives established at the top. This will be made possible by a continuing improvement in administrative skill and experience and, very importantly, by improvements in the technology of handling quantitative information. As suggested earlier, however, this improvement in administration can take two alternative forms: improved control over economic life through better physical planning and administration, or evolution to a type of administration that exploits the interrelation of value and the resource-allocation problem. Under the first, local management would still be bound by a great multiplicity of constraints, in the form of detailed input allocations and production programs expressed in physical quantities. Through the use of mathematical planning methods and greater computational capacity, however, the central planners will make these commands more realistic than they are now. Central allocation of inputs will be more rational, the directives finally assigned to each manager will be mutually consistent, and so on. There will be a great increase in the speed with which physical indicators can be worked out, so that it will be possible to consider continuous revision as errors reveal themselves. Under the second alternative for better administration, the greater computational capacity would be used to determine indices of value for resources and products, and these, together with some relatively simple rules of behavior, would guide managers to make decisions that would serve the objectives of the regime. (The mathematical approaches to planning with which the Russians are now experimenting can provide value information as well as quantity information.) This approach would make it possible to issue commands from the center in much more summary form than at present — that is, "maximize output," subject to only a few constraints, or ultimately perhaps "maximize profits," subject to still fewer constraints. My inclination is to believe that the second is the more likely of the two alternatives.

There are many bits of evidence that the Russians are groping their way toward the value approach in controlling their economy. There is a growing concern with problems of pricing and value. This concern embraces practical efforts to make prices more useful and theoretical probings into the problem of measuring value. Some quite remarkable theoretical works have been published recently that break out of the bounds of Marxist value theory: those by Kantorovich and Novozhilov mentioned in Chapter 2. Kantorovich's work is especially interesting in reference to my thesis. His first approach to the problem of allocation (by way of linear programming) was to calculate rational quantities, but he found that this calculation revealed values as well; his recent writing emphasizes the idea that these values make possible an administrative system in which detailed commands and reporting cast in terms of physical quantities can be reduced in favor of more local decision making, more condensed commands, and fewer performance indicators. There is also an intimation in much recent Soviet writing that the economy has become so complicated that the older methods of simple priority rules and sweeping judgments made at the top must give way to more sophisticated and flexible calculations made on the spot. For instance, an economist, in discussing the problem of rational investment decisions in the electric-power industry (*Planovoe khozyaystvo,* no. 7, 1959), says that the only feasible method of making a simultaneous comparison of all the alternatives is to have prices that reflect real costs, including interest costs. The recent shift to fewer and more aggregative inventory indicators was mentioned in Chapter 9; and, as we have seen in Chapter 8, the Russians have recently dropped the percentage-cost-reduction figure as an indicator of cost performance, replacing it with what is almost a profit index of performance (cost per ruble's worth of output). This is only a small sample of the evidence implying the evolution toward more emphasis on value indicators.

I am well aware that other omens exist which may cast doubt on the significance of these reports of swallows flying north. In some cases, the Russians have moved detailed decision making up the administrative ladder and have tried to bind lower management in a tighter set of constraints. If there is some attempt to encourage more rational decisions about technological change by adjusting value indicators, for instance, there is also an attempt to create a more effective central machinery (in the form of the State Committee for the Coordination of Scientific Research) for making and enforcing the execution of such decisions. The latter may far outweigh the former in significance. Similarly, the reorganization of 1957, in the perspective of several years' operation, seems to have involved very little attrition of detailed physical allocation. Occasionally where there has been some hint that central control was weakening, there was a near-panic reaction to reinforce it. For instance, when a territorially ordered motivation system threatened to supersede commands about interregional deliveries, the commands were quickly given a strong backing of legal sanctions. There has also been some difficulty under the new system in keeping the allocation of investment resources congruent with what the central planners want, and it has been said (by Khrushchev at the Twenty-Second Party Congress, for one) that the center will have to institute more detailed rationing of investment goods in place of rationing of funds. In short, whether by instinct or as the result of concrete experience, the central planners show little disposition to release the strings of direct physical allocation of resources; and, as suggested above, just when they find it increasingly difficult to manipulate all these strings effectively (because of the economy's growth in size and complexity), technological progress in data-handling capacity and computational ability may enhance the longevity of the old system.

Whichever direction the evolution of planning takes, the implications for accounting are evident. If administration is improved by the physical-control approach, then there will be little pressure to improve accounting. The system will require more and better information of other kinds, but it will be able to tolerate relatively crude accounting for purposes of central reporting. Local management will be kept with little enough room for maneuver, and so it will not be strongly affected by weaknesses in accounting. On the other hand, if administration is improved by the placing of more reliance on value indicators, then surely accounting must also be improved. Managerial responsibility would be defined in more generalized terms, less in terms of compliance with detailed orders; at the same time, the impress of central-reporting objectives would fade. In such a situation, accounting could at last develop into a refined and effective tool of local management.

GLOSSARY · NOTES · INDEX

GLOSSARY

Aktiv. The assets side of the balance sheet.

Amortizatsiya (amortization). Amortization has a twofold aspect in the Soviet mind — it is the transfer of value from fixed assets to output and, at the same time, the contribution which an enterprise must make toward making good this loss of society's capital goods. The charges made to exact that contribution are called *amortizatsionnye otchisleniya* (amortization deductions).

Analiz khozyaystvennoi deyatelnosti (analysis of economic performance). Analysis, usually by the next higher level of authority, of the work of economic units on the basis of their annual or even more frequent reports.

Balans (balance sheet). In addition to its specific meaning, this term is also often used with the general meaning of any twosided statement, such as the balance of incomes and expenditures of an enterprise or a consolidated budget for the entire household sector.

Balans izmenenii tsen (balance sheet of price changes). This is a device similar to an input-output table designed to help price planners estimate the direct and indirect impact of price changes for some commodities on the costs of other commodities.

Bukhgalter. Bookkeeper.

Bukhgalterskii uchet (bookkeeping). See *Uchet.*

Dotatsii. Subsidies.

Garantiinyi rezerv (guarantee reserve). A reserve formed in some kinds of industrial enterprises to meet obligations on guarantees concerning their output.

271

Glavk (from *glavnoe upravlenie* — chief administration). An intermediate link in the administrative hierarchy, formerly between the ministry and the enterprise, now between the economic council and the enterprise.

Glavnyi bukhgalter (chief bookkeeper). The chief accounting officer of an enterprise or higher-level organs. In some kinds of institutions he is called *starshii* (senior) *bukhgalter*.

Iznashivanie. See *Iznos.*

Iznos (depreciation). The actual physical wear and tear on an item, used also by engineers in this literal sense. *Iznos* is the state, the process being labeled *snazhivanie* or *iznashivanie.*

Kapitalnyi remont (capital repair). Major repair of assets, the scope of which is defined by specific instructions in each jurisdiction. It is distinguished from current repair (*tekushchii remont*) by the fact that it occurs relatively infrequently and usually involves extensive replacement of components.

Khozyaystvennyi sposob stroitelstva (own-account method of construction). In this form of construction the enterprise acts as its own general contractor. It differs in this respect from *podriadnyi sposob,* where an outside contractor undertakes responsibility for the work. The two methods differ also in that, under the first, actual outlays are taken as the value of the completed work; in the second, a contract price is taken as the value of the work.

Khozraschet (from *khozyaystvennyi raschet* — economic accountability). This concept denotes the degree of freedom and responsibility allowed an enterprise. It means basically a moderate degree of financial and contractual independence, within which the enterprise is responsible for fulfilling the assigned plan. *Vnutrizavodskii khozraschet* is an extension of this administrative technique to smaller units within the enterprise.

Koeffitsient iznosa (coefficient of depreciation). The ratio of the depreciation of an asset in value terms to its original value.

Koeffitsienty defitsitnosti (coefficients of deficitness). Coefficients used by planners to adjust a set of established prices to a new set which will more accurately reflect scarcity.

Moralnyi iznos (obsolescence — literally, intangible wear and tear). Following Marx, Soviet economists distinguish obsolescence of type I, loss of value of old assets through reduction in the cost of producing them, and of type II, loss in value due to the competition of more productive replacement rivals.

Neustoiki (forfeits). See *Peni.*

Normativ (standard). The term customarily used for standard is *norma*, but in inventory planning the standard for inventory holdings has always been described as *normativ*.

Operativno-tekhnicheskii uchet (operating records). See *Uchet*.

Otchetnost (reporting). This term includes the whole process of reporting and the reports themselves.

Own working capital. See *Sobstvennye oborotnye sredstva*.

Passiv. The liabilities and net-worth side of the balance sheet.

Peni, shtrafi, neustoiki (penalties, fines, forfeits). Payments made for violation of contractual obligations or administrative regulations.

Pervonachalnaya stoimost (original value). The cost of an asset at time of acquisition. It is contrasted with *vosstanovitelnaya stoimost* (replacement value), which is some current estimate of value, allowing for price changes and for obsolescence. Both concepts, however, involve no correction for depreciation.

Podriadnyi sposob stroitelstva (contract method of construction). See *Khozyaystvennyi sposob*.

Popennaya plata (stumpage fee). A fee collected from lumbering organizations on the basis of timber cut. It is supposed to be differentiated so as to extract differential rent.

Progressivki. Payments for overfulfillment of output norms under progressive piecerate systems.

Prostoi. Stoppages.

Rentabelnost (profitability). This term sometimes means profitability in a simple accounting sense: a difference between cost and price. In other contexts it may mean something more general: general economic advantageousness.

Sebestoimost. Cost.

Shtrafi (fines). See *Peni*.

Shturmovshchina (storming). The tendency of Soviet enterprises to work feverishly at the end of an accounting period in order to meet the goals for the period. This is followed by a lull during the first part of the following period, and the cycle then begins again.

Snashivanie. See *Iznos*.

Sobstvennye oborotnye sredstva (own working capital). A measure of "own" resources not immobilized in fixed assets or other specified kinds of assets, and so free for the purpose of holding inventory assets. In the balance sheet, the term is often modified as *sobstvennye oborotnye i priravnennye k nim sredstva* (own working capi-

273

tal and items equivalent to own working capital), which includes as resources a few other liability items in addition to the charter fund. This larger concept is called "own and equivalent working capital" in the balance sheet in Chapter 9. Occasionally *fondy* (funds) is substituted for *sredstva,* but that usually then implies the inventory assets themselves. The usage of *fondy* and *sredstva* in the sphere of inventories is inconsistent with most other terminology in which *fondy* represents liability accounts and *sredstva* asset accounts.

Sovnarkhoz (from *sovet narodnogo khozyaystva* — economic council). A territorial administrative subdivision created in the reorganization of 1957. Under this reorganization most enterprises in the fields of industry and construction were removed from the branch ministries and placed under the control of the territorial sovnarkhozes. The latter administer enterprises for the most part through chief administrations.

Starshii bukhgalter (senior bookkeeper). See *Glavnyi bukhgalter.*

Statisticheskii uchet (statistics). See *Uchet.*

Tekhpromfinplan (technical-industrial-financial plan). The basic plan guiding the work of the enterprise, setting forth detailed indicators of its activity, both in physical and value terms.

Tekushchii remont (current repair). See *kapitalnyi remont.*

Tred (from *trudovaia edinitsa* — labor unit). The unit of account into which it has often been proposed that all Soviet accounting in value terms ultimately be translated. The idea obviously is based on the Marxist belief that labor is the measure of value.

Tselevoe finansirovanie (financing for special purposes). Funds given to an enterprise beyond its usual business revenues, usually from the budget, designated for expenditure for a special purpose. Also, the balance-sheet account showing the amount of these funds.

TsSU (from *Tsentralnoe Statisticheskoe Upravlenie* — Central Statistical Administration). The main data-collecting channel in the Soviet economy, through which information collected by territorially organized lower-level units is checked, processed in various ways, and passed up to the center. The TsSU has important responsibilities in the area of framing accounting legislation, approving forms, training bookkeeping personnel, and encouraging the mechanization of accounting. At one point in its history, this organization was called TsUNKhU, from *Tsentralnoe Upravlenie Narodno-Khozyaystvennogo Ucheta* (Central Administration of National-Economic Accounting).

Uchet (recordkeeping). This general term for recordkeeping is subdivided into statistics (*statisticheskii uchet*), bookkeeping (*bukhgalterskii uchet*), and operating records (*operativno-tekhnicheskii uchet*).

Ustavnyi fond (charter fund). The balance-sheet account that designates the original endowment of resources allotted to the enterprise by its charter (*ustav*). The amount subsequently changes as a result of the operations of the enterprise.

Vnutrizavodskii khozraschet. See *Khozraschet.*

Vosstanovitelnaya stoimost (replacement value). See *Pervonachalnaya stiomost.*

VSNKh (from *Vysshii Sovet Narodnogo Khozyaystva* — Supreme Council of the National Economy). A single agency responsible for administering the Soviet economy in the early postrevolutionary years. In the thirties it was replaced by separate commissariats specialized by branches of the economy.

Vyshestoiashchii organ (superior organ or agency). The next level of authority above any given unit in the Soviet administrative hierarchy. For an enterprise it is usually the glavk; for a glavk it was formerly the ministry, but is now the sovnarkhoz.

Zayavka. Requisition.

NOTES

KEY TO ABBREVIATIONS

BU — *Bukhgalterskii uchet* (Bookkeeping)
DiK — *Dengi i kredit* (Money and Credit)
FSSSR — *Finansy SSSR* (Finances of the USSR)
MTITR — *Mekhanizatsiya trudoemkikh i tiazhelykh rabot* (Mechanization of Labor-Intensive and Heavy Work)
NKh — *Neftyanoe khozyaystvo* (The Oil Industry)
PE — *Problemy ekonomiki* (Problems of Economics)
PKh — *Planovoe khozyaystvo* (Planned Economy)
SF — *Sovetskie finansy* (Soviet Finances)
ST — *Sotsialisticheskii trud* (Socialist Labor)
TsSU — Tsentralnoe Statisticheskoe Upravlenie (Central Statistical Administration)
TsUNKhU — Tsentralnoe Upravlenie Narodno-Khozyaystvennogo Ucheta (Central Administration of National-Economic Accounting)
VE — *Voprosy ekonomiki* (Questions of Economics)
VM — *Vestnik mashinostroeniya* (Journal of Machinebuilding)
VS — *Vestnik statistiki* (Journal of Statistics)

CHAPTER 1. *Introduction*

1. P. N. Amosov, *Problema materialnogo ucheta v sotsialisticheskom khozyastve* (The Problem of Physical Accounting in the Socialist Economy; Petrograd, 1921), pp. 26–27, 15–16.

2. See, for instance, I. A. Gorbachev, *Obshchiya poniatiya ob organizatsii i uchete khozyaystva proizvodstvennykh predpriyatii i uchrezhdenii VSNKh* (General Concepts of Organization and Accounting in the Management of Production Enterprises and Estab-

lishments of the Supreme Council of the National Economy; Moscow, 1919), and A. Dembo, *Uchet i preodolenie razrukhi* (Accounting and Escape from Ruin; Kiev, 1921).

3. *KPSS v rezoliutsiyakh i resheniyakh* (The Communist Party of the Soviet Union in Resolutions and Decisions; 7th ed., Moscow, 1954), I, 697–698. Italics in the original.

4. M. V. Nikolaev, *Zakonodatelstvo ob uchete i otchetnosti* (Legislation on Accounting and Reporting; Moscow, 1933), pp. 5–7, 15ff.

5. Decree of September 29, 1932, found in *ibid.*, pp. 137–169.

CHAPTER 2. *The Relation between Cost Accounting and Economic Calculation*

1. K. A. Razumov, *Proektirovanie obogatitelnykh fabrik* (Designing Enrichment Mills; Moscow, 1952), pp. 60–62 and the literature cited therein.

2. There are exceptions to both parts of this generalization, of course. There are many indications in the literature that managers are expected to adjust their output programs in response to prices. Also, the possibilities of determining how to produce the assigned program solely on the basis of cost calculations are limited by the exigencies of physical allocation, arbitrariness in the allocation of capital, and so on. The limitations on the cost-minimization approach are illustrated, for instance, in an article by D. I. Chernomordik on the capital-allocation problem ("Effektivnost kapitalnykh vlozhenii i teoriya vosproizvodstva" [The Effectiveness of Capital Investments and the Theory of Reproduction], *VE*, no. 6, 1949). He considers the problem of finding the most economical variant for a city transportation system on the basis of cost calculations, but then rejects the most economical variant on the grounds that the steel needed for it is not in fact available. What this indicates is that the planning of quantities has gone wrong, not that the monetary calculation gives the wrong answer. If this is the most economical variant, then materials *should* be available for it. The important point here, however, is that the local planner would be unable to make any kind of a decision at all on the basis of physical considerations alone and must perforce use value considerations at least tentatively.

3. Abram Bergson, *The Structure of Soviet Wages* (Cambridge, Mass., 1946), p. 208. Since the thirties, the degree of administrative interference with labor mobility has increased somewhat, but we know that the Russians still place great emphasis on productivity in setting their wage scales and that the scales are

characterized by great differentiation according to grade and kind of labor. So Bergson's conclusions on the basis of the data of the thirties are probably still relevant.

4. This criticism was voiced, for instance, by several speakers at the June 1959 plenum of the Central Committee, which discussed the problem of technical progress.

5. See, for instance, G. Kosiachenko, "Puti povysheniya ekonomicheskogo stimulirovaniya tekhnicheskogo progressa" (Ways of Raising the Economic Stimulus to Technical Progress), *PKh*, no. 8, 1960, pp. 10–12.

6. A. M. Aleksandrov, *Finansy SSSR* (Finances of the USSR; Moscow, 1952), pp. 310–313. Differential rent is explained in this source in a thoroughly "bourgeois" manner, although the emphasis is on the aim of making costs comparable rather than on the pricing objective. Such clarity is far from common, however, and the article on differential rent in the *Bolshaya sovetskaya entsiklopediya* is much more equivocal on the nature of differential rent.

7. As an example of this reasoning, see the article by A. A. Gorev, in *PKh*, no. 3, 1926, p. 148.

8. Sh. Ia. Turetski, *Ocherki planovogo tsenoobrazovaniia v SSSR* (Essays on Planned Price Formation in the USSR; Moscow, 1959), pp. 289–292.

9. The Russian price planners attempt to predict the effect of price changes in the case of some commodities on the costs of other kinds of outputs by using what is called the *balans izmenenii tsen* (balance sheet of price changes). This is a table somewhat like an input-output table, in which the planners try to trace the direct and indirect effects of a price change by successive approximation. To judge from the descriptions of the *balans* in the literature, it is a fairly crude instrument, with which it would be difficult to make any accurate predictions on the ultimate system of prices resulting from a change in some prices. For a description of the *balans* and its use, see L. Maizenberg, *Tsenoobrazovanie v narodnom khozyaystve SSSR* (Price Formation in the National Economy of the USSR; Moscow, 1953), pp. 132–138.

10. V. P. Maslakov, *Kommunalnye tarify v SSSR* (Charges for Municipal Services in the USSR; Moscow, 1951), p. 30.

11. Maizenberg, p. 117.

12. Maizenberg, p. 124.

13. D. Kondrashev, "Tsenoobrazovanie v promyshlennosti SSSR" (Price Formation in the Industry of the USSR), *DiK*, no. 1, 1951, p. 21.

14. Maizenberg, p. 120.

15. I. P. Dobrychin, "Tekhniko-ekonomicheskaya otsenka mashin novykh konstruktsii" (Technical-Economic Evaluation of Machines of New Design), *Avtomobilnaya i traktornaya promyshlennost* (Automobile and Tractor Industry), no. 6, 1954, p. 6. Dobrychin says that trucks are designed which will be efficient at high speeds and at full loads, but that both of these conditions are generally violated in the actual operation of trucks.

16. This view is stated explicitly in Maizenberg, p. 77; and in A. Bachurin, "K voprosu o pribyli i naloge s oborota" (On the Question of Profit and the Turnover Tax), *VE*, no. 3, 1954, p. 52.

17. See, for instance, D. I. Chernomordik, *Zheleznodorozhnye gruzovye tarify SSSR* (Railroad Freight Tariffs in the USSR; Moscow, 1953), pp. 67–73.

18. On the "coefficients of deficitness," see Gregory Grossman, "Industrial Prices in the USSR," *American Economic Review*, May 1959, and V. V. Novozhilov, "Izmerenie zatrat i ikh rezultatoy v sotsialisticheskom khozyaystve" (The Measurement of Expenditures and Their Results in the Socialist Economy), in V. S. Nemchinov, ed., *Primenenie matematiki v ekonomicheskikh issledovaniyakh* (The Application of Mathematics to Economic Research; Moscow, 1959), pp. 42–45.

19. Ia. V. Shukstal, et al., *Transportnye izderzhki v narodnom khozyaystve SSSR* (Transport Expenditures in the National Economy of the USSR; Moscow, 1959).

20. V. Belkin, "Ekonomicheskie raschety s pomoshchiu elektronnykh vychislitelnykh mashin" (Economic Calculations by Means of Electronic Computing Machines), *VE*, no. 10, 1959, p. 143.

21. L. V. Kantorovich, *Ekonomicheskii raschet nailuchshego ispolzovaniya resursov* (Economic Calculation of the Optimum Utilization of Resources; Moscow, 1960), and Novozhilov, "Izmerenie zatrat i ikh resultatov."

CHAPTER 3. *Depreciation Accounting: A General Description*

1. This change was made by a series of decrees in 1938. The first and most important of these, after which all the rest were patterned, was the decree "Concerning the Utilization of Amortization Deductions and the Improvement of Repair in Industrial Enterprises," of January 8, 1938. It can be found in *Pravda*, January 9, 1938.

2. Ia. B. Kvasha, *Amortizatsiya i sroki sluzhby osnovnykh fondov* (Amortization and Service Lives of Fixed Assets; Moscow, 1959).

3. Abram Bergson, *The Real National Income of Soviet Russia since 1928* (Cambridge, Mass., 1961), pp. 46, 48.

4. Ia. B. Kvasha, "O normakh amortizatsii" (On Amortization Norms), *VE*, no. 7, 1957, p. 101. A study of the fixed-asset valuations of the railroads concluded in 1954 that a revaluation of the fixed assets to current prices would raise the value by 57.3 percent. See P. Bunich, *Amortizatsiya osnovnykh fondov v promyshlennosti* (Amortization of Fixed Assets in Industry; Moscow, 1957), p. 57.

5. A. Shevchuk and V. Gorelik, "Nekotorye voprosy podgotovki k pereotsenke osnovnykh fondov" (Some Problems in Preparing for the Revaluation of Fixed Assets), *VS*, no. 8, 1958, p. 33.

6. L. M. Kantor, *Osnovnye fondy promyshlennosti i ikh ispolzovanie* (Fixed Assets of Industry and their Utilization; Leningrad, 1947), p. 17.

7. A fairly complete description of this revaluation may be found in M. Guttsait and M. Persits, "Voprosy planirovaniya i ucheta osnovnykh fondov narodnogo khozyaystva" (Questions of Planning and Accounting for the Fixed Assets of the National Economy), *PKh*, no. 8, 1939, p. 39.

8. A precise definition of large-scale industry may be found in *Slovar-spravochnik po sotsialno-ekonomicheskoi statistike* (Dictionary-Handbook of Social and Economic Statistics; 2nd ed., Moscow, 1948), p. 108. Generally it includes all industrial enterprises except those which employ less than sixteen workers, if mechanical power is used, or less than thirty workers without mechanical power.

9. The revaluation of the fixed assets of the railroads is discussed in K. Iu. Charnetski, *Kalkuliatsiya na zheleznodorozhnom transporte* (Cost Calculation in Railroad Transportation; Leningrad, 1931), p. 95, and A. Arakelian, "K voprosu o pereotsenke osnovnykh fondov narodnogo khozyaystva" (On the Question of Revaluing the Fixed Assets of the National Economy), *PE*, no. 5, 1938, p. 81.

10. Guttsait and Persits, p. 41, and V. Sobol, "K voprosu ob otsenke osnovnykh fondov" (On the Question of Valuing Fixed Assets), *PKh*, no. 4, 1947, p. 59.

11. The results of the 1940 revaluation are used, however, in distributing the total depreciation charge for the railroads among the various enterprises within the railroad system. The total charge is determined by using the book value of assets, but the allocation of this total charge is based on the results of the 1940 revaluation, since they represent a more accurate picture of the relative magnitudes of asset stocks in different enterprises.

12. For a description of this revaluation, see A. Margulis, "Inventarizatsiya na predpriyatiyakh osvobozhdennykh raionov" (Taking Inventory in Enterprise in Liberated Regions), *SF*, no. 1–2, 1944.

13. N. Voznesenski, *Voennaya ekonomika SSSR v period otechest-*

vennoi voiny (The War Economy of the USSR in the Period of the Fatherland War; Moscow, 1948), pp. 46, 65–66. The actual fraction of assets revalued was far less than one third, of course, since much equipment was evacuated to the East and reinstalled at the old values; there was little new investment in the invaded areas during the war, and much of the stock of fixed assets in these areas was destroyed and never revalued.

14. It should be pointed out that the following discussion applies only to the portion of investment outlays connected with construction and installation. Equipment is always acquired and owned by the investor and is capitalized at its cost of acquisition. But equipment has never accounted for more than about 40 percent of total investment outlay, and the following discussion applies to something over half of investment. See, for instance, the tabulations in TsSU, *Narodnoe khozyaystvo SSSR v 1959 godu* (National Economy of the USSR in 1959; Moscow, 1960), p. 546.

15. This cost-price divergence in the case of construction is no different in principle from the subsidies on other types of output, of course. Many other elements of investment are subsidized at one stage or another, but discussion of these subsidies is beyond the scope of this book.

16. See, for instance, Naum Jasny, *Soviet Prices of Producers' Goods* (Stanford, 1952), chap. 8.

17. According to G. M. Malenkov, *Otchetnyi doklad XIX sezdu partii o rabote ts. k. VKP(b)* (Report to the 19th Party Congress on the Work of the Central Committee of the All-Union Communist Party; Moscow, 1952), p. 64, the loss made by the construction organizations was 2.5 billion rubles. The capital-investment plan for 1951 was 132 billion rubles, and, since the share of capital investment going for construction and installation is about 60 percent, this would imply a construction and installation program of about 80 billion rubles. If we subtract the 25 percent of construction and installation which is carried out by the own-account method, this leaves the contract construction organizations with a program of about 60 billion rubles.

18. See, for instance, the 1951 budget speech and discussion in the Supreme Soviet (*Pravda*, March 8, 1951), in which many examples are given of construction organizations which made losses of up to 60 percent of the contract price of the work done.

19. Detailed discussion of how completed assets are valued may be found in any Soviet textbook on cost accounting in construction, such as M. Kh. Zhebrak, *Kurs bukhgalterskogo ucheta kapitalnogo stroitelstva* (Course in Construction Bookkeeping; Moscow, 1948).

20. In Soviet discussions of capital investment, these expenditures are called "outlays not increasing the value of fixed assets." According to K. N. Plotnikov, *Biudzhet sotsialisticheskogo gosudarstva* (The Budget of the Socialist State; Moscow, 1948), p. 307, they amounted to 2.4 percent, 4.2 percent, and 3.3 percent of total investment outlays in 1940, 1943, and 1944, respectively.

21. This calculation is based on information in A. A. Keller, *Neftianaya i gazovaya promyshlennost SSSR v poslevoennye gody* (The Oil and Gas Industry of the USSR in the Postwar Years; Moscow, 1958), T. Gonta, *Neft i prirodnyi gaz Ukrainy* (Oil and Natural Gas of the Ukraine; Moscow, 1957), and M. M. Brenner, *Neft* (Oil; Moscow, 1957).

22. I. A. Nikiforov, *Analiz khozyaystvennoi deyatelnosti stroitelnykh organizatsii* (Analysis of the Economic Performance of Construction Organizations; Moscow, 1951), p. 50, and L. S. Abramson, *Spravochnik po osnovnym voprosam finansovoi raboty i bukhgalterskogo ucheta v stroikakh* (Handbook on the Principal Questions of Financial Work and Bookkeeping in Construction Projects; Moscow, 1947), pp. 83–84.

23. See, for instance, P. Bunich, *Amortizatsiya osnovnykh fondov v promyshlennosti* (Amortization of Fixed Assets in Industry; Moscow, 1957), p. 77.

24. Norman M. Kaplan and William L. White, *A Comparison of 1950 Wholesale Prices in Soviet and American Industry* (Santa Monica, 1955), p. 33.

25. Descriptions of the revaluation procedure and instructions can be found in P. Bunich, *Pereotsenka osnovnykh fondov* (The Revaluation of Fixed Assets; Moscow, 1959), and V. Ostroumov and B. Gorelik, *Organizatsiya raboty po pereotsenke osnovnykh fondov* (Organization of the Work of Revaluing Fixed Assets; Moscow, 1959).

26. See, for instance, VS, no. 6, 1957, p. 67, and a note by A. Mitrofanov, in VE, no. 9, 1957, p. 135.

27. Bunich, *Pereotsenka osnovnykh fondov*, pp. 59–63.

28. Some of the results of the revaluation are described in A. Beliakov, "Nekotorye itogi pereotsenki osnovnykh fondov SSSR" (Some Results of the Revaluaton of Fixed Assets of the USSR), VS, no. 10, 1960, and in TsSU, *Narodnoe khozyaystvo SSSR v 1959 godu*, pp. 65–75.

29. VS, no. 10, 1960, p. 7.

30. *Ibid.*

31. The plans for the revaluation of collective-farm fixed assets are described extensively in a series of articles and consultations in

Vestnik statistiki during 1961. The results have not yet been revealed.

32. A fairly complete discussion of both these sets of rates is given in P. A. Khromov, *Amortizatsiya osnovnykh fondov v promyshlennosti SSSR* (Amortization of Fixed Assets in the Industry of the USSR; Moscow, 1939).

33. *Ibid.*, pp. 51–52.

34. One source says specifically that in the absence of alternative branch instructions this procedure is used. S. Tatur and L. Krasnov, *Uchet osnovnykh fondov promyshlennogo predpriyatiya* (Accounting for Fixed Assets of the Industrial Enterprise; Moscow, 1948), p. 46.

35. A. Margulis, *Voprosy ucheta i otchetnosti* (Questions of Accounting and Reporting; Moscow, 1944), p. 72.

36. Kvasha, "O normakh amortizatsii," p. 104.

37. Kanto, *Osnovnye fondy promyshlennosti i ikh ispolzovanie*, p. 19.

38. L. A. Maizlin, *Khozraschet v tekstilnoi promyshlennosti* (Economic Accountability in the Textile Industry; Moscow, 1956), p. 109.

39. Nauchno-issledovatelskii Finansovyi Institut, *Planirovanie i finansirovanie kapitalnogo remonta osnovnykh fondov* (Planning and Financing of Capital Repair of Fixed Assets; Moscow, 1958), p. 102.

40. A. Arakelian, *Osnovnye fondy promyshlennosti SSSR* (Fixed Assets of the Industry of the USSR; Moscow, 1938), p. 34.

41. L. M. Kantor, *Amortizatsiya i remont v promyshlennosti* (Amortization and Repair in Industry; Moscow, 1949), p. 45, and T. S. Khachaturov, *Osnovy ekonomiki zheleznodorozhnogo transporta* (Economic Principles of Railroad Transportation; I, Moscow, 1946), p. 57. The same objection is made in G. Ia. Roshal, "Finansirovanie kapitalnogo remonta" (Financing Capital Repair), *SF*, no. 6, 1947, p. 26, and in Sh. Turetski, *Vnutripromyshlennoe nakoplenie v SSSR* (Intraindustrial Accumulation in the USSR; Moscow, 1948), pp. 206–207.

42. The new norms are given in E. I. Gleikh, *Otraslevoi kurs bukhgalterskogo ucheta* (Course in Bookkeeping of Economic Branches; 2nd ed., Moscow, 1951), p. 61, and in E. P. Lebedev, *Transportnaya statistika* (Transportation Statistics; Moscow, 1953), p. 216.

43. See, for instance, V. A. Goloshchapov, *Bukhgalterskii uchet* (Bookkeeping; 5th ed., Moscow, 1950), p. 133.

44. P. Ivanov, "Novye edinye normy amortizatsii osnovnykh

fondov SSSR" (New Uniform Depreciation Rates for the Fixed Assets of the USSR), *PKh*, no. 12, 1961, p. 27.

45. It is obvious that reliance on composite rates must also make difficult the allocation of depreciation within the enterprise. Probably this is not a serious problem in the Soviet economy, however, because of the failure of Soviet cost accountants to develop a detailed cost-center approach to cost accounting. Even if class rates existed, depreciation would probably still be treated as a general overhead to be distributed on a more or less arbitrary basis.

46. "O razrabotke novykh norm amortizatsionnykh otchislenii i pereotsenke osnovnykh fondov" (On Working Out New Norms for Amortization Deductions and the Revaluation of Fixed Assets), *PKh*, no. 3, 1957, p. 95.

47. N. P. Grachev, "Voprosy amortizatsii i khozyaystvennogo rascheta na promyshlennykh predpriyatiyakh" (Questions of Amortization and Economic Accountability in Industrial Enterprises), *VE*, no. 6, 1957, p. 106.

48. G. Ia. Burshtein, "Amortizatsiya osnovnykh sredstv ugolnoi promyshlennosti" (Amortization of the Fixed Assets of the Coal Industry), *Ugol* (Coal), no. 6, 1959, p. 38.

49. See Ivanov, "Novye edinye normy."

CHAPTER 4. *Soviet Depreciation Charges: A Statistical Appraisal*

1. The omission of a charge in agriculture, in particular, has a very important effect on the ratio of depreciation to gross national product in view of the large share of Soviet national income originating in agriculture. In terms of Bergson's calculations of national income in "adjusted rubles" for 1937, approximately 30 percent of net national income originated in agriculture. Abram Bergson, *Soviet National Income and Product in 1937* (New York, 1953), p. 76.

2. P. Pavlov, *Snashivanie i amortizatsiya osnovnykh fondov* (The Depreciation and Amortization of Fixed Assets; Moscow, 1957), pp. 242–268.

3. I. M. Broide, *Finansirovanie i kreditovanie predpriyatii neftianoi i gazovoi promyshlennosti* (Financing and Crediting Enterprises of the Oil and Gas Industry; Moscow, 1958), p. 140.

4. For a typical discussion of the method of figuring Soviet depreciation rates, see L. Kantor, "Printsipy postroeniya norm amortizatsii v sotsialisticheskoi promyshlennosti" (Principles of Constructing Amortization Norms in Socialist Industry), in Ministerstvo Finan-

sov SSSR, *Amortizatsiya v promyshlennosti SSSR* (Amortization in the Industry of the USSR; Moscow, 1956).

5. A. Dodonov, *Amortizatsiya i remont osnovnykh sredstv* (Amortization and Repair of Fixed Assets; Moscow, 1960), p. 107.

6. P. A. Khromov, *Amortizatsiya osnovnykh fondov v promyshlennosti SSSR* (Amortization of Fixed Assets in the Industry of the USSR; Moscow, 1939), p. 53.

7. Expenditures on capital repair are expressed in current prices, of course, and this fact would tend to mitigate the effect under discussion. In the period involved, however, expenditures on capital repair were probably quite small in relation to retirements.

8. The only critical commentary on the subject before the late 1950s that I know of is P. P. Nemchinov, "K voprosu ob unifikatsii ucheta likvidatsii osnovnykh sredstv" (On the Question of Unifying Accounting for the Liquidation of Fixed Assets), Kievskii Finansovo-ekonomicheskii Institut, *Uchenye zapiski* (Scientific Notes), no. 2, 1950.

9. A. Kolosov, "O vozmeshchenii iznosa osnovnykh fondov" (On Recouping the Depreciation of Fixed Assets), *Nauchnye doklady vysshei shkoly, Ekonomicheskie nauki* (Scientific Reports of Higher Education, Economic Sciences), no. 1, 1958.

10. G. Safrai, "Nekotorye voprosy vosproizvodstva osnovnykh fondov promyshlennosti" (Some Problems of the Reproduction of Fixed Assets of Industry), *VE*, no. 7, 1957, p. 47.

11. P. Bunich, *Amortizatsiya osnovnykh fondov v promyshlennosti* (Amortization of Fixed Assets in Industry; Moscow, 1957), p. 110.

12. N. S. Norkin, *Bukhgalterskii uchet i analiz khozyaistvennoi deyatelnosti na predpriyatiyakh vodnogo transporta* (Bookkeeping and Analysis of Economic Performance in Enterprises of Water Transportation; Leningrad, 1950), p. 225, and A. Dodonov, "Uchet i ischislenie iznosa osnovnykh sredstv" (Accounting and the Determination of Depreciation of Fixed Assets), *VE*, no. 1, 1958, p. 122. The second source suggests that in the retirement calculations the accountant will simply compare the expenditures for capital repair made for the asset with the original value. The former often exceeds the former, and in such cases the accountant will not assign any depreciation to the asset.

13. Dodonov, p. 109.

14. Bunich, *Amortizatsiya osnovnykh fondov*, p. 101.

15. P. Bunich, "Ob amortizatsionnykh otchisleniyakh v promyshlennosti SSSR" (On Amortization Deductions in the Industry of the USSR), in Ministerstvo Finansov SSSR, *Amortizatsiya v promy-*

shlennosti SSSR, p. 28, and Bunich, *Amortizatsiya osnovnykh fondov*, p. 101.

16. These figures are taken from Pavlov, p. 122.

17. Ia. B. Kvasha, "O normakh amortizatsii" (On Amortization Norms), *VE*, no. 7, 1957, p. 103.

18. According to Bunich, *Amortizatsiya osnovnykh fondov*, p. 100, "In the years of the great Patriotic War, capital repair of fixed assets was scarcely carried out at all. The funds intended for capital repair for the most part were handed over to the budget." It is also said that after 1953, a number of ministries were given the right to use unspent capital repair funds to add to working capital (A. Dodonov, "Uchet i ischislenie iznosa osnovnykh sredstv" (Recording and Computing Depreciation of Fixed Assets), *VE*, no. 1, 1958, p. 121).

19. Safrai, p. 45.

20. Safrai, p. 41, and Dodonov, "Uchet i ischislenie," p. 122.

21. Bunich, *Amortizatsiya osnovnykh fondov*, p. 102, and Pavlov, p. 192.

22. Dodonov, "Uchet i ischislenie," p. 122.

23. See, for instance, Dodonov, *Amortizatsiya i remont*, p. 170.

24. Ia. B. Kvasha, *Amortizatsiya i sroki sluzhby osnovnykh fondov* (Amortization and Service Lives of Fixed Assets; Moscow, 1959), p. 75.

25. *Ibid.*, p. 76.

26. P. Filippov, "Sovershenstvovat planirovanie amortizatsionnykh otchislenii" (Perfect the Planning of Amortization Deductions), *PKh*, no. 11, 1960, p. 42.

CHAPTER 5. *Some Problems of Cost Allocation*

1. These are the main ledger accounts; the subsidiary ledger contains a finer classification, varied according to the branch.

2. There is nothing surprising in this similarity, since Soviet overhead accounting was originally based on American practice. An American cost accountant who was employed in the Institut Tekhniki Upravleniya (Institute of Management Technology) of the NKRKI in the early 1930s, when this organization was responsible for working out accounting instruction, says: "The writer has not in his experience in the Russian field come across any new methods of treating or distributing burden. Indeed it is the American methods that are looked upon and copied with the utmost seriousness." J. L. Wurman, "Cost Accounting and Management in Soviet Russia," *N.A.C.A. Bulletin*, February 1931.

3. Sh. Ia. Turetski, "Zadachi perestroiki sistemy kalkulirovaniya

i ucheta sebestoimosti" (Problems of Reconstructing the System of
Cost Calculation), *PKh*, no. 5, 1938, p. 63; Iu. O. Liubovich,
Ekonomika mashinostroitelnogo zavoda (Economics of a Machinebuilding Factory; Moscow, 1948), p. 201; A. Margulis, *Voprosy
ucheta i otchetnosti* (Problems of Accounting and Reporting; Moscow, 1944), p. 8.

4. Under the simple piecerate system, the worker is paid at a
rate per unit of output whatever the size of output. Under the
progressive piecerate system, units of output above the norm are
paid for at increasing rates.

5. P. Mashkovski, "Voprosy ucheta nakladnykh raskhodov v
promyshlennosti" (Questions of Accounting for Overhead Costs in
Industry), *BU*, no. 1, 1954; and M. Kh. Zhebrak, "Metody raspredeleniya kosvennykh raskhodov" (Methods of Distributing Indirect Expenses), *BU*, no. 4, 1954.

6. N. N. Ivanov, *Normativnyi uchet proizvodstva v promyshlennykh predpriyatiyakh* (Standard Cost Accounting in Industrial
Enterprises; Moscow, 1951), p. 109; S. E. Kamenitser, *Organizatsiya
i planirovanie sotsialisticheskogo promyshlennogo predpriyatiya* (Organization and Planning of the Socialist Industrial Enterprise; Moscow, 1950), p. 381; M. Kh. Zhebrak, *Kurs promyshlennogo ucheta*
(Course in Industrial Accounting; Moscow, 1950), p. 222; V. Kontorovich, *Tekhpromfinplan promyshlennogo predpriyatiya* (The
Technical, Industrial, and Financial Plan of an Industrial Enterprise;
Moscow, 1953), p. 381.

7. Margulis, pp. 17–26.

8. *Ibid.*, p. 31.

9. "Novaya instruktsiya po uchetu sebestoimosti promyshlennoi
produktsii" (The New Instruction on Accounting for Cost of Industrial Output), *VS*, no. 3, 1953, p. 90.

10. Kontorovich, p. 309.

11. The precise content of this account may be found in
S. Shchenkov, *Otchetnost promyshlennykh predpriyatii* (Reporting by
the Industrial Enterprise; Moscow, 1952), pp. 131–134.

12. "According to the instruction of the RKI, the distribution of
. . . general factory overhead expenses should be made in proportion to full shop value of the given items," S. G. Strumilin,
"Protsessy tsenoobrazovaniya v SSSR" (Processes of Price Formation in the USSR), *PKh*, no. 7, 1928, p. 33.

13. A. S. Konson, *Ekonomicheskie voprosy proektirovaniya mashin*
(Economic Problems of Machinery Design; Moscow-Leningrad,
1950), p. 144.

14. G. V. Teplov, *Planirovanie na mashinostroitelnykh zavodakh*

(Planning in Machinebuilding Plants; Moscow, 1949), p. 357. This reference to limits per thousand rubles of gross output appears frequently in the literature on cost planning.

15. V. A. Goloshchapov, *Bukhgalterskii uchet* (Bookkeeping; Moscow, 1950), pp. 177–180.

16. For instance, Margulis, pp. 27–29.

17. For two examples, see A. A. Afanasev, *Osnovy postroeniya bukhgalterskogo balansa* (Principles of Constructing the Bookkeeping Balance Sheet; 3rd ed., Moscow, 1952), pp. 38–41; and D. Kondrashev, in a review of Margulis, *SF*, no. 8–9, p. 46.

18. N. N. Ivanov, "Uluchshit uchet sebestoimosti promyshlennoi produktsii" (Improve Accounting for the Cost of Industrial Output), *BU*, no. 9, 1947, pp. 8–9.

19. This question is discussed more fully in Chapter 7.

20. This rule was first introduced in 1940 along with a number of others intended to improve the valuation of unfinished production. Goloshchapov, pp. 177–180.

21. Margulis, p. 85.

22. L. Ia. Rozenberg, *Tekhnika ucheta subestoimosti promyshlennoi produktsii* (Technique of Accounting for the Cost of Industrial Output; Leningrad, 1949), p. 56.

23. Goloshchapov, p. 178; S. V. Meshalkin, *Finansirovanie kapitalnogo remonta osnovnykh sredstv* (Financing the Capital Repair of Fixed Assets; Moscow, 1949), pp. 8–9.

24. L. M. Kantor, "K voprosu ob ekonomicheskoi prirode sebestoimosti pri sotsializme" (On the Question of the Economic Nature of Cost under Socialism), *VE*, no. 10, 1954, p. 101.

25. Afanasev, pp. 62–3.

26. Zhebrak, *Kurs promyshlennogo ucheta*, p. 224.

27. For a summary of American thought on practice on costing joint products, see National Association of Cost Accountants, *Costing Joint Products*, Research Series No. 31, April 1, 1957.

28. Strumilin, "Protsessy tsenoobrazovaniia v SSSR."

29. Zhebrak, *Kurs promyshlennogo ucheta*, p. 266.

30. A. I. But, *Planirovanie v tsvetnoi metallurgii* (Planning in Nonferrous Metallurgy; Moscow, 1946), pp. 230–232.

31. S. Kobyzev, *Bukhgalterskii uchet v sovkhozakh, MTS i kolkhozakh* (Bookkeeping in State Farms, Machine-Tractor Stations, and Collective Farms; Moscow, 1946), pp. 130–131.

32. I. M. Prokofev, *Bukhgalterskii uchet v sovkhozakh* (Bookkeeping in State Farms; Moscow, 1947), p. 306.

33. Zhebrak, *Kurs promyshlennogo ucheta*, pp. 255-260. In his

examples, the costs benefiting both outputs are more than two thirds of the total.

34. B. I. Weitz, *Electric Power Development in the USSR* (Moscow, 1936), 232–233.

35. N. F. Sedykh, "Metody kalkuliatsii v neftedobyvaiushchei promyshlennosti Soedinenykh Shtatov" (Methods of Cost Calculation in the Oil Industry of the USA), *NKh*, no. 6, 1928, pp. 798–907. An examination of the context in which these rules were set up suggests the absence of any theoretical basis for them. The cost-accounting conference which drafted them studied the accounting of American firms and, to judge from the description of the two systems given in the source, patterned the Russian rules on the American practice.

36. The switch to a coefficients method was proposed in S. F. Marshev, "Ob opredelenii sebestoimosti produktsii v pererabotke nefti" (On Determining the Cost of Output in Oil Refining), *NKh*, no. 8–9, 1931, pp. 83–88; and later articles say that the coefficients method is the one used. See, for instance, A. S. Eigenson, A. I. Skoblo, and P. A. Ilin, "K voprosu o metodologii kalkuliatsii sebestoimosti nefteproductov" (On the Question of the Method of Calculating the Cost of Oil Products), *Azerbaidzhanskoi neftianoe khozyaystvo* (The Azerbaidjan Oil Industry), no. 10–11, 1940, pp. 52–57. Just when the change was made is not known.

37. A brief résumé of the succession of methods together with some of the reasoning behind each of them is given in L. A. Kashnitski, "K voprosu o metodike kalkulirovaniya sebestoimosti nefteproduktov" (On the Question of the Method of Calculating the Cost of Oil Products), *NKh*, no. 2, 1956, pp. 8–13.

38. P. Nikitin, *Lespromkhoz as an Administrative and Production Unit* (New York, 1953), p. 70; and N. F. Fugelzang, *Posobie po sostavleniyu promfinplana derevoobrabatyvayushchego predpriyatiya* (Handbook for Drawing Up the Financial Plan of a Woodworking Enterprise; Moscow, 1950), p. 65.

39. A detailed description of the method and the coefficients is given in D. S. Levin and M. G. Poliakov, *Kalkulirovanie sebestoimosti produktsii miasnoi promyshlennosti* (Calculation of the Cost of Production in the Meat Industry; Moscow, 1936), pp. 90–93. The following source confirms that the coefficient system is still used. M. Poliakov and V. Bogomolov, "Uluchshit kalkulirovanie sebestoimosti na predpriyatiyakh miasnoi promyshlennosti" (Improve Cost Calculation in Enterprises of the Meat Industry), *VS*, no. 4, 1953.

40. D. Vainshenker, "Voprosy analiza sebestoimosti promyshlennoi

produktsii" (Questions of Analysis of the Cost of Industrial Output), VS, no. 1, 1954, p. 42.

41. V. I. Stotski, *Osnovy kalkuliatsii i ekonomicheskogo analiza sebestoimosti* (Principles of the Calculation and Economic Analysis of Cost; Moscow-Leningrad, 1932), pp. 135ff.

42. A. B. Chirkov, *Osnovy balansovogo ucheta i kalkuliatsii na predpriyatiyakh tselliuloznoi i bumazhnoi promyshlennosti* (The Principles of Balance-Sheet Accounting and Cost Accounting in Enterprises of the Cellulose and Paper Industry; Moscow, 1948), p. 304.

43. N. P. Rastorguev, *Bukhgalterskii uchet i kalkuliatsiya v chernoi metallurgii* (Bookkeeping and Cost Calculation in Ferrous Metallurgy; Moscow, 1949), p. 210.

44. Stotski, p. 140.

45. *Ibid.*, p. 135.

46. Rozenberg, p. 85. Rastorguev, p. 210, says that the coefficients reflect value (*tsennost*).

47. Turetski, "Zadachi perestroiki."

48. In planning calculations this principle can lead to serious error, however, and its use in project-making calculations has recently been criticized. It is said that project-making organizations, in laying out their investment programs on the basis of some sort of cost-saving approach, valued byproducts at current prices and thus attributed all the cost savings to the main product. Thus the relative profitability of these investment variants was overstated. This is supposed to have been done in the chemical industry, in ferrous metallurgy, and in nonferrous metallurgy. "Itogi diskussii ob opredelenii ekonomicheskoi effektivnoisti kapitalnykh vlozhenii v promyshlennost SSR" (Results of the Discussion on Determining Economic Effectiveness of Capital Investments in Industry of the USSR), VE, no. 3, 1954, p. 107.

49. Kashnitski, p. 9.

CHAPTER 6. *Allocation of Outlays to Central Overhead*

1. Strictly speaking, the budget-financed capital repair does not disappear from the balance sheet, but is credited to the charter fund and debited to the depreciation account. Nevertheless, it never affects the cost accounts or the profit and loss account.

2. S. G. Strumilin, *K perestroike sovetskogo ucheta* (Toward a Reconstruction of Soviet Accounting; Moscow, 1936), p. 37.

3. S. Mekhanik, "Zatraty predpriyatiya i sebestoimost produktsii"

(Outlays of the Enterprise and the Cost of Production), *SF*, no. 6, 1947.

4. N. A. Blatov, *Osnovy promyshlennogo ucheta i kalkuliatsii* (Foundations of Industrial Accounting and Cost Calculation; Moscow, 1936), pp. 322–337.

5. V. I. Pereslegin, *Otchetnyi balans dokhodov ministerstva i glavka* (The Budget Report of Ministries and Glavks; Moscow, 1948), p. 52.

6. Not all labor-training expense is charged off to the budget, but, according to Pereslegin, most such expenses are.

7. A. Ia. Stepanov, *Planirovanie finansov mashinostroitelnogo zavoda* (Planning the Finances of a Machinebuilding Factory; Moscow, 1955), p. 161, says that the institute of the machine-tool industry, for instance, is supported by the budget.

8. V. A. Goloshchapov, *Bukhgalterskii uchet* (Bookkeeping; Moscow, 1950), p. 455.

9. D. Kondrashev, *Balans rashhodov i dokhodov predpriyatii i obedinenii promyshlennosti* (Income and Expenditure Statements of Enterprises and Combines in Industry; Moscow, 1948), p. 82.

10. Mekhanik, p. 20.

11. This is only a partial list, and a detailed search would undoubtedly reveal others.

12. The reference here to losses and outlays is not strictly correct, since several of the items may be either a profit or a loss in specific cases. However, many of them can be only losses and, even when they may be either, they are in fact usually losses. If the item does turn out to be a profit, the question is simply reversed — is this income a deduction from costs or is it purely revenue, that is, windfall income for the head office? In most cases my conclusions below are applicable, *mutatis mutandis*, to either case. We will consider this problem specifically as we discuss each item separately.

13. A. A. Afanasev, *Osnovy postroeniya bukhgalterskogo balansa* (Principles of Constructing the Bookkeeping Balance Sheet; Moscow, 1952), pp. 53–54.

14. Goloshchapov, p. 181.

15. Kondrashev, in a review of Margulis' *Voprosy ucheta i otchetnosti* (Problems of Accounting and Reporting; Moscow, 1944), in *SF*, no. 8–9, 1944, p. 46.

16. See, for instance, N. S. Norkin, *Bukhgalterskii uchet i analiz khozyaystvennoi deyatelnosti na predpriyatiyakh vodnogo transporta* (Bookkeeping and Analysis of Economic Performance in Enterprises of Water Transportation; Leningrad, 1950), where a detailed explanation is given of how the year-round expenses of river-transport

organizations are reserved for charging to production in the period of navigation.

17. This was the treatment under the 1936 statute concerning the balance sheet. The new statute introduced in 1952, however, decreed that any profits arising from such cancellations of debt were to be extracted directly to the budget. The losses were still to be reflected in the profit and loss account. V. I. Pereslegin, *Novoe polozhenie o bukhgalterskikh otchetakh i balansakh* (New Statute on Bookkeeping Reports and Balance Sheets; 2nd ed., Moscow, 1952), p. 23.

18. Afanasev, p. 54; Goloshchapov, p. 182.

19. Mekhanik, p. 19; Margulis, p. 11.

20. *Ibid.*

21. Norkin, p. 332.

22. V. Stepanova, "Berezhno ispolzovat taru v narodnom khozyaystve" (Use Packing Materials Sparingly), *FSSSR*, no. 8, 1954, p. 24.

23. *Ibid.*, p. 25.

24. B. B. Veselovski, *Kurs ekonomiki i organizatsii gorodskogo khozyaystva* (A Course on the Economics and Organization of the Municipal Economy; Moscow, 1950), p. 160.

25. Stepanov, p. 163.

26. S. A. Shchenkov, *Otchetnost promyshlennykh predpriyatii* (Reporting by Industrial Enterprises; Moscow, 1952), p. 98.

27. D. A. Datovski, *Planirovanie zhilishchno-kommunalnogo khozyaystva stroitelnykh organizatsii* (Financing the Housing and Municipal Operations of Construction Organizations; Moscow, 1952), pp. 4–5.

28. I. I. Zimin, *Organizatsiya finansov lesozagotovitelnogo predpriyatiya* (Organization of the Finances of a Lumbering Enterprise; Moscow-Leningrad, 1954), p. 8.

29. Mekhanik, p. 19.

30. Kondrashev, p. 33.

31. A. V. Voronin, *Kalkuliatsiya i analiz sebestoimosti produktsii tekstilnykh predpriyatii* (Calculation and Analysis of Cost of Output of Textile Enterprises; Moscow, 1958), p. 129.

32. Apparently it is recognized that this practice is a form of taking money out of one pocket and putting it into the other, and in 1947 some steps were taken to eliminate these losses by easing the rates of turnover tax on such produce. A. K. Suchkov, *Gosudarstvennye dokhody SSSR* (Revenues of the Soviet State; Moscow, 1949), p. 93. But the accounting texts still speak of losses.

33. It is not clear just how broad a class losses from natural disasters is defined to be. However, in addition to the kinds of losses listed above, it is known that in the river-transport industry, losses of fixed assets through collisions and other such accidents are considered losses from natural disasters. Norkin, p. 209.

34. S. G. Strumilin, "Protsessy tsenoobrazovaniya v SSSR" (Processes of Price Formation in the USSR), *PKh,* no. 6, 1928, p. 49.

35. V. P. Raikher, "Strakhovoi fond" (The Insurance Fund) in N. V. Orlov, ed., *Trudy Leningradskogo Finansovo-Ekonomicheskogo Instituta* (Transactions of the Leningrad Financial-Economic Institute; 2, Moscow-Leningrad, 1941).

36. I. M. Prokofev, *Bukhgalterskii uchet v sovkhozakh* (Bookkeeping in the State Farms; Moscow, 1947), pp. 216–217.

37. Incidentally, by this argument it would be better to write off last year's losses to the charter fund directly rather than through the profit and loss account. This is undoubtedly not done because it would open up possibilities of falsification which would be difficult to control.

38. I have seen no discussion of how a revaluation is reflected in the accounts of the Gosbank. The liabilities side of the Gosbank balance sheet is more or less identical with the stock of money, and so if the balance sheet is to remain in balance a revaluation of short-term credit means a change in the stock of money. How this is effected is never explained.

39. Shchenkov, p. 207f.

40. E. I. Gleikh, *Otraslevoi kurs bukhgalterskogo ucheta* (Course in Bookkeeping of Economic Branches; 2nd ed., Moscow, 1951), pp. 267–268.

41. E. G. Penkov, *Inventarizatsiya v predpriyatiyakh gosudarstvennoi torgovli* (Taking Inventory in Enterprises of State Trade; Moscow, 1949), p. 93.

42. N. N. Ivanov, *Normativnyi uchet proizvodstva v promyshlennykh predpriyatiyakh* (Standard Cost Accounting in Industrial Enterprises; Moscow, 1951), p. 113.

43. Incidentally, the Russians' concept is much broader than the Western concept of transfer payments. In accordance with Marxist economic theory, they include here all taxes, interest, rent, and social-insurance deductions. Shchenkov, p. 95.

44. L. M. Kantor, "K voprosu ob ekonomicheskoi prirode sebestoimosti pri sotsializme" (On the Question of the Economic Nature of Cost under Socialism), *VE,* no. 10, 1954, pp. 95–97.

CHAPTER 7. *The Impact of Accounting Data on Decisions: Some Illustrations*

1. M. V. Nikolaev, *Zakonodatelstvo ob uchete i otchetnosti* (Legislation on Accounting and Reporting; Moscow, 1933), pp. 89–114.

2. *Ibid.*

3. L. M. Kantor, *Amortizatsiya i remont v promyshlennosti* (Amortization and Repair in Industry; Moscow, 1949), pp. 17–18.

4. P. Ivanov, "Novye edinye normy amortizatsii osnovnykh fondov SSSR" (New Uniform Depreciation Rates for the Fixed Assets of the USSR), *PKh*, no. 12, 1961, p. 31.

5. A. G. Omarovski, "Ekonomika remonta mashin i razmeshchenie remontnykh predpriyatiya" (Economics of Machinery Repair and the Location of Repair Enterprises), *VM*, no. 6, 1958, p. 68. Actually this is a very common assertion and can be found in many other sources as well.

6. Some discussions of the "balance of equipment" and its relationship to replacement decisions may be found in V. Vorotilov, "Modernizatsiya oborudovaniya i rost proizvoditelnosti truda" (Modernization of Equipment and the Growth of Labor Productivity), *ST*, no. 5, 1958, p. 35; A. Kolosov, "O vozmeshchenii iznosa osnovnykh fondov" (On Recouping the Depreciation of Fixed Assets), *Nauchnye doklady vysshei shkoly, Ekonomicheskie nauki* (Scientific Reports of Higher Education, Economic Sciences), no. 1, 1959, p. 49; and a note by Mitrofanov in *VE*, no. 9, 1957, p. 137.

7. Ia. B. Kvasha, *Amortizatsiya i sroki sluzhby osnovnykh fondov* (Amortization and Service Lives of Fixed Assets; Moscow, 1959), pp. 67–75.

8. For one typical example, see F. G. Petrov, "Ekonomicheskoe obosnovnanie primeneniya spetsialnykh stanochnykh prisposoblenii" (The Economic Basis for Using Special Attachments for Machine Tools), *VM*, no. 2, 1958, p. 70.

9. See, for instance, I. Shubkina, "Sravnitelnyi analiz ekonomicheskoi effektivnosti avtomatizirovannogo i neavtomatizirovannogo proizvodstva" (Comparative Analysis of the Economic Effectiveness of Automated and Nonautomated Production), *Nauchnye doklady vysshei shkoly, Ekonomicheskie nauki*, no. 2, 1958, p. 51; V. I. Ganshtak and E. K. Smirnitski, "Ekonomicheskie voprosy modernizatsii oborudovaniya" (Economic Questions in the Modernization of Equipment), *VM*, no. 12, 1958; and G. I. Samborski, "Ekonomicheskie voprosy kompleksnoi avtomatizatsii proizvoidstva v mashino-

stroenii" (Economic Questions of Complex Automation of Production in Machinebuilding), *VM*, no. 11, 1958, p. 12.

10. A. V. Fortunatov, *Ekonomicheskaya effektivnost ratsionalizatorskikh meropriyatii* (The Economic Effectiveness of Suggestions for Rationalization; Moscow, 1956), pp. 20–23.

11. N. P. Bannyi, *Tekhniko-ekonomicheskie raschety v chernoi metallurgii* (Technical-Economic Calculations in Ferrous Metallurgy; Moscow, 1958), pp. 24–28.

12. G. E. Edelgauz, "O nekotorykh voprosakh planirovaniya i ucheta sebestoimosti produktsii v mashinostroenii," (On Some Problems of Planning and Accounting for the Cost of Production in Machinebuilding), *VM*, no. 8, 1954.

13. E. D. Khanukov, *Transport i razmeshchenie promyshlennosti* (Transportation and the Distribution of Industry; Moscow, 1955), p. 336.

14. For a description of this approach, see S. K. Danilov, *Ekonomika transporta* (Economics of Transportation; 2nd ed.; Moscow, 1957), pp. 548–561.

15. Khanukov, p. 331.

16. This is implied in V. N. Orlov, *Kalkuliatsiya i analiz sebestoimosti zheleznodoroznykh perevozok* (Calculation and Analysis of the Cost of Railroad Haulage; Moscow, 1949), chap. 11.

17. See Gregory Grossman, "Industrial Prices in the USSR," *American Economic Review*, May 1959.

18. D. A. Tarasov and I. I. Tatarinov, "Ratsionalnoe ispolzovanie topliva i teploenergetiki na neftepererabatyvaiushchikh zavodakh" (Rational Utilization of Fuel and Heat Energy in Refineries), *Promyshlennaya energetika* (Industrial Energy), no. 1, 1959.

19. I. P. Krapin, "Kalkulirovanie sebestoimosti para utilizatsionnykh ustanovok" (Calculation of the Cost of Steam from By-product Installations), *Stal* (Steel), no. 3, 1958.

CHAPTER 8. *Accounting for Cost Control*

1. A good description of these cost plans and the cost reports may be found in S. A. Shchenkov, *Otchetnost promyshlennykh predpriyatii* (Reporting by Industrial Enterprises; Moscow, 1952), chap. 9.

2. P. A. Khromov, A. A. Arakelian, and A. V. Vorobeva, *Ekonomika promyshlennosti SSSR* (Economics of the Industry of the USSR; Moscow, 1956), p. 209.

3. *Pravda*, March 1, 1947.

4. "Average-progressive" norms are norms set on the basis of the

average performance of the best workers, shops, etc., engaged in any activity.

5. P. I. Zlobin, *Bukhgalterskii uchet, otchetnost i analiz deiatelnosti stroitelnykh organizatsii* (Bookkeeping, Reporting and Analysis of the Performance of Construction Organizations; Moscow, 1950), p. 109; A. A. Afanasev, *Osnovy postroeniya bukhgalterskogo balansa* (Principles of Constructing the Bookkeeping Balance Sheet; 3rd ed., Moscow, 1952), p. 24; N. N. Ivanov, "O metodike proizvodstvennogo ucheta i o kontrole za zatratam na proizvodstvo" (On the Methodology of Production Accounting and on Control of Expenditures on Production), *BU*, no. 6, 1953, p. 21. According to M. Kh. Zhebrak, *Kurs promyshlennogo ucheta* (Course in Industrial Accounting; Moscow, 1950), p. 312, it is used in the furniture industry, the shoe industry, the leather industry, and a number of other branches. This method is obligatory for all enterprises of regional, city, and oblast jurisdiction and for industrial cooperatives. V. A. Goloshchapov, *Bukhgalterskii uchet* (Bookkeeping; Moscow, 1950), pp. 71, 93.

6. "Novaya instruktsiya po uchetu sebestoimosti produktsii" (The New Instruction on Accounting for Cost of Production), *VS*, no. 3, 1953, p. 89, and D. Vainshenker, "Voprosy analiza sebestoimosti promyshlennoi produktsii" (Questions of Analyzing the Cost of Industrial Production), *VS*, no. 1, 1954, p. 42.

7. See, for instance, A. Margulis, *Voprosy ucheta i otchetnosti* (Problems of Accounting and Recording; Moscow, 1944), p. 27–31. A 1938 source describes a case in which an audit showed that the plant had 3.5 million rubles of undisclosed losses in its unfinished production account. *Mashinostroenie* (Machinebuilding), October 2, 1938. A large number of such cases are discussed in an article in *BU*, no. 2, 1947. One of these concerns a machinebuilding enterprise in which the costs of operating a subsidiary mine had been left in the unfinished-production account until they finally reached 570 million rubles. There are also a large number of examples given in L. Semenov, "Kak dolzhno uchityvatsia i otsenivatsia nezavershennoe proizvodstvo promyshlennogo predpriyatiya," (How Unfinished Production Should be Determined and Valued in the Industrial Enterprise), *DiK*, no. 5–6, 1941, pp. 44–49.

8. See, for instance, "Povysit kachestvo ucheta proizvodstva i kalkulirovaniya sebestoimosti produktsii" (Raise the Quality of Accounting for the Cost of Industrial Output), *BU*, no. 3, 1954, p. 5.

9. S. Mekhanik, "Finansirovanie raskhodov budushchikh let" (Financing Expenditures of Future Years), *SF*, no. 10–11, 1943, p. 20; N. N. Ivanov and V. I. Pereslegin, "Ob uluchshenii planirovaniya,

ucheta i kalkuliatsii sebestoimosti produktsii" (On Improving Planning, Recording and Calculation of the Cost of Output), *BU*, no. 11, 1953, p. 19.

10. Mekhanik, p. 17. The books on "cost analysis" also hint that this account is likely to be inflated and that the rate at which the enterprise writes it off must be checked very carefully. I. I. Poklad, *Analiz sebestoimosti produktsii i finansov na mashinostroitelnom zavode* (Analysis of the Cost of Production and Finances in the Machinebuilding Plant; Moscow, 1953), p. 53.

11. *Mashinostroenie* (Machinebuilding), October 2, 1936.

12. It should be mentioned that these expense shifts often take place in the reverse direction. The minimizing of costs is only one of the goals of management, and there are often instances in which other motives conflict with the aim of meeting a cost goal. Outlays on capital repair and capital construction are often charged to the cost of current output, because the other sources of funds for repair and investment are so restrictive. G. Etchin, "Likvidirovat otvlechenie oborotnykh sredstv na kapitalnoe stroitelstvo i kapitalnyi remont" (Stop the Transfer of Working Capital to Construction and Capital Repair), *Finansy i kredit SSSR* (Finances and Credit of the USSR), no. 3, 1953; and L. Eliashov, "Rezultaty beskontrolnosti" (The Results of Lack of Control), *SF*, no. 9, 1947, p. 30.

13. Afanasev, p. 47; P. A. Khromov, *Amortizatsiya osnovnykh fondov v promyshlennosti SSSR* (Amortization of Fixed Assets in the Industry of the USSR; Moscow, 1939), p. 60.

14. S. Meshalkin, *Finansirovanie kapitalnogo remonta osnovnykh sredstv* (Financing the Capital Repair of Fixed Assets; Moscow, 1949), pp. 8–9.

15. Afanasev, p. 47; *BU*, no. 5, 1947, p. 1.

16. For some examples, see the following. N. N. Ivanov, "Uluchshit uchet sebestoimosti promyshlennoi produktsii" (Improve Accounting for the Cost of Industrial Output), *BU*, no. 9, 1947, p. 10; G. G. Bocharov, *Normativnyi uchet v mashinostroenii* (Standard Cost Accounting in Machinebuilding; Moscow, 1949), p. 105; editorial, "Povysit otvetstvennost za kachestvo ucheta i balansa" (Increase Responsibility for the Quality of Accounting and the Balance Sheet), *BU*, no. 5, 1947, p. 2; and F. Semochkin, "K rassmotreniyu godovykh otchetov za 1946 g." (On Examining the Annual Reports for 1946), *BU*, no. 2, 1947, p. 46.

17. G. G. Bocharov, "Osnovy kalkuliatsii v mashinostroenii" (Principles of Cost Calculation in Machinebuilding), *BU*, no. 6, 1952, p. 46.

18. Some examples are given in *BU*, no. 9, 1947, pp. 5–6; "Povy-

sit kachestvo dokumentalnykh revizii" (Raise the Quality of Documentary Audits), *BU*, no. 4, 1954, pp. 1–4; S. S. Ostroumov, *Osnovy bukhgalterskogo ucheta i subebno-bukhgalterskoi ekspertizy* (The Principles of Bookkeeping and Legal Expertise; Moscow, 1953), p. 141.

19. S. S. Geidish, *Tretia vsesoiuznaya konferentsiya po unutrizavodskomu planirovaniyu v mashinostroenii* (Third All-Union Conference on Intraplant Planning in Machinebuilding; Moscow, 1949), p. 53.

20. The decrees outlining the responsibilities of these two organs is to be found in Goloshchapov, pp. 6–11.

21. The decree, "On Intrabranch Financial Control and Documentary Audit of Institutions, Enterprises, Economic Organizations, and Construction Projects," may be found in Goloshchapov, pp. 9–10.

22. D. I. Alenchikov, "Nazrevshie voprosy vnutrivedomstvennogo finansovogo kontrolia" (Some Pressing Problems of Intradepartmental Financial Control), *SF*, no. 8, 1945, p. 29. This practice still exists, as indicated in *BU*, no. 7, 1954, p. 18.

23. S. Mikhailov, "Ustranit nedostatki v uchete i kontrole" (Eliminate Deficiencies in Accounting and Control), *BU*, no. 7, 1954, p. 29.

24. The most recent legislation defining the responsibility and functions of the chief bookkeeper is the 1947 "Statute Concerning the Chief (Senior) Bookkeepers of State, Cooperative, and Public Institutions, Organizations, and Enterprises." It may be found in Goloshchapov, pp. 13–18.

25. Afanasev, p. 76.

26. A. S. Konkov, *Ekonomiya materialov na zavode* (Economy of Materials in the Plant; Moscow, 1952), p. 7.

27. See, for instance, Stanley Henrici, *Standard Costs for Manufacturing* (New York, 1953), for a description of some of these methods; and OEEC, *Cost Accounting and Productivity* (Paris, 1952), for the impressions of a group of European experts concerning their use in the United States.

28. "Nauchno-proizvodstvennaya konferentsiya po voprosam vnutrizavodskogo khozrascheta" (Scientific-Production Conference on Questions of Intraplant Economic Accountability), *VE*, no. 6, 1951.

29. Akademiya Nauk Latviiskoi SSR, Insitut Ekonomiki, *Voprosy vnutrizavodskogo khozrascheta* (Questions of Intraplant Economic Accountability; Riga, 1954), pp. 12–18.

30. L. M. Kantor, "K voprosu ob ekonomicheskoi prirode sebestoimosti pri sotsializme" (On the Question of the Economic Nature of Cost under Socialism), *VE*, no. 10, 1954, p. 101.

31. A. Vorobeva, "Puti ukrepleniya tsekhovogo khozrascheta"

(Ways of Strengthening Economic Accountability in the Shop), *VE*, no. 4, 1951, pp. 48–49; and "Nauchno-proizvodstvennaya konferentsiya," p. 106.

32. S. K. Tatur, *Khozraschet i rentabelnost* (Economic Accountability and Profitability; Moscow, 1951), p. 146.

33. Vorobeva, pp. 48–49.

34. Much of the accounting literature used in the Soviet Union in the late 1930s consisted of translations of American and German works. The visit of a Soviet delegation to the Sixth International Congress on Accounting in New York in 1929 and a subsequent tour of some American plants gave a great impetus to the Soviet enthusiasm for American accounting methods. This delegation recommended among other things that American accounting experts be engaged to improve Russian accounting. One such expert, who worked for the Institute of Management Technique in the early 1930s, said that this organization made great use of American literature and experience in working out recommendations for Soviet plants. J. L. Wurman, "Cost Accounting and Management in Soviet Russia, *N.A.C.A. Bulletin*, February 1931, p. 908.

35. L. Zernov and V. Kuts, "Sovershenstvovat uchet proizvodstva i kalkulirovanie sebestoimosti produktsii" (Perfect Accounting and Cost Calculation), *BU*, no. 2, 1958, p. 23.

36. *VS*, no. 4, 1957, p. 29.

CHAPTER 9. *Inventory Control*

1. Robert W. Campbell, "A Comparison of Soviet and American Inventory-Output Ratios," *American Economic Review*, September 1958.

2. A. F. Rumyantsev, V. I. Pereslegin, and G. V. Teplov, eds., *Ekonomika sotsialisticheskogo promyshlennogo predpriyatiya* (Economics of the Socialist Industrial Enterprise; Moscow, 1956), p. 155.

3. M. V. Dmitriev, *Voprosy formirovaniya i snizheniya sebestoimosti produktsii v legkoi promyshlennosti* (Questions of Cost Composition and Cost Reduction in Light Industry; Moscow, 1957).

4. For a more detailed discussion of the supply and marketing system in the Soviet economy, see Joseph Berliner, *Factory and Manager in the USSR* (Cambridge, Mass., 1957), and David Granick, *Management of the Industrial Firm in the USSR* (New York, 1954).

5. These categories have been somewhat altered since the reorganization of 1957.

6. For an extended explanation of these difficulties, see *Ekono-*

mika sotsialisticheskoi promyshlennosti, pp. 154ff, and V. Sitnin, "Voprosy organizatsii i ispolzovaniya oborotnykh sredstv" (Questions of Organization and Utilization of Inventories), *FSSSR*, no. 1, 1956, pp. 19–23.

7. On the difficulties of refusing unwanted materials, see, for instance, A. Petrov, "Kreditovanie predpriiatii legkoi promyshlennosti" (Crediting Enterprises of Light Industry), *DiK*, no. 5, 1958, p. 39, and Sitnin, p. 19.

8. Sitnin, p. 20, and L. A. Maizlin, *Khozraschet v tekstilnoi promyshlennosti* (Economic Accountability in the Textile Industry; Moscow, 1956), pp. 66–67.

9. *DiK*, no. 9, 1955, p. 5.

10. V. Kazarnovski, *Analiz khozyaystvennoi deiatelnosti promyshlennogo predpriyatiya* (Analysis of Economic Performance of the Industrial Enterprise; Moscow, 1954), p. 107.

11. An article in *DiK*, no. 5, 1956, mentions a plant under pressure from both the glavk and the Gosbank to unload excessive inventories. When it finally drew up a list of surplus commodities, it listed for disposal only minimal amounts. On one important commodity it reserved for itself a two and a half years' supply.

12. The statute on the rights of the glavks and ministries in this regard are given in *Direktivy KPSS i sovetskogo pravitelstva po khozyaystvennym voprosam* (Directives of the Communist Party of the Soviet Union and the Soviet Government on Economic Questions; Moscow, 1958), IV, 11 and 14, and on the rights of the sovnarkhozes in *ibid.*, IV, 784–805. Typical discussions of the abuses of these rights appear in *DiK*, no. 10, 1958, p. 64, and B. I. Ganshtak, *Ocherki po ekonomike mashinostroitelnoi promyshlennosti* SSSR (Essays on the Economics of the Machinebuilding Industry of the USSR; Moscow, 1957), p. 282.

13. M. Eidelman, "Uluchshit uchet materialov v narodnom khoziaistve" (Improve Materials Accounting in the National Economy), *VS*, no. 2, 1954.

14. See, for instance, Z. S. Katsenellenbaum, *Oborotnye sredstva v promyshlennosti* SSSR (Working Capital in the Industry of the USSR; Moscow, 1955), p. 91, and V. Kontorovich, *Tekhpromfinplan promshlennogo predpriyatiya* (The Technical, Industrial and Financial Plan of an Industrial Enterprise; Moscow, 1953), p. 262, and *FSSSR*, no. 6, 1958, pp. 35–36.

15. *Ekonomika sotsialisticheskoi promyshlennosti,* p. 154.

16. S. Kutyrev, *Proverka ispolzovaniya oborotnykh sredstv na promyshlennom predpriyatii* (Checking on the Use of Working Capital in the Industrial Enterprise; Moscow, 1954), p. 37.

17. V. Kotov, "Uchet materialnykh tsennostei na promyshlennykh predpriyatiyakh" (Accounting for Material Values in the Industrial Enterprise), *BU*, no. 3, 1958, pp. 13–18.

18. Howard T. Lewis and Wilbur England, *Procurement, Principles and Cases* (Homewood, 1957), p. 276.

19. *DiK*, no. 5, 1958, pp. 55–56.

20. *Ibid.*

21. O. Kadinski, "Za pravilnoe normirovanie oborotnykh sredstv" (For Correct Setting of Norms for Working Capital), *DiK*, no. 6, 1957, pp. 27–28.

22. *Ibid.*, p. 26.

23. *Ibid.*, p. 25.

24. *DiK*, no. 10, 1958, p. 66.

25. *DiK*, no. 5, 1958, p. 56, and no. 2, 1958, p. 29.

26. *DiK*, no. 3, 1958, p. 44.

27. For good discussions of these problems with many illustrative examples, see A. Ivanov, "Uskoriaem oborachivaemost oborotnykh sredstv" (Speed Up Inventory Turnover), *FSSSR*, no. 6, 1958, and M. Serebriannyi and S. Chistiakov, "Uluchshit planirovanie i organizatsiyu oborotnykh sredstv promyshlennykh predpriyatii" (Improve the Planning and Organization of Working Capital of Industrial Enterprises), *FSSSR*, no. 7, 1957.

28. For some typical discussions, see *DiK*, no. 3, 1956, p. 56, and no. 1, 1957, pp. 9–11.

29. I. Dolgin, "Uluchshit planirovanie oborotnykh sredstv" (Improve the Planning of Working Capital), *DiK*, no. 11, 1955, p. 35; no. 3, 1958, p. 57; and E. Mitelman, *Finansirovanie i kreditovanie sotsialisticheskoi promyshlennosti* (Financing and Crediting of Socialist Industry; Moscow, 1955), pp. 144–145.

30. See, for instance, *DiK*, no. 2, 1956, p. 20, and N. Sakov, *Sebestoimost i metody ee snizheniya* (Cost and Methods of Lowering It; Moscow, 1957), p. 109.

31. *Spravochnik finansovogo rabotnika* (Financial Workers' Handbook; Moscow, 1940), p. 679.

32. *VE*, no. 4, 1950, p. 95.

33. *VE*, no. 4, 1950, p. 96.

34. A. M. Birman, *Planirovanie oborotnykh sredstv* (Planning Working Capital; Moscow, 1950), pp. 150–151.

35. *VE*, no. 7, 1950, p. 86.

36. *DiK*, no. 7, 1958, p. 27; no. 5, 1956, p. 57; no. 11, 1955, p. 35; *FSSSR*, no. 6, 1958, p. 34.

37. V. Gerashchenko, "Nekotorye voprosy ukrepleniya khozya-

ystvennogo rascheta" (Some Problems of Strengthening Economic Accountability), *DiK*, no. 7, 1957, p. 5.

38. I. Dolgin, "Ukrepliat khozyaystvennyi raschet na predpriyatiyakh" (Strengthen Economic Accountability in the Enterprise), *DiK*, no. 6, 1958, p. 43.

39. The data for this conclusion are given in A. Zverev, "Gosudarstvennyi biudzhet pervogo goda semiletki" (The State Budget for the First Year of the Seven Year Plan), *PKh*, no. 1, 1959, p. 8; A. Zverev, *Voprosy natsionalnogo dokhoda i finansov* (Questions of the National Income and Finances; Moscow, 1958), p. 144; and TsSU, *Narodnoe khozyaystvo SSSR v 1959 godu* (The National Economy of the USSR in 1959; Moscow, 1960), p. 807.

40. The objection that a single normativ will promote differential hoarding is in *DiK*, no. 5, 1956, p. 56, and proposals for giving premiums for reducing inventories may be found in *FSSSR*, no. 5, 1958, p. 57, and in *DiK*, no. 3, 1958, p. 46.

CHAPTER 10. *The Mechanization of Accounting*

1. The schety is the Russian abacus, used by bookkeepers since very early times. It is in one way an appropriate and productive tool: it is cheap, of simple foolproof construction, and a skilled user can add and subtract on it with great rapidity. However, it is on a completely different level from modern mechanical aids in which the machinery does all the work of computing and at the same time makes the record. The arithmometer is a small, lever-set calculator, operated with a hand crank. It was invented by V. T. Odner, a Russian, in 1874. Because it is lever-set and hand-operated, it is relatively unproductive, especially for addition and subtraction.

2. P. Nosov and T. Tirzbanurt, "Mekhanizatsiya ucheta i uluchshenie administrativno-upravlencheskogo apparata" (Mechanization of Accounting and Improving the Administrative Apparatus), *PKh*, no. 4, 1953, p. 94.

3. Moskovski Ekonomiko-statisticheskii Institut, *Voprosy statistiki i ucheta* (Questions of Statistics and Accounting; 2, Moscow, 1959).

4. *KPSS v rezoliutsiyakh i resheniyakh* (The Communist Party of the Soviet Union in Resolutions and Decisions; 7th ed., Moscow, 1954), II, 444.

5. *Ibid.*, II, 599.

6. The text of this report may be found in *Tekhnika upravleniya* (Management Technology), no. 6, 1930, pp. 253–261.

7. This decree may be found in M. V. Nikolaev, *Zakonodatel-*

stvo ob uchete i otchetnosti (Legislation on Accounting and Reporting; Moscow, 1933), pp. 12–14.

8. *Ibid.*

9. F. V. Drozdov, "K voprosu o proizvodstve v SSSR schetnykh mashin" (On the Question of the Production of Accounting Machines in the USSR), *Tekhnika upravleniya* (Management Technology), no. 2, 1929, p. 32.

10. A. Popov, "Zo sovershennuyu teknicheskuyu bazu ucheta" (For a Modern Technical Basis for Accounting), *PKh*, no. 3, 1935, p. 122.

11. I. Kolychev, "Vazhnoe izobretenie" (An Important Invention), *DiK*, no. 4–5, 1940, p. 90.

12. Popov, p. 123. The similarity of the Russian machine to the American is underlined by an incident related by one Soviet writer. He explains indignantly that the Germans looted the KSM from the occupied Russian territories, removed the markings, and sold them in Prague as American machines. G. P. Evstigneyev, "Mashinizirovannyi uchet v SSSR" (Machine Accounting in the USSR), *BU*, no. 12, 1947, p. 17.

13. G. P. Evstigneyev, *Organizatsiya mekhanizirovannogo ucheta* (The Organization of Mechanized Accounting; Moscow, 1949), p. 8.

14. Popov, p. 48.

15. The figure for the United States is obtained by subtracting from output, as shown in the 1937 *Census of Manufactures*, the exports shown in U.S. Department of Commerce, *Foreign Trade and Navigation of the United States*, 1937.

16. For instance, it is reported in *Mashinostroenie* (Machine-building), April 14, 1939, that the monthly goal for KSM was only 175 machines in 1939. Another article says that a planned expansion of the Moscow SAM plant to permit production of 125 complexes of punched-card machinery in 1938 had not even been started in 1939 (*Mashinostroenie*, November 15, 1939).

17. I. Globa, "Mashinizirovannyi uchet v 1940 godu" (Machine Accounting in 1940), *DiK*, no. 1, 1940, p. 49.

18. *Za industrializatsiyu* (For Industrialization), October 10, 1930.

19. *Finansovaya gazeta* (The Financial Newspaper), April 8, 1938.

20. *Mashinostroenie*, April 29, 1938.

21. *Ibid.*, January 9, 1939.

22. Popov, p. 119.

23. *Mashinostroenie*, February 9, 1938.

24. Kolychev, p. 90.

25. For instance, the 38 complexes of punched-card machinery which had been in operation in the Ministry of Aviation and the Ministry of Shipbuilding before the war were no longer being used at the end of the war. S. S. Geidish, "Zhurnal ignoriruyushchii voprosy mekhanizatsii" (A Journal Which Ignores Questions of Mechanization), *MTITR*, no. 10, 1948, p. 48.

26. Earlier decrees were those of May 1945 and October 1947. The texts of these decrees were never published, but the general nature of their provisions is found in some of the general discussions of postwar mechanization. See, for instance, I. S. Bulgakov, *Schetnye mashiny* (Accounting Machines; Moscow, 1950), p. 4; Evstigneyev, p. 17; A. M. Fisson, "Sereznyi khozyaystvennyi vopros" (A Serious Economic Question), *MTITR*, no. 4, 1949, and the editorial in *MTITR*, no. 7, 1949.

27. D. Zhak and T. Tirzbanurt, "O sostoianii mekhanizatsii ucheta i vychislitelnykh rabot" (On the Status of Mechanization of Accounting and Computing Work), *VS*, no. 2, 1952, p. 65.

28. Editorial in *MTITR*, no. 7, 1949.

29. See U.S. Department of Commerce, Business and Defense Services Administration, *World Trade in Adding Machines, Calculators, Cash Registers, 1953–1959* (Washington, 1960).

30. Nosov and Tirzbanurt, p. 95, and *Pravda*, November 27, 1953.

31. Moskovski Ekonomiko-statisticheskii Institut, *Voprosy statistiki i ucheta*, p. 13, and *Promyshlenno-ekonomicheskaia gazeta* (The Industrial-Economic Newspaper), April 1, 1959.

32. A list of the plants claimed as reparations may be found in G. W. Harmssen, *Am Abend der Demontage* (Bremen, 1951), pp. 95–101. The dismantled plants included the Astra-werke and the Wanderer-werke in Chemnitz, the Archimedes plant and a cash-register factory in Glasshutte. There is no specific information on what happened to the dismantled plants, but the fact that the Soviet plant in Riazan, which did not exist before the war, has been producing since the war a line of machines copied from the prewar Astra machines suggests that the dismantled plant may have formed the basis for the Riazan plant.

A list of the plants which are included in *Tochmash* may be found in G. W. Harmssen, *Reparationen, Sozialprodukt, Lebensstandard* (Bremen, 1947), p. 122, and a later list appears in Deutsches Institut für Wirtschaftforschung, *Wirschaftprobleme der Besatzungzonen* (Berlin, 1948). The most important accounting-machinery plant was the former Rheinmetall-Borsig plant in Sommerda.

33. Ministerstvo Vneshnei Torgovli, *Vneshniaya torgovlia Soyuza*

SSR za 1959 god (Foreign Trade of the USSR in 1959; Moscow, 1960).

34. Moskovski Ekonomiko-statisticheskii Institut, *Voprosy statistiki i ucheta*, p. 11.

35. *Ibid.*, p. 15, and VS, no. 7, 1960, p. 6.

36. *VE*, no. 11, 1959, p. 154.

37. See, for example, the editorial in VS, no. 12, 1959, and the entire issue no. 8, 1960, which is devoted in large part to the reports made at a conference on the subject.

38. For instance, M. Kh. Zhebrak, one of the outstanding Soviet authorities on accounting, says that "the task of industrial accounting consists first of all in the control of plan fulfillment." *Kurs promyshlennogo ucheta* (Course on Industrial Accounting; 6th ed., Moscow, 1950), p. 4.

39. Voikorovski, "Ob uluchshenii raboty upravlencheskogo apparata" (On Improving the Work of the Administrative Apparatus), *Sakharnaya promyshlennost* (The Sugar Industry), no. 4, 1954, p. 8.

40. See, for instance, A. Vorobeva, "Puti ukrepleniya tsekhovogo khozrascheta" (Ways of Strengthening Economic Accountability in the Shop), *VE*, no. 4, 1951, pp. 48–49; "Nauchno-proizvodstvennya konferentsiya po voprosam vnutrizavodskogo khrozrascheta" (Scientific-Production Conference on Questions of Intraplant Economic Accountability), *VE*, no. 6, 1951, p. 106; and S. K. Tatur, *Khozraschet i rentabelnost* (Economic Accountability and Profitability; Moscow, 1951), p. 146.

41. See, for instance, *Legkaya promyshlennost* (Light Industry), no. 10, 1949; A. V. Voronin, *Kalkuliatsiya i analiz sebestoimosti produktsii tekstilnykh predpriyatii* (Calculation and Analysis of the Cost of Production in Textile Enterprises; Moscow, 1948), p. 81; and Vorobeva, pp. 48–49.

42. *BU*, no. 2, 1954, p. 5, and no. 8, 1954, p. 1.

43. "Po puti sokrashcheniya apparata" (On the Way to Reducing the Apparatus), *BU*, no. 2, 1955, p. 6.

44. A. I. Lozinski, *Grafik — Osnova ratsionalnoi organizatsii ucheta* (A Timetable — Basis for Rational Organization of Accounting; Moscow, 1946), p. 8.

45. *Ibid., passim.*

46. See, for instance, the editorials in *BU*, no. 1, 1954, p. 7, and no. 10, 1954, p. 2.

47. Lozinski, p. 9.

48. United States figures for 1940 and 1950 are based on U.S. Bureau of the Census, *U.S. Census of Population*, II: *Characteristics of the Population*, part I, U.S. Summary, chap. C (Washington,

1953). The figure is adjusted to the Soviet coverage by subtracting from the total: (1) cashiers (known for 1950 and estimated as the same proportion of the cashiers and bookkeepers for 1940); (2) an estimate of those engaged in public accounting (estimate taken from U.S. Department of Labor, Bureau of Labor Statistics, *Employment Outlook in Accounting*, Washington, 1951, p. 5, for 1950, and a similar proportion of the accountants and auditors category in 1940); and (3) on a purely guesswork basis, one fourth of the office machine operators. The 1930 figure is based on data in U.S. Bureau of the Census, *Sixteenth Census of the United States: 1940*, "Population, Comparative Occupation Statistics for the United States, 1870 to 1940" (Washington, 1943), p. 51, which adjust the data of previous censuses to the 1940 occupational classification. The 1930 adjusted figure is obtained by again subtracting one fourth of the office machine operators and reducing the bookkeeper, accountant, and cashier category by the same fraction as in 1940.

The Soviet figures are from the respective census publications: Gosplan SSSR, *Vsesoyuznaya perepis naseleniya 1926 goda*, XXXIV, Soyuz sovetskikh sotsialisticheskikh respublik, II, *Zaniatia* (Moscow, 1930), p. 180; I. Sautin, "Naselenie strany sotsializma," *Bolshevik*, no. 10, 1940, p. 22; TsSU, "O raspredeleniya naseleniya SSSR po obshchestvennym gruppam, otrasliam narodnogo khozyaystva, i zaniatiyam . . ." *VS*, no. 12, 1960; the 1947 figure, from N. A. Kiparisov, "Podgotovka uchetnykh kadrov v SSSR," *BU*, no. 11, 1947, p. 31, is not a census figure but appears to be consistent in concept with the others. The Russian concept is "bookkeepers and ledger clerks" (*bukhgaltera i schetovody*) and, according to the definition in the 1926 census, does not include such auxiliary accounting workers as auditors, cashiers, timekeepers, and so on.

49. U.S. Bureau of the Census, *U.S. Census of Population: 1950*, IV, Special Reports, part 1, chap. C, "Occupation by Industry" (Washington, 1955).

50. TsUNKhU, *Sotsialisticheskoe stroitelstvo* (Socialist Construction; Moscow, 1936), pp. 630–631.

51. For instance, there were only 1,980 bookkeepers, accountants, cashiers, and ticket agents in all of American agriculture in 1940 (U.S. Bureau of the Census, *Sixteenth Census of the United States: 1940*, "Population, The Labor Force, Occupational Characteristics," Washington, 1943, p. 15); in the Soviet economy in 1938 there were 248,390 bookkeepers in the collective farms alone, without the state farms and machine-tractor stations (*PKh*, no. 7, 1939, p. 147).

52. Evstigneyev, "Mashinizirovannyi uchet v SSSR," p. 16.

53. Ministerstvo Mashinostroeniya i Priborostroeniya, *Preiskurant*

optovykh tsen na poligraficheskie i schetnye mashiny (Price List of Wholesale Prices for Printing and Accounting Machines; Moscow, 1949), pp. 37–40.

54. V. A. Ginodman, *Mekhanizatsiya ucheta i vychislitelnykh rabot* (Mechanization of Accounting and Computational Work; Moscow, 1950), p. 240.

55. *Ibid.*

56. It is said that the productivity of labor rises at least by 2.5 times when punched-card machines are used, as is shown by the experience of the MSS (*BU*, no. 11, 1954, p. 1). Since it takes 8 operators to run the complex, the number displaced would theoretically be 12.

INDEX

Abacus. See *Schety*

Accounting: scope of, 2–3; concepts for understanding the Soviet economy, 4–5; as control instrument, 8; as a source of economic information, 7–8; objectives, 16, 19–22; and economic rationality, 17–19, 23, 26, 44–45; head office, 27–29; future evolution, 47–48, 268; labor force, 189, 225, 246–247

Accounting machinery: imports, 227, 231–232, 236, 238, 240; production, 228–231, 234–239; punched card, 230–231, 234, 237, 239; types, 230, 237–238; United States, 230–231; repair problems, 231–233, 239; stocks, 231–233, 239–240; problems in mastering, 237, 240; Seven Year Plan goals, 240

Administrative friction: and cost concept, 41–42, 131; characteristic of Soviet system, 41–42, 44–45; and allocation of overhead, 103–104

Administration, future improvements, 265. See also Organization

Allocation: overhead costs 33–37, 103–112; joint costs, 117–124;

material, 200–201, 265. See also Depreciation

All-Ukrainian Institute of Labor, 226

Amortization deductions. See Depreciation

Analysis of economic performance, 175–176, 260–262

Applicability of Soviet accounting ideas to United States problems, 6–7

Arithmometer: production, 230; stocks, 233; description, 303

Assets. See Fixed assets; Inventories

Auditing: weaknesses, 181–183; internal, 182; pay of auditors, 182; in United States, 183

Balance of equipment, 159–160

Balance sheet: distinctive features, 13; explanation of account headings, 197–200; illustration, 198; use in inventory control, 199–200

Balans izmenenii tsen, 279

Bias in accounting rules, 135, 151

Bookkeepers: rights and duties, 14, 184, 299; role in enterprise, 184; training, 253; unattractiveness of occupation, 253–254; conservatism, 263

Budget: as part of income account, 29; as source of financing, 34, 36; as source of repair funds, 71; assignment of outlays to, 127–131

Bukhgalterskii uchet: definition of concept, 3; periodical, 181, 243

By-products, cost allocation, 124–125; in project-making calculations, 291

Capital, charges for, 47. *See also* Own working capital

Capital intensity, 37

Capital repair: definition, 51, 77–78; accounting entries, 77–79; in depreciation-rate formula, 79–80; assignment of outlays to, 179

Central Administration of National-Economic Accounting. *See* Central Statistical Administration

Central planning: influences on accounting, 6, 13, 188–189; allocation of resources, 19–21; deficiencies in, 173–175, 259–260; conflict with local needs, 257

Central Statistical Administration: responsibility for accounting practice, 14–15; as control organ, 35; stock of accounting machinery, 239

Changes over time in Soviet accounting, 9

Charter fund: in depreciation accounting, 80–84; outlays written off to, 83, 141, 143–144; definition, 197; related to own working capital, 197

Chief bookkeeper. *See* Bookkeepers

Coal industry: cost distortions, 74; losses on fixed assets, 89, 95–96; inventory classification, 209–210, 257–258

Coefficients of deficitness, 46

Coefficient of depreciation, 92–93, 95–96

Collective farms: failure to do accounting, 66; revaluation of fixed assets, 66, 283–284

Commissariat: of agriculture, 57; of communications, 57; of fishing industry, 57; of heavy industry, 108, 113; of finance, 111, 178. *See also* Ministry

Communist Party: statements on accounting, 12; Fifteenth Congress, 227; Sixteenth Conference, 227; Twenty-Second Congress, 268

Computational capacity: inadequate for detailed cost calculation, 185; hinders rapid inventory accounting, 202; keeps quality of accounting low, 253; and improvement in administration, 265

Control and Audit Administration, Ministry of Finance, 180

Control by the ruble, 214

Cost: alternative concepts, 23–26; marginal, 25, 166; variable-fixed distinction, 25, 162–164; opportunity, 29, 255; as performance indicator, 53, 97, 135, 150–151, 171–172, 176, 267; of accounting machinery, 251. *See also* Joint products

Cost planning. *See* Central planning

Cost-price residuals, 29, 39, 41–42

Credit, bank: short-term, 145, 214–218, 221; for modernization projects, 158; reform of 1931, 196

Data processing. *See* Computational capacity

Depreciation: changes over time, 9; accounting, objectives, 50–54; differs from capitalist forms, 50; as allocator of funds, 51–52, 69; decree of 1938, 51, 68–69; in national income accounting, 52, 96; estimated in 1960 revaluation, 65; allocation among firms, 68–71, 73; distortions in cost accounting, 73; underestimation,

73, 75–77; as share of GNP, 75–77; accounting entries, 80–84; allocation among assets, 90–92; concepts, 100. *See also* Replacement; Repair

Depreciation rates: assigned from above, 67; decree of 1930, 67; differentiation by asset class, 69, 71, 74; changed in 1950, 72–73; revised January 1962, 74; division into repair and replacement, 96–101

Detail: in assignment of depreciation, 82, 91; in overhead accounting, 116–117; related to undermechanization, 241–244; determined by needs of outside control, 258–259

Double entry: distinguishing accounting data, 3; identified with capitalism, 11–12

Economic calculation: in ore-enriching projects, 21; partial optimization, 21–22; influenced by costs and prices, 22–23, 25, 33–35, 43, 45–46, 73, 125; input index, 22, 25; bookkeeping costs ignored, 26, 46, 165–169; capital intensity, 37, 278; errors in, 43; investment, 156–157; innovations, 161–162; make-or-buy decisions, 162–163; need for accurate prices recognized, 170. *See also* Replacement

Economic council: as collector of funds for development expenses, 35; right to distribute working capital, 205, 223; inventory policy, 223

Economic Research Institute, Ministry of Ways of Communication, 164

Enterprise: definition, 12–13; accounting distinguished from head-office accounting, 27. *See also* Management, lower level

Falsification, accounting: current vs. capital repair, 99, 113; costs, 99, 176, 180, 298; as reflection of managerial attitudes, 175; inventory indicators, 221–222

Financial plan, description, 29

Financing for special purposes, 83–84, 127, 129–30

Fines and penalties, 109, 133, 137–138, 149

Fixed assets: heterogeneity in valuation, 55; retirement losses, 83, 88–90, 94–95; average age, 93–94, 95; modernization, 158; distinguished from inventory assets, 210. *See also* Revaluation; Valuation of fixed assets

Foreign influences, 188, 263–264, 287, 300

Formula: for estimating obsolescence, 64; for depreciation charges, 79; for calculating normativs, 208–209

Funds: for assistance to inventions, 128; directors, 147; premium, 147–148; enterprise, 158. *See also* Charter fund; Investment; Capital repair; Own working capital

General plant expenses, 108–109

Glavk: assignment of depreciation rates by, 69; cost planning and control, 173, 212–213; auditing responsibilities, 181; inventory planning and control functions, 209

Gleikh, E. I., 147

Gosbank: as illustration of khozraschet, 35–36; functions, 35; supervision of capital repair, 99; control over modernization of assets, 158; as source of working capital, 199–200; in inventory control, 205–206, 215, 218, 221; credit for goods shipped, 221; stock of accounting machinery, 233–234, 239; mechanization of accounting, 239; responsible for analyzing reports, 261

Gosplan: responsible for accounting practice, 14–15; control functions, 35; allocation of materials, 201; establishment of normativs, 207

Hoarding, 93, 215, 217

Households, relationship to state economy, 28, 32–33

Inflation: repressed, 32; effect on fixed asset valuation, 56, 62; effect on repair costs, 70, 79, 88, 99

Input-output techniques, 47

Institute of Management Technique, 226, 227

Institute of Precision Mechanics and Computational Technique, Academy of Sciences, 234

Insurance, Soviet treatment of, 130–131, 141

Interest charges: omitted in pricing, 37; proposed inclusion in pricing, 47; disguised as depreciation, 54

Inventories: control system, 4, 192–193; revaluation, 144–146; in planned vs. market economy, 192–194; excessive holdings, 194–195; rate of turnover, 194–195; maldistribution among firms, 195; normed vs. nonnormed, 198–199; disposal of excess, 202, 204

Inventory taking: fixed assets, 57, 63, 66, 253; effect on cost calculation, 176–177, 179–180, 185

Investment: organization, 57–58; uncapitalized outlays, 59–60; magnitude, 83, 91; centralization of funds, 158

Joint products: cost allocation, 117–124, 166–168; in capitalist firms, 118; in agriculture, 121–

122; in mining, 121; in power generation, 122–123; in oil industry, 123–125

Kantor, L. M., 56, 149–150

Kantorovich, L. V., 47, 266

Kettle method of cost calculation, 116, 175

Khozraschet: concept, 12–13; objectives, 33–34, 127; intraplant, 186–188, 242, 244

Khrushchev, N. S., 268

Kvasha, Ia. B., 93, 100

Labor-training expenses, 129

Labor unit of account, 12

Legislation, accounting: as basis of study, 10; duties of bookkeepers, 14, 184, 299; uniformity, 14–15; depreciation, 51, 68–69

Losses: in construction, 58; retirement, 83, 88–89; on housing, 139–140, 151; from natural disasters, 141–142, 294. See also Profits

Lumber industry: depreciation rates, 70; losses on retirement, 89; cost calculation, 96; inventory normativs, 211, 213

Management, lower level: control over repair, 97, 99–100, 159; degree of authority, 99–100, 205, 209; use of accounting reports, 187–191, 242, 264; inventory attitudes, 215

Management attitudes: toward costs, 172; on inventories, 193–194, 208–209, 215, 224; of glavks, 203, 215; on liquidity, 205–206; toward financial indicators, 214; of ministries, 215; of sovnarkhozes, 223

Managerial accounting, 183–184

Marxist concepts: value theory, 23, 37–38, 125, 255; of depreciation, 100; impact on accounting, 115, 149, 154, 255–256; and joint-

RUSSIAN RESEARCH CENTER STUDIES

° Publications of the Harvard Project on the Soviet Social System.
† Published jointly with the Center for International Affairs, Harvard University.
‡ Out of print.